United States Government US Senate

Table of Contents

waste not, want not.

Washington has reversed the wisdom of the old cliché that less is needed when less is wasted. Every branch of government bickered this year over the need to spend more (while continuing to misspend) with an attitude of "waste more, want more!"

Confronted with self-imposed budget cuts necessary to trim years of trillion dollar shortfalls, Washington protested that it could not live within its means. It attempted to take hostage the symbols of America to exact ransom from taxpayers. Public tours of the White House were canceled and Medicare payments for seniors' health care were cut.

While the President and his cabinet issued dire warnings about the cataclysmic impacts of sequestration, taxpayers were not alerted to all of the waste being spared from the budget axe.

The Department of Defense (DOD) developed a plan this year to constrain pay and benefits for our brave men and women in uniform, who risk their lives to protect us from terrorists,[1] for example, while at the same time continuing to pay the salary and other government benefits for the Fort Hood shooter,[2] responsible for the worst terrorist attack on American soil since 9-11.[3]

> As you read each of the 100 projects costing nearly $30 billion outlined in this report, ask yourself:
>
> Can we afford this at this time?
>
> Could this money have been better spent or not spent at all?
>
> Is this a national priority or is this something benefiting a special interest?
>
> Does this fit the role of the federal government as outlined in the U.S. Constitution?

DOD grounded the Air Force Thunderbirds and Navy Blue Angels,[4] yet still spent $432 million to construct aircraft they never intend to fly.[5]

The Army National Guard spent $10 million on Superman movie tie-ins while plans were being made to cut the strength of the Guard by 8,000 soldiers, the *real* supermen and women who fight for truth, justice and the American way.

As the Smithsonian was closing exhibits at its world renowned museums,[6] the federal government was funding the creation of "play zones" at the National Museum of Play, an inventory of toys at the Denver Museum of Miniatures, Dolls and Toys, and a website celebrating romance novels.

The U.S. Department of Agriculture (USDA) cut housing assistance for the disabled elderly while subsidizing thousands of risky mortgages, including more than 100 homes (that cost in excess of half-a-million dollars each) within walking distance of the ocean in Hawaii. And while nutrition assistance was being reduced for many needy families, USDA was spending money on celebrity chef cooks-offs and running up the taxpayer tab on Bloody Marys, sweet potato vodka, and red wine tastings from here to China.

The Department of Interior was counting sheep with high-tech unmanned aerial drones[7] after delaying the opening of some national landmarks and closing others early.

This lack of common sense was only accentuated in October when the government shut down, in part because Congress failed to approve even one regular appropriations bill. Agency heads were forced to decide what constituted essential and nonessential activities. As a result, veterans' memorials were locked down and "closed" signs were put up. No similar dramatic notice was given to the government boondoggles that continued to waste of taxpayer money.

NASA ultimately paid more than 17,700 employees—97 percent of its staff— to do nothing for 16 days as a result of the shutdown.[8] These hardworking employees, caught in factors outside of their control, should not be confused with the "pillownauts" the space agency hired to lie around in bed and do nothing for 70 days.[9]

Even the government shutdown could not shut down Obamacare, but the failure of its $319 million website nearly did.[10] Millions of dollars more were spent to urge taxpayers to visit the website that did not work—at whiskey festivals and on TV with ads featuring Elvis impersonators. Yet, even the hundreds of thousands who had their plans canceled struggled to sign up for the plans they did not want in the first place. At least one dog was able to enroll, however.

And just days before the impending shutdown, when much of Washington was bracing for a protracted closure of most government offices and activities, USDA decided to celebrate Christmas early by funding six Christmas trees projects and—in the spirit of holiday cheer—35 different wine initiatives, including the creation of two smart phone apps to help "navigate to the next winery."

These are only a few of the 100 examples of government mismanagement and stupidity included in *Wastebook 2013*. Collectively these cost nearly $30 billion in a year when Washington would have you believe everything that could be done has been done to control unnecessary spending. Had just these 100 been eliminated, the sequester amount would have been reduced nearly a third without any noticeable disruption.

As you glance at each of the entries presented in this report, place your personal political persuasion aside and ask yourself: Do each of these represent a real national priority that should be spared from budget cuts or are these excesses that should have been eliminated in order to spare deeper cuts to those services and missions that should be performed by the federal government?

When it comes to spending your money, those in Washington tend to see no waste, speak no waste, and cut no waste.

Sincerely,

Tom A. Coburn, M.D.
U.S. Senator

1. Paid to Do Nothing – (Government wide) At least $400 million

The first session of the 113th Congress will likely go down as the least productive in history, more notable for what it did not do than what it did. A mere 57 laws were enacted, no budget could be agreed upon, and not a single regular appropriations bill to fund government operations passed on time, resulting, in part, in a 16 day government wide shutdown in October. Through it all Congress was paid. And eventually, so were all the other federal employees, including many deemed non-essential and therefore not permitted to report to work.

The White House estimates it cost $2 billion to provide back pay to federal employees "for services that could not be performed" during the shutdown. "Total compensation costs, including benefits, are about 30 percent larger, in the range of $2.5 billion."[11]

Of course, it is not the fault of employees who are non-essential, formally deemed "non-exempt,"[12] for the failure of Congress to do its job.

More than 100,000 federal employees being paid a salary of at least $100,000 were furloughed as non-essential. Each of these were paid $4,000 for the time off of work during the shutdown.

Again, it is not the fault of these civil servants that Congress did not do its job and, like everyone else, they have bills to pay. But it is truly unfair to charge billions of dollars to pay others not to work to taxpayers working to cover their own bills and the bills of the government. This is especially true when the non-essential federal employee is being compensated more than twice the average U.S. family income of $51,000.[13]

A sampling of just three federal agencies found more than 35,500 federal employees earning $100,000 or more who were furloughed for performing non-essential duties (and then paid for not performing those duties).

More than 100,000 federal employees being paid a salary of at least $100,000 were deemed non-essential and not required to work during the government shutdown.

The Department of Treasury "furloughed 21,751 non-excepted/non-essential employees with an annual salary of $100,000.00 or more during the government shutdown."[14] This adds up to nearly $84 million spent to pay just these employees to do nothing. Meanwhile, the Administration furloughed as non-essential "nearly all of the Treasury Department's Office of Foreign Asset Control (OFAC), which implements the U.S. government's financial sanctions against countries such as Iran and Syria."[15] And while taxpayers continued to file returns and make payments during the shutdown, they "could not receive assistance" from the IRS.[16]

"During the shutdown of the federal government in October 2013, the Department of Veterans Affairs furloughed 1,406 employees who are paid an annual salary of $100,000 or more (356 in the Office of Information & Technology, 832 in the Veterans Benefits Administration, and 218 in the Office of the Inspector General)."[17] This means $5.6 million was spent to pay $4,000 or more to each of the employees for not performing any duties. Over this same period, some services to veterans were halted or curtailed and progress to reduce the veterans' disability claims backlog was stalled.[18]

The National Aeronautics and Space Administration (NASA) deemed as non-essential and furloughed approximately 12,300 employees earning an annual salary of $100,000 or more during the government shutdown.[19] The cost to pay these employees for a paid vacation of 16 days exceeded $47 million.

At these three agencies alone, more than $135 million was spent to pay employees with salaries exceeding $100,000 to do nothing for two weeks. With 15 departments and at least 25 independent agencies within the executive branch, more than 100,000 federal employees earning $100,000 or more were likely furloughed and paid to do nothing, costing taxpayers $400 million. This is one-fifth of the total back pay for furloughed non-essential federal employees.

Many who perform what most of us consider essential occupations earn on average far less than $100,000. A full-time public school teacher, for example, is paid about $56,000 a year.[20] A registered nurse is compensated about $68,000 a year.[21] And a police officer is paid about $58,000 a year.[22]

At least six state governors are also paid less than $100,000, including the chief executives of Arizona, Arkansas, Colorado, Kansas, Maine, and Oregon.[23]

Any federal employee collecting an annual salary of $100,000 or more should be performing essential work and considered exempt from furlough during a government shutdown. Likewise, Congress, which is expected to perform essential work, should not be paid when it fails to pass an annual budget as required by law.

2. It's a Bird. It's a Plane. It's Superman! – (National Guard) $10 million

Sequestration, the across-the-board spending cuts agreed to by Congress and the President, will reduce the strength of the Army National Guard by more than 8,000 soldiers.[24] So perhaps it shouldn't be surprising that in the face of these cuts, the National Guard is turning to Superman for help.

Faster than a speeding bullet, more powerful than a locomotive, able to leap tall buildings in a single bound, not even the menacing threats of sequester or a government shutdown could furlough the caped crusader and his fight for truth, justice, and the American way.

The real super men and women fighting for truth, justice, and the American way don't wear red capes.

This year, the Army National Guard teamed up with Superman on a $10 million "Soldier of Steel" promotional campaign, intended "to increase awareness and consideration of service opportunities in the National Guard."[25] The recruitment ads "dovetailed with the release of the Warner Bros. blockbuster movie, 'Man of Steel,'" the latest Superman movie[26] and, strangely enough, with a downsizing of the National Guard.

"The centerpiece of this awareness campaign were two theater spots airing in 90 percent of theater screens nationwide," according to the National Guard.[27] Signs and video monitors were placed in more than 1,500 theaters "and supporting elements included in-gym networks ads, ads placed with targeted high school magazines/websites, and online/mobile/video ads."[28]

Players "crack the codes, pilot the experimental helicopter and test your aim on the firing range with prototype weaponry" as part of the Army National Guard's Soldier of Steel video game.

The promotional campaign also included online video games,[29] a series of work out and fitness videos,[30] and sports cars design wraps. Dale Earnhardt Jr. drove the National Guard "Man of Steel" Chevrolet SS on June 16th at the Michigan International Speedway.[31] Panther Racing's No. 4 National Guard Chevrolet IndyCar was repainted blue and red with Superman's iconic "S" placed prominently on the nose of the car for the 97th Running of the Indianapolis 500 Mile Race as part of the National Guard's "Soldier of Steel" recruiting campaign.[32]

Theater and social media placement for the Superman tie-in recruitment campaign cost the Army National Guard $8 million for development, and production cost another $2 million.[33] These costs do not include the "motorsport car wraps" because the cars were already partnering with the National Guard.[34]

In addition to taxpayer cash, the "Man of Steel" collected more than $160 million from over 100 other promotional tie-ins.[35] The movie itself, *Superman: Man of Steel* has grossed over $662 million worldwide to date[36] and it will earn more with its DVD release.

The Army National Guard's budget did not fare as well as Superman's. As a result of the spending restraints imposed by the Budget Control Act of 2011, "the Army may have to reduce at least 100,000 additional personnel across the Total Force – the Active Army, the Army National Guard and the Army Reserve. When coupled with previously planned cuts to end strength, the Army could lose up to 200,000 soldiers over the next ten years," according to Army leadership.[37]

Yet, the Army still spent $10 million to subsidize the promotion of *Superman* with the hopes of enlisting new recruits. This money could have been better spent on the real life supermen and superwomen in the Army National Guard who are courageously risking all in the fight for truth, justice, and the American way.

As Superman flies away with massive profits from sponsors and ticket sales and the force size and budget of the Army National Guard shrinks, the U.S. national debt continues to go up, up and away.

A car in the Indianapolis 500 Mile Race was repainted blue and red with Superman's iconic "S" on the nose as part of the National Guard's "Soldier of Steel" recruiting campaign.

3. Uncle Sam Looking for Romance on the Web – (NEH) $914,000

More and more people are looking for love online and now Uncle Sam is paying to make the web a little more romantic.

The Popular Romance Project has received nearly $1 million from the National Endowment of the Humanities (NEH) since 2010 to "explore the fascinating, often contradictory origins and influences of popular romance as told in novels, films, comics, advice books, songs, and internet fan fiction, taking a global perspective—while looking back across time as far as the ancient Greeks."[38] In addition to the funds provided by NEH, the Library of Congress

The Popular Romance Project has received nearly $1 million from the federal government since 2010 to promote romance novels, which may leave many taxpayers feeling jilted for subsiding an industry that generates over $1 billion a year.

Center for the Book is also a participant in the project.[39]

According to the Popular Romance Project, "with this funding, we will develop an expanded website—including hundreds of new video interviews and blog posts, games that explore branding and marketing, and archival materials—as well as a mobile version."[40]

"Taking love and its stories seriously, wherever they may be found, the Popular Romance Project will spark a lively, thoughtful conversation between fans, authors, scholars, and the general public about the writing, production, and consumption of popular romance, including its history and transformation in the digital age."[41]

The Popular Romance Project aims to "bring new audiences into the conversation about the nature of love, romance, and their expression in novels and popular culture more broadly" through four programs:

- A documentary entitled "Love Between the Covers";
- An interactive website dedicated to romance and romance novels;
- An academic symposium on "the past and future of the romance novel" hosted by the Library of Congress Center for the Book; and
- A "nationwide series of library programs dealing with the past, present, and future of the romance novel" with a traveling exhibit.[42]

Some of the recent website topics include:

- **Team Edward or Team Jacob?** "Are heroes like Edward romantic or controlling?" ponders the Popular Romance Project website, referring to the vampire character in the *Twilight*.[43]
- **Call Me Maybe:** The Popular Romance Project website celebrates Carly Rae Jepsen's hit song "Call Me Maybe" as a "fun, flirty invitation to a dreamy crush" and examines how the song's video has provokes some "very interesting conversations about contemporary romance."[44]
- **The Spy Who Loved Me:** The romance of British Secret Service Agent James Bond, 007, is examined by the Popular Romance Project website, noting that "the recurrent death of romance is fundamental to the 007 franchise. What can popular romance scholars make of this motif?"[45]

While supporters note that "in some ways, romance novels are the dirty little secret of the literary world" and "largely ignored by mainstream critics, regularly maligned by academics, and sometimes hidden away even by their readers," they hope this project will change that impression–all with the assistance of the federal government.[46] In addition to the NEH financial aid, the Library of Congress is planning symposium to "explore the past and future of the romance novel form, scheduled to coincide with the release" of the "Love Between the Covers" documentary "around Valentine's Day 2015."[47]

"Are heroes like Edward romantic or controlling?" is one of the many topics related to love and romance the Popular Romance Project website explores.

NEH has invested nearly $1 million in this project over the past three years. In September, NEH issued a $250,000 grant for the "production of an interactive, multifaceted website that would serve as an anchor for the Popular Romance Project, a multimedia project on the writing, production, and consumption of popular romance literature."[48] Last October, NEH provided $616,000 for the "production of a two-hour documentary about the history and context of the romance novel and the global community built around a mass-produced popular cultural product" to be spent this year and next.[49] In 2010, NEH awarded a two year grant totaling $48,000 for the "planning and scripting for a film, a symposium, and reading and discussion programs on how romance literature reflects universal themes of courtship, love, and intimacy"[50] as well as travel to conferences about romance novels.[51]

NEH may love to waste money on this project, but taxpayers are likely to feel jilted about subsidizing the promotion of a billion dollar industry that generated over $1.4 billion in 2012, and remains as hot as ever.[52]

4. Obama Administration Studies American's Attitudes Towards Filibuster as Senate Majority Leader Eliminates the Longstanding Senate Right to Debate – (MO) $251,525

What makes the world's greatest deliberative body so deliberative?

Up until last month, every member of the U.S. Senate had the right to speak for as long as he or she wished, even if doing so delayed votes or other business.

The iconic 1939 movie *Mr. Smith Goes to Washington* dramatized the power of the filibuster to influence public opinion by utilizing unlimited debate to bring truths to light.

While the majority often grumbles that the filibuster is nothing more than an obstructionist tactic, it is one that has long been utilized to force open debate, improve legislation, bring consensus, and even halt legislation or nominations. As designed, only a supermajority could cut off deliberations by invoking cloture, after which an additional 30 hours of debate time still remained, thereby empowering any senator's viewpoint to be heard.

While control of the Senate and the White House has changed over the past decade, opinion polls during this period have consistently indicated there is no overwhelming desire from the public to eliminate the filibuster.

But in November, the Senate Majority Leader broke the longstanding rules of the Senate that require 67 votes to change these procedures and killed the filibuster with a bare majority of 51 other senators. The filibuster was eliminated for consideration of most presidential nominations requiring Senate confirmation, thereby "eliminating the ability of the Senate

The classic American movie *Mr. Smith Goes to Washington* dramatized the power of the filibuster to influence public opinion by utilizing unlimited debate to bring truths to light. Today's Senate majority would essentially tell Mr. Smith to "shut up and sit down." The Obama Administration is spending a quarter-of-a-million dollars to examine the public's opinion of the parliamentary tactic, which the President supports eliminating, while cutting off federal support for hundreds of scientific proposals.

minority to filibuster executive branch nominees and any judgeship below the Supreme Court."[53] The Senate Majority Leader has since hinted "that at some point the filibuster may end entirely, and not just for nominations," but also for legislation. He stated if the leader of the Senate "decides that's what they want to do, then they can have a vote before the full Senate and decide if that's what they want to do." He noted "the Senate is a democratic body; it always has been. We work on collegiality just like judges do. But there comes a time when collegiality breaks down and you have to do something."[54]

While the Majority Leader believes it is democratic to end this longstanding right of all senators, a majority of voters feels the opposite. Quinnipiac University conducted two polls in recent years on the subject and both found a lack of majority support for killing the filibuster. Most Americans believed it would be a "bad idea" to eliminate the filibuster.[55] Another poll found the lack of support for ending the filibuster statistically unchanged, with just 42 percent saying it would be a good idea.[56]

When George W. Bush was president and Republicans held a majority in the Senate in 2005, 43 percent favored eliminating the filibuster.[57]

Regardless of what party controlled the White House or the Senate, the public has never rallied to end the filibuster.

"There is no groundswell of support for changing the filibuster rule," notes Peter Brown, assistant director of the Quinnipiac University Polling Institute.[58]

The point of this, however, is not to dispute the merits of the filibuster or actions of the Majority Leader; rather, it is to debate the necessity to spend federal funds to gauge Americans attitudes towards the parliamentary procedure.

The Obama Administration, which supported the move to end the filibuster,[59] is spending more than a quarter-of-a-million dollars out of the budget of the National Science Foundation (NSF) to study **"attitudes toward the Senate filibuster among the American public."**[60]

Researchers at Washington University in St. Louis received a $251,525 NSF grant for the project, which is now in its fourth year.[61]

According to NSF, "this research examines public attitudes about majority rule and minority rights in the United States. It does so by focusing on public views about prominent legislative battles involving the Senate filibuster - extended debate intended to prevent a vote. The Senate's cloture rule provides that a three-fifths majority of elected senators is required to close debate and move to a vote on a motion, a rule that allows a large minority to prevent majority action. This study exploits an existing survey panel to assess the public's views of majority rule and minority rights both in the abstract and in response to major legislative episodes. The study examines the effect of abstract views of majority rule, minority rights, and the filibuster, policy preferences, party preferences and other factors such as political sophistication and education on evaluations of legislative outcomes involving the filibuster."[62]

The filibuster has already been surveyed at length by public opinion polls going back to the 1930s. Gallup first looked at Americans' attitudes in 1937, when President Roosevelt sought to pack the Supreme Court and opponents filibustered the change in the Senate.[63] CNN, CBS News, Quinnipiac, *National Journal*, *The New York Times* and others have all sponsored independent surveys of the public's attitude toward the filibuster.[64]

NSF notes the findings of its study "will be reflected in on the investigator's textbook on congressional politics, which is one of the most widely-read textbooks by undergraduates on the subject."[65]

Regardless of whether or not the government's findings reflect the decades of polls taken without federal funds, all of these opinions may already be irrelevant. The right to filibuster nominations has largely been dismantled without the backing of public opinion and both the Majority Leader and President have left open the possibility of eliminating the legislative filibuster in the future.[66]

It is difficult to justify funding this politically motivated project while cutting off federal support for hundreds of scientific proposals. NSF announced earlier this year that a result of sequestration "the total number of new research grants will be reduced."[67] Approximately 600 new NSF grants were not funded.[68] But the filibuster research project continues to go on and on just like a real filibuster, which just happened to be partially eliminated.

5. Beachfront Boondoggle: Taxpayer's on the Hook for Paradise Island Homes – (HI) $500 million

Ever dream of escaping it all and owning a dream home on a remote island paradise? Didn't think you could afford it? Think again. There is now a U.S. Department of Agriculture (USDA) home loan program here to help you. Created to assist those with low and moderate incomes in rural areas obtain "safe and sanitary dwellings,"[69] the program has expanded to cover "mortgages for millionaires" and homes in suburban and urban areas, as well as seaside "resort communities."[70]

This year more than 100 individuals or families received loan guarantees for $500,000 or more from the U.S. Department of Agriculture to purchase a residence in Hawaii.[71] If these new homeowners later cannot afford their new homes, it's no problem; the federal government will protect the banks from losses by repaying 90 percent of the loans.[72]

These and thousands of other loan guarantees were issued this year by the USDA Rural Housing Service (RHS) Section 502 loan programs. The "Section 502 guarantee program and Section 502 direct loan program provide loans to low and moderate income individuals for the purchase of modest housing in a rural area. The programs had authority to guarantee $24 billion in privately sourced loans and make $900 million in new direct loans for FY2013."[73]

"There is no down payment requirement" for the loans,[74] "no maximum purchase price,"[75] and— according to USDA—the government "is *required* to serve all borrowers who meet eligibility requirements and seek to purchase homes in eligible areas" (emphasis added).[76] And despite the name of the program, it serves more than just rural areas. An independent analysis found that, "today, the program covers nearly the entire U.S. land mass. That has helped turn the program into one of the sweetest deals available."[77]

The program issued nearly 166,000 loan guarantees in FY 2013 and more than 100 of those were for "amounts greater than, or equal to $500,000." Nearly all of these half-a-million dollar home loans were in Hawaii.[78]

Many of the most scenic parts of Hawaii, including Maui and Kauai, are eligible areas for USDA rural loan assistance. Maui has been selected as the top island in the world for 20 consecutive years in the annual Condé Nast Traveler Readers' Choice Awards.[79] Providing a "combination of tropical ambience and American comforts," this island paradise offers "an abundance of activities offered, from whale-watching to nature hikes to watersports" with "unending natural beauty."[80] The entire island of Kauai, described as "a little slice of heaven,"[81] is considered rural by USDA.[82]

Since property values in Hawaii exceed the national average, buying a home there may seem to be out of reach for most, but everyone from risky borrowers to the wealthy are benefitting from this USDA loan program. The USDA rural housing program's "income guidelines are generous," notes a senior loan officer in Hawaii.[83] Likewise for those with more modest incomes, "the Federal Government will reimburse up to 90 percent of the original loan amount to the lender if a borrower defaults on a loan."[84]

Thousands of borrowers do foreclose every year, costing the federal government hundreds of millions of dollars, and the number and cost have skyrocketed over the past five years. In 2008, the program had 3,369 foreclosures costing in $103 million in loss claims paid. By 2011, there were 18,808 foreclosures costing $295 million. Last year, the program paid $496 million in loss claims, according to the USDA Office of Inspector General.[85] If trends continue, this loss will have exceeded half-billion dollars in 2013.

The department acknowledges default rates "vary throughout the year" and "during 2012, the delinquency rate for loans 30 or more days past due ranged from 7.65 percent to 10.44 percent."[86] By comparison, the delinquency rate "in a typical housing market is around 3 percent."[87]

USDA is subsidizing thousands of risky and questionable mortgages, including more than one hundred half-a-million dollar homes in Hawaii, while threatening to evict thousands of poor disabled elderly residents.

While designed to operate off of loan fees, the program's delinquency rates make a taxpayer bailout more likely according to experts who predict "it's likely the program isn't covering its costs and will probably require taxpayer funding."[88]

While USDA was putting taxpayers on the hook for generous and increasingly risky loan guarantees, housing assistance to low-income individuals across the country, including in Hawaii, was being cut. In March, USDA threatened the "elimination of rental assistance for more than 10,000 very low income rural residents, generally elderly, disabled, and single female households."[89] In July the Department notified hundreds of borrowers that their contracts would be cut off before the end of FY 2013,[90] including a housing unit for disabled elderly in Kailua-Kona, Hawaii.[91]

And while USDA is quick to threaten assistance for the poor, elderly and disabled, the Inspector General found the Rural Development program "did not identify and review loss claims from loans with questionable eligibility prior to payment," resulting in millions of dollars in improper payments.[92]

Before USDA kicks out low income elderly and disabled from rural housing, the department should first discontinue its risky loan practices that are costing nearly half-a-billion dollars a year in loss claims.

6. Pimping the Tax Code – (NV) $17.5 million

Through the tax code, Uncle Sam is assisting the operation of the legal brothels in Nevada. These businesses are antiquated practices from the days of the state's silver boom starting in the 1850s, yet they still manage to get special treatment in the tax code through exemptions designed for businesses.

Though prostitution is illegal almost everywhere in the nation, the federal tax code still allows brothels to qualify for standard business deductions and expenses.[93] These deductions significantly reduce a brothel's overall federal income tax liability, even though annual revenues for the industry have been approximately $50 million.[94] All while other sectors of the economy shriveled.

Brothels can take deductions for groceries, "salaries and wages of prostitutes, rent, utilities and taxes and licenses."[95] [96] The Mustang Ranch brothel, which was Nevada's oldest, reduced its income tax liability by also deducting costs of "promotion," which included "free passes." Workers are also allowed business deductions. "[B]reast implants and...costumes" have also been ruled allowable deductions by the Internal Revenue Service (IRS).[97] Workers can also deduct the cost of "equipment for that specialized stuff," noted one tax expert.[98]

About 19 legal brothels currently exist in Nevada.[99] Only 10 counties out of 3,007 in the United States allow prostitution, and all are in Nevada.[100] The counties alone have just 300,000 people. Brothels are hardly economic drivers for communities since most "are in rural areas with few people."[101]

Even though prostitution is deemed illegal under nearly every law in the nation, Congress must explicitly disallow businesses – legal or illegal – from making such deductions from their tax liability. The IRS argued before the Supreme Court that illegal activities should qualify for normal deductions, but the Court placed the buck on Congress to make that point explicit, which it has failed to do. A number of federal laws already limit the scope of what businesses are allowed to deduct, but brothels are not mentioned.

At least one prominent Nevada lawmaker has noted that allowing the practice gives the Silver state a bad name: "Nevada needs to be known as the first place for innovation and investment – not as the last place where prostitution in still legal."[102]

7. Mass Destruction of Weapons – (DoD) $7 billion

As the U.S. war effort in the Middle East winds to a close, the military has destroyed more than 170 million pounds worth of useable vehicles and other military equipment.[103] The total amount of equipment eventually to be scrapped—the equivalent of 77,000 metric tons—is approximately 20 percent of the total war material the U.S. military has in Afghanistan. [104,105]

The military has decided to simply destroy more than $7 billion worth of equipment rather than sell it or ship it back home.[106]

"We have a lot of stuff there. Inevitably, we overbought," stated Gordon Adams, a professor at American University and former defense official in the Clinton administration. "We always do when we go to war."[107]

Why just not leave the excess equipment in country for use by the Afghan military? A major concern is that Afghanistan's forces would be unable to maintain it. Moreover, there is worry the defense industry might suffer if the Pentagon unloads tons of used equipment on the market at vastly reduced prices.[108] This should be viewed as market correction and a positive outcome of the drawdown, not a reason to send valuable equipment to the scrap heap.

The most controversial aspect of the disposal is the mass destruction of Mine-Resistant Ambush Protected (MRAP) vehicles—the massive beige personnel carriers the Pentagon raced to build starting in 2007 to counter the threat of roadside bombs in Iraq and Afghanistan.[109]

The Pentagon has determined it will no longer require about 12,300 of its 25,500 MRAPs.[110]

In Afghanistan alone, about 2,000 of roughly 11,000 MRAPs have been labeled excess by the military. About 9,000 will be shipped to the United States and U.S. military bases in Kuwait and elsewhere, but thousands of remaining vehicles, each worth at least $500,000, will simply be shredded.[111]

The MRAPs were once in hot demand, especially by members of Congress. In 2007, Congress appropriated $4 billion for the MRAP program, which was ten times more than the $400 million requested by the Pentagon. The vehicles were as difficult to manufacture as they were popular. The 3/8-inch steel on the vehicles is difficult to produce, and only a few contractors provide it.[112]

In 2007, the Department of Defense made the acquisition of MRAPs its highest priority. More than 24,000 MRAPs were built for troops in Iraq and Afghanistan, costing taxpayers an estimated $45 billion.[113]

Congress' excess is now on display, however.

What was once the Defense Department's highest priority is now the Afghanistan scrap market's flavor of the month. Much of the military's equipment will continue to be shredded for pennies per pound on the Afghan scrap market. U.S.-made war scrap will likely be worth $80 million on the international market.[114]

The Army has roughly $25 billion worth of equipment in Afghanistan. Some military leaders simply wanted to bring most of it home, but they were overruled because the cost of shipping heavy equipment out of Afghanistan was too high. However, at least one top Army logistics official disagreed.

Lieutenant General Raymond Mason, Army deputy chief of staff for logistics, contended that since the estimated cost of shipping home and repairing the gear tops out at $14 billion, it makes sense to bring it back. "For an investment of $12 to $14 billion, we get $25 billion worth of stuff," he stated. [115]

According to Mason, "We are very good at getting in, but no so good at getting out."[116]

8. Let Me Google That for You: National Technical Information Service – (Department of Commerce) $50 million

One federal agency is charging other offices and taxpayers to provide government reports that are largely available free of charge on the Internet. It is essentially the "let me Google that for you" office of the federal government.

Home to more than three million records,[117] the Department of Commerce's National Technical Information Service (NTIS) collects "government-funded scientific, technical, engineering, and business-related information" and reports and sells them to other federal agencies.[118] Only it turns out most of what it sells can also be found for free on the Internet with little effort.

Established more than 60 years ago, NTIS is a vestige of the pre-Internet era when a lot of the reports the agency collects were not widely available; however, as times have changed agency has not.

Required by law to be largely self-sustaining,[119] NTIS charges other federal agencies to access its collection of reports. However, a November 2012 review of the office by GAO uncovered that about three-quarters of the reports in the NTIS archives were available from other public sources. Specifically, "GAO estimated that approximately 621,917, or about 74 percent, of the 841,502 reports were readily available from one of the other four publicly available sources GAO searched."

GAO explains, "The source that most often had the reports GAO was searching for was another website located at http://www.Google.com."[120] In addition, reports could be found on the website of the issuing federal department, the Government Printing Office's website, or USA.gov.[121]

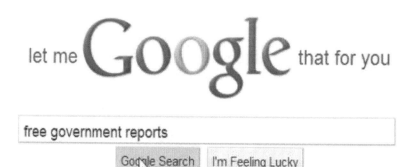

Yet, federal departments continue to send taxpayer dollars to NTIS for reports they could get for free with a simple web search. NTIS notes that one of its best-sellers[122] is the Armed Forces Recipe Service, available on CD-ROM for $79.[123] However, the Armed Forces Recipe Service recipe index is also available online and can be downloaded for free directly from the Quartermaster Corps Website.[124] Further, a recipe index that offers "1,700 convenient recipes for groups of 100 that can be easily adjusted up or down,"[125] likely falls outside the scope of technical, scientific, and engineering reports the office should be collecting.

Another report sold by NTIS is the 2009 Public Health Service Food Code produced by the Department of Health and Human Services (HHS), which is available for $69.[126] Alternatively, the report is available for free on the Food and Drug Administration's website.[127]

Moreover, GAO found much of the work outdated because NTIS has focused largely on growing its repertoire of older reports. "Specifically, NTIS added approximately 841,500 reports to its repository during fiscal years 1990 through 2011, and approximately 62 percent of these had publication dates of

2000 or earlier." While the office worked to accumulate reports older than those dated 2000, GAO reports that only 21 percent of the reports distributed from 2001 to 2011 were dated older than 1989.[128] Meanwhile, nearly 100 percent of the reports from 2009-2011 were distributed. However, these are also the most likely to be available online elsewhere.[129]

More than 12 years ago, GAO issued two different reports explaining NTIS would need to soon reconsider its function and fee-based model, as the Internet made of the reports it sold available for free.[130],[131] Shuttering the NTIS entirely was first suggested in 1999, by the Clinton administration's Secretary of Commerce William Daley, who contended "declining sales revenues soon would not be sufficient to recover all of NTIS' operating costs."[132] The Secretary "attributed this decline to other agencies' practice of making their research results available to the public for free through the Web."[133]

According to GAO, "the decline in revenue for its products continues to call into question whether NTIS's basic statutory function of acting as a self-financing repository and disseminator of scientific and technical information is still viable."

As the actual "let me Google that for you" website (http://lmgtfy.com/) explains, "this is for all of those people who find it more convenient to bother you with their question than google it for themselves." But when NTIS is doing the Googling, the search response comes with a price tag for taxpayers.

Federal agencies pay NTIS millions of dollars each year to provide government reports can are available for free online and can be found with a simple Google search.

9. Millions Spent Building, Promoting an Insurance Plan Few Want and a Website that Doesn't Work – (Department of Health and Human Services) At least $379 million

With nearly half-a-billion dollars in government funding put behind promoting a product relatively few people seem interested in purchasing from a website that doesn't work, Obamacare is perhaps the biggest marketing flop since Coca-Cola introduced the world to "New Coke" in 1985.

The cost to build Healthcare.gov is estimated at $319 million so far.[134] "The total amount to be spent nationally on publicity, marketing and advertising will be at least $684 million, according to data compiled The Associated Press from federal and state sources."[135]

As the Washington Post reported on Obamacare's infamous website Healthcare.gov, "when the Web site went live Oct. 1, it locked up shortly after midnight as about 2,000 users attempted to complete the first step."[136]

As time went by, things did not much improve.

Fewer than 107,000 people had enrolled in Obamacare as of early November,[137] even though more than 4.8 million Americans were notified their health insurance plans were canceled as a result of the new Obamacare rules and regulations.[138] There were only 23 people per day that enrolled during the first month in the Federal Exchange.[139] And the latest polls show growing opposition to the program, with 57 percent of Americans now opposing the Affordable Care Act, better known as "Obamacare."[140]

President Obama candidly acknowledged what millions of Americans had concluded after trying to use the new HealthCare.gov website: it was not working:

> "The rollout of the new health care [website] has been rough, to say the least... We always knew that that was going to be complicated and everybody was going to be paying a lot of attention to it," he said. "We should have done a better job getting that right on day one -- not on day 28 or on day 40."[141]

A significant part of the response to Healthcare.gov's failures, however, has been an intensifying ad campaign. "Ads based on research about the uninsured" have already been "popping up on radio, TV and social media. The pitch: If you don't make much money, the government can pick up some of the cost of your health insurance. If you can afford a policy, by law you have to get one." [142] The unintended punch line is the ads direct the uninsured to sign up for a plan on the website.

One health insurance company executive questioned "why would you spend $1 million sending people to a website that's broken."[143] A very good question since administration officials were warned by consultants in March that the healthcare.gov website was "at risk of failure."[144] Yet the Administration went ahead and signed lucrative contracts with a number of big name Washington PR firms for more than $60 million to promote the site anyway.

"In July, HHS inked a $33 million contract with PR giant Weber Shandwick. Centers for Medicare and Medicaid had already signed a $3 million and $8 million contracts. Porter Novelli also has a $20 million contract with the agency."[145]

As one Washington PR veteran noted, "you can have the greatest PR program imaginable on all different platforms — social, media, advertising and earned media — but you have to have a product that is functioning."[146]

The states setting up their own health care exchanges "will receive proportionally more federal money for outreach, advertising and marketing than" the states where the federal government is running the program.[147] In those states, "community groups with federal grants will lead the effort" to convince people to sign up.[148]

ABC News showcased what it labeled "The Strangest Ads to Promote Obamacare Sign-Ups."[149] Topping the list is Minnesota's ads "using legendary folklore hero Paul Bunyan (and his blue ox Babe) to show Minnesotans that the land of the north is also 'the land of 10,000 reasons to get health insurance.'" The two appear in a series of ads[150] "in which the famous lumberjack suffers some kind of typical Minnesota injury -- an axe wound, a water ski collision."[151]

Nearly $28 million will be spent promoting Obamacare in Washington.[152] One of the state's ads has a woman playing "paper, rock, scissors" to escape the attack of a rabid raccoon.[153]

Oregon is spending $10 million advertising Obamacare[154] with advertisements that don't even mention the program or how to enroll in it. One of the television ads, produced by the Portland advertising agency North, Inc., does not mention the word "insurance" or how or why to enroll in the program. Another Oregon ad does not mention the word "insurance," but features what appears to be Gumby riding on the Beatles' yellow submarine.[155] Between Oct. 1 to Nov. 30, however, just 44 residents were able to sign up for private insurance through Cover Oregon."[156]

AIN'T NOTHING BUT A HOUND DOG: Colorado's $20 million Obamacare campaign, which features an Elvis impersonator, has signed up fewer than 4,000 enrollees including one dog named Baxter.

Colorado is spending more than $20 million to promote the program[157] hoping to enroll 136,000 patients in health exchange network by the end of March.[158] So far, fewer than 4,000 have been enrolled,[159] though one of the enrollee's turned out to be a man's pet dog.[160] The state's ad campaign compares enrolling in Obamacare to winning at a casino and features an Elvis impersonator.[161]

Baxter.

In Kentucky, outreach workers attended a number of bourbon festivals and visited college campuses across the state to make young people aware of the program.[162]

California is spending $94 million on its Obamacare enrollment campaign, including "radio and television commercials, highway billboard advertisements, and a number of Twitter and Facebook posts" and promotion at county fairs and street festivals.[163]

10. Cost of Unused Mega-Blimp Goes Up, Up and Away – (Army) $297 Million

In an era of technological advances that make the machines of war smaller and more agile, the Army spent three and a half years developing a football field-sized blimp that would provide continuous surveillance of the Afghan battlefield – called by some an "unblinking eye."[164]

In 2013, however, the Army closed the blimp's eye forever when it brought the project to a halt after spending nearly $300 million.[165] The Army sold the airship back to the contractor that was building it for just $301,000.

The blimp, also known as the Long Endurance Multi-Intelligence Vehicle (LEMV), was intended to fly without a human pilot for up to three weeks at a time, recording everything on the ground. With an expected total cost of $517 million, an aggressive schedule was set to launch the helium-filled airship.

Army officials hoped to see the blimp flying over the Afghan battlefield by December 2011, but instead the aircraft made its first and only voyage in August 2012 – for 90 minutes over Lakehurst, New Jersey.[166]

Immediately following the flight – which was manned – the Army issued a release declaring the test "successful," saying the blimp, "can operate at altitudes greater than 22,000 feet above mean sea level, has a 2,000 mile radius of action, can carry a 2,750 pound [intelligence, surveillance, reconnaissance] payload for more than 21 days," and is highly fuel efficient.[167]

The Pentagon's Mega Blimp was a mega waste of money for taxpayers. After $300 million and only one flight, it was sold back to the contractor for 0.10 percent of what it cost to build.

Less than two months later, however, GAO released a report which showed the project had been plagued with severe problems.

GAO found the LEMV "did not meet their originally scheduled launch dates and have experienced cost overruns ..."[168] Despite its intended ability to fly at 20,000 feet for 21 straight days, GAO noted the airship was "12,000 pounds overweight" and would only be able to fly at 16,000 for "4 to 5 days."[169]

The blimp sat parked in Hangar 6 at Joint Base McGuire-Dix-Lakehurst until the Army decided to shut the project down in 2013.[170]

In addition to the cost and schedule mishaps, some noted how the blimp had an uncertain mission with the Afghan war winding down.[171]

It was not the first airship to be grounded by the military, however.

According to *Defense* News, "The Defense Department has spent more than $1 billion on at least nine programs in recent years, yet the military owns just one working airship, a piloted Navy blimp called MZ-3A, which is used for research."[172]

Army officials, with no more use for an enormous blimp, decided to salvage what they could and sold the aircraft back to the contractor for $301,000 – a fraction of its cost to build.[173]

After nearly $300 million invested in its design and construction, the Army was left with nothing but an empty hangar bay.

11. Pillownauts, Paid to Lie Around and Do Nothing – (NASA) $360,000

With 97 percent of its staff laid off, NASA became the most shut down agency during this year's government shutdown.[174] More than 17,700 of NASA's 18,250 employees were furloughed for weeks.[175] And the NASA administrator has said furloughs may occur again in 2014 if sequestration continues.[176]

Yet the space agency is paying 20 individuals $18,000 each to literally do nothing more than lie around for a couple months.[177] Subjects of NASA's Countermeasure and Functional Testing study "will spend 70 days lying in bed" with their "body slightly tilted downward (head down, feet up)."[178]

While participants in the study have been called "pillownauts," NASA does not want "couch potatoes" for the study, says researcher Ronita Cromwell.[179]

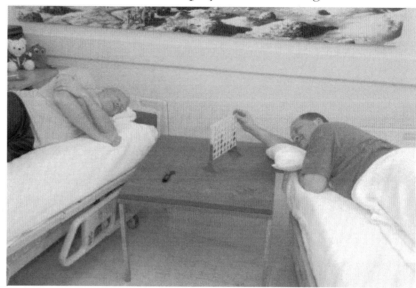

Two participants in NASA's bed rest research project. (photo courtesy of NASA)

Since the test subjects have lots of free time while lying around, participants are free to watch TV or play games. Some "write books or try to learn foreign languages, and some even continue to work if they have Internet-based occupations."[180]

The NASA Flight Analogs Project Team at the Johnson Space Center "maintains a dedicated bed-rest study facility" at the University of Texas Medical Branch in Galveston where NASA has been conducting bed rest research for years.[181]

A participant in one study said "the day I got up, after being in bed for 54 days [the study was cut short by Hurricane Ike], my feet hurt like crazy walking for the first time! But, I reminded myself, this is what astronauts go through, too."[182]

"A few people take a liking to the study and come back for more." John Neigut, a researcher with the Flight Analogs Project says "we have numerous repeat requests for people to come back to the study."[183]

Who wouldn't want to be paid to lie in bed all day?

NASA says the bed rest study "will help scientists learn how an astronaut's body will change in weightlessness during space flight in the future,"[184] presumably on a mission to Mars, which is the top priority of the space agency according to the administrator.[185]

No manned space missions to Mars—or anywhere else—are planned, scheduled or even possible in the foreseeable future, however, and NASA no longer has an active manned space program. But even in the event such a mission does occur, a lack of physical exercise during a long trip to Mars pales in comparison to the much larger health threat posed to astronauts by cosmic rays which can cause acute radiation sickness.[186]

Paying people to lie in bed and daydream of flying to Mars may be as close as NASA gets to sending a manned mission to the red planet. Perhaps the agency might get there sooner if it prioritized paying rocket scientists and engineers rather than people to just lie around.

Duplication? NASA has conducted the pillownaut study numerous times since the 1960's. But back then, NASA had real plans for long term space travel.

12. Indie Rock Music Execs' World Tour – (ITA) $284,300

With aging rock stars now old enough to collect Social Security, perhaps it should not be so shocking a genre of music that once represented rebellion and counter-culture is now taking government welfare and handouts.

The American Association of Independent Music (A2IM) received $284,300 this year from the International Trade Administration (ITA) Market Development Cooperator program.[187] This is "the first time" the federal government's "trade arm" has funded the promotion of the U.S. music industry.[188]

With the government subsidies, independent music label executives have been traveling around the globe promoting rock music in foreign markets[189] on what might be called "the Indie Rock Music Execs World Tour." Last year, ITA officials accompanied A2IM members on a trip to Asia.[190] This year the group was rocking in Rio.

Rock and roll—despite declining revenues—is still big business, generating $7.1 billion in the U.S. last year[191] and independent music sales now make up one-third of the U.S. market, according to Billboard magazine.[192]

Indie music execs rocking in Rio.

So why would those who represent indie rock—an alternative form of rock that resists the commercial influences of big money—ask Uncle Sam to sponsor their tour?

"We need to find new revenue streams," explained Rich Bengloff, president of the American Association of Independent Music.[193]

Whatever the excuse, the group is having a rocking good time courtesy of taxpayers. Government official joined 12 independent music industry execs—once cultural adversaries—on a multi-city trip to Brazil from April 18-22, 2013.[194] The agenda included a conference on independent music[195] and "marathon one-on-one meetings in Rio De Janeiro and Sao Paulo over four days, with a little R&R in between."[196] This included a side trip to Sugarloaf Mountain.[197]

Alec Bemis, the managing partner at Brassland label, spent time on the trip to Brazil "comparing the record stores, club districts and facial expressions of locals at the mention of his bands." He "spent a day strolling through a six-story São Paulo mall of tiny mom-and-pop shops devoted to rock music, posters and fashion." He concluded in Brazil, "lots of kids are into in Goth rock and hard-core, underground rock forms."[198] When asked about the success of his trip, Mr. Bemis said he "didn't ink any deals" but thought the trip it was a great opportunity, noting, "Oh, this could work."[199] While his label's bands and their fans may not have got to join him on the trip, Bemis points out "the internet has been creating a smaller, more connected world for over a decade."[200] This is a good point that further raises the necessity of government support for this and other trips.

As a result of the government funded junkets, Mr. Bengloff said some labels have "signed foreign distribution and licensing deals that will generate hundreds of thousands of dollars a year."[201] Coincidentally, that is the amount taxpayers shelled out to pay for the tickets of this tour that did not even get to attend.

With a growing market share, becoming the first genre of rock to ask for a government hand out, and even raising money for politicians,[202] indie rock and roll is sounding less independent these days and more like a special interest collecting corporate welfare.

The Indie Rock Music Execs World Tour may not have sold out, but the labels who participated surely did.

13. Status Update: Facebook Pays No Taxes, Instead gets a Tax Refund – (IRS) $295 million

With a status update no one will "like," the social media giant Facebook, is likely to avoid paying taxes in 2013, with $2.17 billion of net operating loss carry-forwards, while earning over a billion dollars in the United States last year.

Here is a status update no one will "like" – one of America's largest companies avoided paying federal or state income taxes, and is poised to do so again this year. In fact, they will likely receive a check from the federal government in the form of a tax *refund*.

Despite bringing in more than $1 billion[203] in U.S. pretax profits last year[204], the social-media giant Facebook reported a combined $429 million refund from their federal and state tax filings.[205] Uncle Sam cut a check to Facebook for roughly $295 million in 2012, according to one analysis of the company's 10-K filing.[206]

Facebook's first annual 10-K report filed with the Securities and Exchange Commission for 2012 details the company's use of the employee stock option tax deduction, which lowered the company's income taxes owed to federal and state authorities by $1.03 billion last year.

By providing stock options as a major form of their compensation, to date, Facebook has claimed $3.2 billion[207] in federal and state stock option deductions, $1.03 billion of which was used to offset their total U.S. pretax profit of $1.1 billion in 2012, and $429 million was refunded from its 2010 and 2011 tax bills.

The remaining $2.17 billion in stock option tax deductions can now be carried forward by the company and used to offset future tax liabilities. This rollover, in addition to currently outstanding employee stock options, may once again make this year's tax bill disappear.

Taxpayers gave Facebook a gift card worth an estimated $295 million in 2012, and Uncle Sam will likely cut the billion-dollar company another big check in 2013.

If Facebook has the same U.S. pretax profit in 2013 as last year ($1.1 billion), the company will be able to zero out their tax bill for the next year.[208]

14. Government Study Finds Out Wives Should Calm Down – (NIH) $325,525

If your wife is angry at you and you don't want her to stay that way, you might avoid passing along the findings of this government study.

Wives would find marriage more satisfying if they could calm down faster during arguments with their husbands, according to government-funded research.

The researchers observed 82 married couples. "The marriages that were the happiest were the ones in which the wives were able to calm down quickly during marital conflict," explained one researcher.[209]

"When couples encounter strongly negative emotional events (e.g., anger arising from disagreements, disappointments, and perceived betrayals) they often fall into primitive, survival-oriented mode of interaction," the study says. "In these interactions, spouses repeatedly attempt to justify their own behavior; criticize the other spouse in a harsh, contemptuous ways; make broad, negative attributions; and engage in nonproductive cycles of demand-withdraw behaviors."[210]

Those unions where wives calmed down quicker were associated with "greater current levels of marital satisfaction for both wives and husbands" as well as "greater marital satisfaction over time for wives." However, "husbands' downregulation of negative emotion (i.e. experience, behavior, and physiology) was not associated with wives or husbands' marital satisfaction."[211]

Men who want a happy marriage are probably wise to avoid telling their wives the government's advice to resolving marital conflicts is for her to calm down.

One example provided in the study of "negative events during conflict conversation" focuses on a stereotypical exchange between a husband and wife regarding how she looks in a dress. She says it is "pretty" and elicits "many compliments" when she wears it. He says he doesn't "think they are sincere" and that he "tolerates" her suit because it doesn't look "neat." He prefers a different outfit which she says is "for a teeny bopper."[212]

The researchers admit the study "had several limitations."[213]

The National Institutes for Health spent $335,525 to conduct the study.[214]

Regardless, men who want a happy marriage are probably wise to avoid telling their wives the government's advice to resolving marital conflicts is for her to calm down.

15. Lifestyle Coaching for Senate Staff -- (Senate Office of Education and Training) $1.9 million

Sometimes working in the Senate is stressful and means staying up all night to get your projects done.

Fortunately, overworked and under-slept staffers can take one of dozens of lifestyle coaching classes offered by the Senate to ensure they're okay.

The Senate Office of Education and Training offers Senate employees a wide variety of free courses on everything from the "Benefits of a Good Night's Sleep"[215] to "Pressure Point Therapy Workshop," in which students are taught "how to locate and relieve active pressure.[216] For its efforts, the office was provided $1.9 million in 2013 according to information provided by the office of the Senate Sergeant at Arms.

Oops! The Senate Office of Education and Training could use a crash course in editing and proofreading.

With little getting done in Washington this year, many taxpayers may think Congress is spending too much time sleeping on the job. Still, the Office of Education and Training provided a seminar regarding the "Benefits of a Good Night's Sleep" for the Senate community.

While the office is little known, even within the Senate, it made national headlines briefly in 2012 over a typo on the cover its course catalog.

After misspelling the word "training" by leaving out the first "N," one staffer remarked, "Ooh! They've got an editing and proofreading class!"[217]

According to its website, the Office "provides a variety of ways for you [a Senate staffer] to enhance your professional development and increase your performance and technical skills." These include such offerings as, "Assert Yourself: Speak Up with Tact Rather than Suffer in Silence," which will teach Senate employees the recognize the difference between assertive, aggressive, and passive behavior "without being a steamroller or a pushover." [218]

Other classes for the more reserved include, "Small Talk: Breaking the Ice in Social Situations"[219] and "That's Not What I Meant!," a one hour class that "explore[s] the difference between your intention and the impact of your words and behavior on the other person." It teaches the important lesson that "[c]ommunication is difficult and complex."[220]

In "Be Curious, Not Furious" students are taught how to examine a difficult work relationship, discuss the difference between labeling people and understanding them, and discuss five ways for understanding challenging behavior.[221]

Should that fail to do the trick, the class on "Forgiveness," defines the concept and explains the "[c]onsequences of holding a grudge."[222]

Some classes are there for Senate staff who slept through elementary, middle and high school such as "Making Subjects and Verbs Agree."[223]

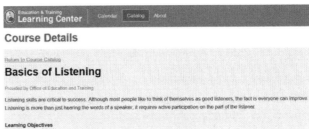

"The Basics of Listening" is one of the courses offered by the Senate Office of Education and Training. It is uncertain if the lessons were actually heard since senators seemed to talk past each other more than ever this year.

16. Money-Losing Sugar Loans Leave Taxpayers With Bitter Taste – (USDA) $171.5 million

When Americans borrow money from banks, they are usually also required to pay them back with money. When U.S. sugar producers borrow money from the taxpayer, however, they can pay it back with sugar.

It's all part of a convoluted, money-losing scheme to sweeten sugar producers' bottom lines – known as the U.S. Sugar Program.

In 2013 alone, the government lost $171.5 million because sugar companies could not pay back the government for money it borrowed.[224]

The 2008 Farm Bill created the Feedstock Flexibility Program (FFP) to increase the use of ethanol and biofuels. Under this program, the government is required, in times of surplus, to buy sugar from processors and to re-sell the sugar to ethanol plants.[225] Since the 2012-2013 sugar harvest season is the first to yield a surplus, taxpayers are witnessing the program's wastefulness for the first time. In August, the first use of the FFP, the USDA bought only 7,118 tons out of 100,000 tons of sugar offered for resale.[226]

USDA then sold this sugar to an ethanol maker at a $2.7 million loss.[227]

In its second purchase, USDA paid $65.9 million for 136,026 tons of sugar, and then sold it to ethanol makers for $12.6 million–a $53.3 million loss.[228] Facing a global surplus of sugar for the foreseeable future, the Congressional Budget Office forecasted the FFP to cost taxpayers at least $239 million over the next ten years.[229]

So how does the USDA end up with this surplus sugar to sell at a loss to ethanol makers? Because the USDA has lent over $1.2 billion to sugar processors in exchange for sugar in collateral.[230] In a move to protect U.S. sugar processors from foreign competition, USDA disperses loans for price support to ensure that U.S. domestic sugar prices are higher than the global markets and that Big Sugar keeps bringing in big profits. In the 2012-2013 season, 20,000 sugar farmers received $1.7 billion in net gains.[231]

Instead of repaying the USDA with cash from their profits, U.S. sugar processors and producers are actually defaulting on their loans and forfeiting the sugar they put up as collateral. American Crystal Sugar, the leading American sugar processor with 15.1% of the market, defaulted on its loan of $71.2 million, which is one-fifth of the government loans held by sugar processors who may also default.[232] While defaulting on a loan has serious financial consequences for the American taxpayer, American Crystal's President and CEO, David Berg, called it "beneficial to [American Crystal's] financial health," and "the way the sugar program is intended to work."[233]

American Crystal is not the only sugar processor not paying its bill to American taxpayers. Earlier in September 2013, USDA accepted 85,000 tons of sugar as payment for a loan due in August.[234] Although USDA swapped the sugar for import credits, the government had to swallow the $34.6 million cost of the loan.[235] As of September 30, 2013, 20 percent of the USDA loans, over $233 million, to U.S. sugar processors were outstanding.[236]

17. Tax-Payer Funded "Pole Dancing": NEA makes it rain for Austin performance group – (NEA) $10,000

"This feels like art," said one performer in the PowerUP Project, which features a troupe of Austin Energy employees who engage in performance art in Austin, Texas, "not so much like work."[237] But taxpayers are partially funding the choreographed "pole dancing" courtesy of a $10,000 dollar grant from the National Endowment of the Arts. In other words, the group's choreographed pole-dancing is being conducted at ta xpayer expense.

PowerUP is the an artistic venture of Forklift Danceworks, a performance group that "celebrates the extraordinary in the ordinary" by creating performances that focus on finding the artistic value in the mundane.

According to their website, the performance includes more than fifty linemen, electrical technicians and Austin Energy employees in a choreographed ninety minute dance with bucket trucks, cranes and field trucks, and a set of 20 utility poles, all set before a live audience – accompanied by the aforementioned pole-dancing[238].

A utility worker plays the accordion while another climbs a pole.

"The NEA funding really helps," says Allison Orr, Artistic Director of Forklift Danceworks, "First of all, it's a vote of confidence, it gives us a certain amount of respect and credibility that helps us to bring in dollars from other organizations."[239]

The creators of the program have said the show is to give tribute to the unseen men who provide and secure the power lines to one of Texas's greatest cities. But in an age of austerity and cuts to government services, the government might consider that one of the best ways to show support for blue-collar workers like these is to put more money in their pocket – not make it rain for pole-dancing linemen.

18. The Million Dollar Bus Stop – (VA)

"Is it made of gold?" asked one commuter after learning a single bus stop in Arlington County, Virginia, cost $1 million.[240]
The answer is no.

The SuperStop is, however, complete with heated benches and sidewalks, "wireless zones for personal computers." Yet it has one shortcoming—a roof that hardly protects from the rain, snow, wind or blazing sun.

With a total cost was $1 million,[241] the bus stop cost more than most single-family homes.[242]

It is large enough to accommodate two buses at a time, but has room to shelter only 15 people.[243] And where it lacks practicality, it seems to make up for in presentation: "The glass-and-steel roof swoops up like a bird taking flight" and "a wall made of etched glass opens the rear vista to newly planted landscaping."[244]

The buck—and the bus—stops here. In fact, one million bucks were dropped off here to construct the "SuperStop," complete with heated benches and sidewalks but little protection from rain, snow, or the blazing sun.

Can't take the heat: the SuperStop's high-tech screen couldn't stand up to a July heat wave.

One patron decried the high cost in an era of more important domestic challenges: "How much steel? How much cement? How much glass? One million [dollars]? Bring them to court. People are hungry. People are sleeping on the street. It doesn't need $1 million."[245]

"Where we're from, they built a whole highway rest stop for $1.5 million," noted one tourist.

The former chairman of the Arlington County Democratic Committee agreed with the sentiment, labeling the bus stop's construction "extravagant and wasteful spending on non-essential design elements."[246]

Some have questioned the open-air design of a roof slanted upward and minimal walls. The bus shelter is "pretty," one County Board member said, "but I was struck by the fact that if it's pouring rain, I'm going to get wet, and if it's cold, the wind is going to be blowing on me."[247] He questioned even calling the structure a shelter at all. "It doesn't seem to be a shelter. It doesn't really shelter you very much...you can get pretty soaked in two minutes."

Future Super Stops costs were budgeted at $904,000, but public outcry about the cost of the first was so high the county had to temporarily halt the process.[248]

The county is hoping to build 23 similar SuperStops and has received $8 million in federal funding since Fiscal Year 2004 to do so.[249] To date, only $1.5 million in federal funds has been spent on the project, leaving $6.5 million in the bank.[250] In FY2013, $102,986 in federal funds were spent on the SuperStop project.[251]

The bus stop is now under investigation. Arlington County has hired an independent contractor to conduct a "comprehensive review" of the project.[252] The investigation, which is adding more cost to the bus stop boondoggle, is likely to come to the same conclusion as the commuters and taxpayers in Arlington County: The SuperStop is a super waste of money.

Can't take the cold: the SuperStop can hardly be described as a bus "shelter." A December storm left the bench dusted with snow

19. Comic Book Superheroes Documentary – (NEH) $125,000

Americans have been holding out for a hero for a long time to go to Washington and straighten out the mess. But alas there are not many supermen within the halls of power these days willing to put the nation's interests above their own, so why shouldn't turn to imaginary heroes from the pages of comic books instead?

That is exactly what two government agencies are doing to celebrate the 75th anniversary of the debut of Superman, considered by many to be the first comic book superhero, in *Action Comics #1*.

To mark the milestone, the National Endowment for the Humanities (NEH) and the National Endowment for the Arts (NEA) have financed the production of a documentary, "*Superheroes: A Never-Ending Battle*," looking back at the history of comics and their impact.[253] The three part documentary aired on Public Broadcasting Service (PBS) in October[254] and is now available for purchase.

That's right, you paid to produce the series and now you can purchase your own copy for $24.99).[255]

The *Superheroes* project has received three federal grants totaling $825,000 over the past three years: A $125,000 NEH grant provided in July,[256] another $675,000 NEH grant awarded in September 2010 and a $25,000 NEA grant in August 2010.[257]

Despite the existence of several other similar documentaries produced over the years, NEH claims

2013 marks the 75th anniversary of the first comic book superhero, Superman, in *Action Comics #1*. To celebrate, two federal agencies have funded a documentary, *Superheroes: A Never-Ending Battle*, looking back at the history of comics and their impact over the years.

"*Superheroes: A Never-Ending Battle*" is the first documentary to examine the dawn of the comic book genre and its powerful legacy."[258] The History Channel aired "Comic Book Superheroes Unmasked" in 2005, for example, and "Comic Book Confidential," released in 1988 and re-issued on its 20th anniversary, won an award for Best Feature Length Documentary.[259]

This documentary is not the first time the federal government has recognized the cultural impact and influence of the heroes and creators of comic books. In 2008, President George W. Bush awarded the National Medal of Arts to Stan Lee, for "his groundbreaking work as one of America's most prolific storytellers, recreating the American comic book," noting Lee's "complex plots and humane super heroes celebrate courage, honesty, and the importance of helping the less fortunate, reflecting America's inherent goodness."[260]

Comic books have come a long way. In the 1950s, a U.S. Senate Committee investigated a possible link between comic books and juvenile delinquency. Today, comic books are big business and many of the characters they spawned star in the hottest summer flicks at the box office. Just last year, comic book publication sales exceeded $474 million.[261] The same year, "Marvel's Avengers," based on the superhero comic book featuring Captain America, Thor, Iron Man, and others grossed over $623 million in movie ticket sales.[262]

While there is no denying the influence of comic books and superheroes, taxpayers deserve real heroic action to confront the debt monster that continues to grow evermore menacing as a result of Washington's whimsical and wasteful spending on projects like this. Coincidentally, in *Action Comics* #1, Superman confronts nefarious behavior in Washington, D.C.[263]

20. Denali Commission Official Asks to be Fired and for Agency to be Eliminated Because "It Hasn't Worked Out" – (AK) $10.7 million

It's not every day an official with a leadership role within a federal agency asks to be fired and for his agency to be eliminated.

It happened this summer.

"I have concluded that [my agency] is a congressional experiment that hasn't worked out in practice," wrote Mike Marsh, the Inspector General for the Denali Commission.[264] Marsh said the commission's mission had "run its course"[265] and that it was time to cut it off from federal funding.

The request did not go unnoticed.

"**Fire Me**" proclaimed the front page headline of the print edition of *The Washington Post* reporting on the unusual request.[266]

Yet Congress ignored his request and the agency continues to receive federal funds. No hearings were held about the future of the agency or even to defend the money it had spent or work it has done over the past 15 years.

Few federal agencies have the distinction now being worn by the Denali Commission. In 2013, the agency's inspector general said the commission's mission had "run its course"[267] and that it was time to cut it off from federal funding.[268]

Washington Post after the inspector general asked for his agency to be eliminated because it was a 15 year old failed "experiment that hasn't worked out in practice." Congress ignored his request and the agency

Denali was established by Congress through the Denali Commission Act of 1998[269] to promote rural development in the State of Alaska,[270] also known as the "bush" communities. Projects include power generation, transition facilities, communication systems, water and sewer systems and other infrastructure needs.

The Commission's goal is to deliver services of the federal government in the most cost-effective manner by reducing administrative and overhead costs.[271] In 2013, the commission received $10.7 million in federal funds and for fiscal year 2014, the Obama Administration requested $7.4 million.[272]

Despite these goals, and 15 years of existence, the Inspector General for Denali urged Congress to "sunset Denali as a federal entity and convert it into a nonfederal entity."[273]

Much of the Inspector General's concerns lie with his belief that many bush communities cannot financially sustain the Commission's investments, and thus the money is wasted and the communities do not benefit. Most of the commission's money has gone towards supplying the towns with powerhouses, tank farms, and medical clinics, but in many cases there is not additional funding, staff, and upkeep expertise to keep these facilities running.

According to the Inspector General, Denali records show it has spent around $200 million on facilities in 81 Alaskan locations with populations of less than 250 people. [274] Further, the total population served in these 81 locations totaled less than 10,000 people – or less than two percent of the state's population.[275]

Denali is run by roughly 15 full-time employees who interface with the federal government and Alaskan state agencies, among other entities. The Inspector General described Denali, however, as nothing more than a "middleman" that provides an unnecessary link in the funding chain. Further, the Inspector General believes the Alaskan State agencies are "far more technically sophisticated" than the small Denali staff and can deal with cabinet-level personnel in a more effective way.[276]

After more than a decade on the job overseeing the commission, Inspector General Mike Marsh asked that "Congress no longer send Denali an annual 'base' appropriation" but instead find ways to help it "leave the federal nest."[277]

21. Federal Program Plays Secret Santa to Special Interests – (USDA) $50 million

While the U.S. Department of Agriculture (USDA) sounded a lot like Scrooge this year by threatening to cut nutrition assistance for low income women and children,[278] it was behaving like a secret Santa to special interests spreading good cheer and taxpayer dollars through the Specialty Crop Block Grant Program. Here are more than a few other examples how the program spent $50 million to ring in the holidays early in 2013:

Rockin' Around the Christmas Tree. Yes, Virginia, there is a Santa Clause. And the Virginia Christmas Tree Growers Association is one of the six projects involving Christmas trees that was funded. These included shearing, marketing and promoting Christmas trees.[279] The program also supported at least five ornamental plant initiatives, including a project to "to increase consumers' awareness and preference for Florida-grown ornamental plants by investigating determinants of consumer purchasing behavior such as personal health and wellness benefits and environmental and economic benefits and by developing contextually relevant marketing strategies to increase plant sales" and another to support seminars on ornamental plants at the South Carolina Nursery and Landscape Association conference.[280]

Visions of Sugar-plums Dancing in Their Heads. The Specialty Crop Block Grant Program had a sweet tooth for sugar producers this year and gave the plum growers reason to dance. The California Dried Plum Board received taxpayer dollars "to enhance the market for" prunes in Japan and South Korea. Funding was provided for "developing and implementing a comprehensive social media marketing campaign" for the Vermont Maple Sugar Makers' Association, "organizing and promoting a Maple Weekend including a recipe contest, tours of sugarhouses, restaurant participation, and promotional activities" with the Massachusetts Maple Producers Association, and partnering with the Michigan Maple Syrup Association "to increase the profitability of Michigan maple syrup producers by developing planting stock for new sugar bushes with a higher sap sugar."[281]

While blaming sequestration for being a Grinch to poor women and children, USDA played secret Santa to special interests.

Global Santa Tracker. Just like Santa with his bag full of toys, the USDA Specialty Crop Block Grant Program traveled around the world this year spreading joy, with more than ten grants paying for international junkets. These included conducting the "USA Pear Road Show" in China, sending representatives from the Oklahoma Pecan Growers Association to international tradeshows, bringing wine connoisseurs from China to Washington state, supporting the participation of Puerto Rican coffee producers in the Specialty Coffee Association of Europe trade shows, hosting seminars on "cooking with pistachios and prunes" in Japan and South Korea, putting on "meetings, product showcases, trade tastings, and educational seminars" for Oregon producers in Asia, facilitating a bean grower field day in Mexico, supporting attendance at domestic and international trade shows for Michigan groups and companies, and assisting with a "trade development mission" to Vietnam, the Philippines and Hong Kong.[282]

Holiday Wine and Spirits. Santa may enjoy a glass of milk with cookies to get him through a busy evening of delivering holiday gifts and cheer, but the Specialty Crop Block Grant Program showed a preference for wine. The program funded 35 wine related projects this year. These included creating two smart phone apps to help "navigate to the next winery," promoting wine trails and sales, improving wine tasting room satisfaction, and developing a West Virginia wine trail publication, and hosting a Wine Pavilion at the South Dakota State Fair.[283]

Making a List and Checking It Twice. When making a list of duplicative government programs, the Specialty Crop Block Grant Program is sure to be on it at least twice since it mirrors in many ways at least two other USDA programs, the Market Access Program and Value-Added Producer Grants.

While not all of the projects funded by the Specialty Crop Block Grant Program were wasteful, nearly all were eligible for funding from other federal programs making the program unnecessary. The largest proportion of grants was provided for marketing and promotion, such as social media for strawberries and a YouTube video about the proper handling of watermelons.

And a Partridge in a Pear Tree: The "USA Pear Road Show," promoting pears as far away as China, was one of the two pear related projects funded this year by the Specialty Crop Block Grant Program. While a flight to China was included, no partridge was actually involved in either project.[284]

22. Federal Government Spends Millions on Apartments for Deaf Seniors, Then Decides They Can't Be Used by Deaf Seniors – (HUD) $1,236,500

After spending $2.6 million on needed apartments for the deaf, government lawyers now say the Tempe, Arizona based Apache ASL Trails (Apache) apartment facility violates the law because it has too many deaf residents. According to the Department of Housing and Urban Development (HUD), the apartment facility does not do enough to also attract non-deaf residents.[285] However, HUD funded this award winning project "knowing" the property was designed and built "for seniors who are deaf, hard of hearing, and deaf-blind."[286]

About eight years ago, a federal study found that deaf and hard of hearing persons face pervasive discrimination in the rental housing market.[287] So projects like the 75-unit apartment, designed specifically for the deaf started to be funded and built.[288] The Tempe, Arizona building is highly successful. According to reports, more than 85 percent of the units are occupied by deaf, deaf-blind and hard of hearing tenants.[289] Currently there is a long waiting list.

The apartments offer a much needed "independent living community for seniors 55 years of age located close to everything in the East Valley."[290] Most importantly, the apartments create a barrier free environment that facilitates communication among residents and between residents and staff. Additional amenities include a "video phone that allows residents to talk with friends,"[291] light-equipped fire alarms, and "blinking lights signal when the doorbell rings and when utilities like the garbage disposal and air conditioning are running."[292] It is worth noting that these additional amenities far exceed the minimal accessibility requirements mandated by HUD for persons who are deaf.

A community for seniors who 👋🤟✋🤲 to live with people who understand.

Apache ASL Trails Advertisement with Sign Language

HUD is now threatening to pull all Arizona housing aid unless the managers of Apache reduce the number of deaf residents to no more than 18 of the complex's 75 apartments or 25 percent of the available units. The National Association for the Deaf has described these actions as unprecedented, saying "There is no statute or regulation that mandates any such 25 percent quota, and the imposition of any such quota is an ideological principle that ignores the reality of housing needs for many people with disabilities including deaf and hard of hearing individuals."[293]

Apache residents say living at facility has positively transformed their lives and that they would be devastated if this housing were not available. One resident in sign language told a reporter that "I would be devastated. I would cry. I want to stay here, we need this place."[294]

Bernie Horwitz, A 73-year old Apache tenant, told *Arizona Family* in 2012, "I get the sense HUD is almost coming in here saying they want to get rid of deaf people."[295] A bipartisan coalition of members of the Arizona Congressional Delegation is leading efforts to resolve this matter in a manner that protects the current residents of Apache and the purpose for which the building was built.

HUD officials claim to have no plans to kick any of the tenants out, but their proposed actions will deny this type of supportive housing to future residents who need and would benefit from the accessibility features of the building. Also, the $1.2 million cost of retrofitting the apartments for deaf residents will have been wasted.

The federal government invested $2.6 million in American Recovery and Reinvestment Act (ARRA) funding and HUD grants into a $16.7 million project.

23. Terrorist Who Killed 13 and Injured 32 at Fort Hood Continued to Collect Government Paycheck – (Army) $52,952

When retired Army Specialist Logan Burnett is asked to describe the Fort Hood shooting he uses language that evokes both the immediate horror of combat and how the trauma of that day still echoes in his life. He remembers blood everywhere—his blood, and the blood of fellow soldiers—and thinking he was going to die. [296,297]

Now three years later, Burnett and other victims of that day are still dealing with the repercussions of the worst terrorist attack on American soil since 9/11. [298]

Thirteen people were murdered and 32 others were wounded in the one-man terrorist attack on Fort Hood, Texas, in 2009, making it "the worst mass murder at a military installation in U.S. history." [299]

While the families of the survivors and victims were fighting to receive military benefits, the Fort Hood shooter Major Nadal Hasan was cashing his paycheck. Since the shooting, Hasan has received over $278,000 in military benefits because the Military Code of Justice doesn't allow a soldier to be suspended until they are found guilty. [300]

"[It] makes me sick to my stomach," said Burnett of the Hassan salary payments. [301] "There have been times when my wife and I cannot afford groceries... gas in our car... times where we ate Ramen noodles for weeks on end." [302]

While soldiers like Burnett and others victims of the Fort Hood terrorist attack have had to fight the Defense Department tooth and nail to receive benefits, taxpayers have spent more than half a million dollars – $548,000, in total – on Hasan's imprisonment, and that number doesn't include his military benefits. [303]

These soldiers and the victims of the Fort Hood terrorist attack deserve better.

They deserve to know that their country values respects them more than it respects the man who tried to end their lives.

Retired Army Specialist Logan Burnett has faced physical, psychological, and economic hardships since surviving what was the largest terrorist attack since 9/11 at Fort Hood, while the perpetrator continued to receive a paycheck (and other military benefits) from the Army.

While Hassan was found guilty in August, Congress needs to act to ensure this type of mistake will not be made in the future.

24. NASA Searches for Signs of Intelligent Life ... in Congress – (NASA) $3 million

One of NASA's next research missions won't be exploring an alien planet or distant galaxy. Instead, the space agency is spending $3 million to go to Washington, D.C. and study one of the greatest mysteries in the universe—how Congress works.[304]

> "In collaboration with Georgetown University's Government Affairs Institute, NASA presents its annual Congressional Operations Seminar on Capitol Hill. Over the course of a week, attendees will be provided a comprehensive look at how Congress is organized, the key players and their roles, how the legislative process really works, and how Congress directly affects the daily operations of every department and agency in the Executive Branch. The seminar will be presented with a particular focus on NASA. Participants will receive briefings from experts in the field, have the opportunity to attend committee hearings, and observe floor action. Participants will also be provided a hands-on understanding of the congressional process and procedures as well as the culture that is the United States Congress."[305]

The space agency says there is a "high demand for this seminar" and it "is open to all NASA HQ civil servants."[306] NASA will be spending $3 million on this mission over five years from December 2012 through December 2017.[307]

"Many government agencies, including NASA, are continuing to experience restructuring, budget cuts, new missions, and numerous other changes. To help federal employees better understand the ways in which congressional actions affect the daily operations of every department and agency in the executive branch, NASA has a need to provide a first-hand understanding of congressional processes and procedure, as well as the 'culture' that is the United States Congress," according to NASA.[308]

Beam me up, Mr. Speaker! NASA is spending millions of dollars to study one of the greatest mysteries of the universe—how Congress works.

There is no question that the inner workings of Congress are as baffling and confounding as the other big mysteries of the universe, such as whether or not life exists on other planets. **The truth is, Congress does very little work these days and even when it does it is often unexplainable. Only 56 bills had been passed by both chambers and signed into law as of December 5, 2013,[309] putting the current Congress on pace to be the least productive *ever*.[310]**

These include the production of National Baseball Hall of Fame commemorative coins, the naming of a bridge, and the renaming of a previously passed law. But perhaps this Congress is better known for what it did not pass— a 2014 budget and not a single regular appropriations bill to set spending levels for agencies, including NASA.

This dysfunction is reflected in Americans' dismal attitudes towards the job performance of the legislative branch. Congress's job approval for 2013 is "on track to be the lowest yearly average" in the four decades that the Gallup polling company has been surveying Americans' attitudes. Only 9 percent of Americans surveyed approved of the job Congress was doing.[311] A poll by *The Economist* rates Congress even lower, with an approval rating of 6 percent.[312] [313]

Most college graduates have taken a course in American Government (or at the very least, seen *Schoolhouse Rock*) and are familiar with how a bill becomes a law. It doesn't take a degree in rocket science, however, to know that the current Congress has failed to perform its most basic tasks. NASA would be far better off looking for intelligent life elsewhere in the universe.

25. Parking Center Stuck in Park – (DOT) $50 million

A child born in 1997—the same year the construction of the Paul S. Sarbanes Silver Spring Transit Center began—is now old enough to drive to and park at the center. That is if the parking center was actually completed and open to pedestrians.

In 1997, local officials in Montgomery County, Maryland announced plans to spend $20 million and build a transit hub in downtown Silver Spring, just outside Washington, D.C.[314] The center was intended to allow easier pedestrian, vehicle and mass transit access to the DC Metro train system, Amtrak and the local commuter train, MARC.[315] The original plans expected the transit center to open in 1998.[316] Sixteen years later, the center remains shuttered and the costs have skyrocketed to more than $112 million.[317] In March 2013, local officials requested an additional $7.5 million.[318] Despite sixteen years in delays and cost increases

A child born in 1997—the same year the construction of the $120 million Paul S. Sarbanes Silver Spring Transit Center began— is now old enough to drive to and park at the center. That is if the parking center was actually completed and open to pedestrians.

approaching 500 percent, the federal government has provided 49 percent of the total funding to date.[319]

Sometimes it costs a lot of money and takes a lot of time to build something great. It took one year and 45 days, for example, to complete New York's Empire State Building for a cost of $41 million in 1931.[320] Maryland's Chesapeake Bay Bridge took 3 ½ years to complete in 1952, costing $45 million. But should it take more than 16 years and $120 million to complete a parking garage?

Construction of the transit center was completed in 2011, though it has sat vacant since. The latest round of delays and cost increases have been attributable to allegations that it was not built correctly, and may not even pass a basic safety test. Post-construction safety inspectors for Montgomery County found "concrete poured by private contractors [Foulger-Pratt] on the reinforcing bars on the top floor was not compliant with industry standards."[321] Another report released in March 2013 by a third-party, KCE Structural Engineers, found additional safety problems and said the structure may only last 12 years, rather than having "a minimum 50-year service life."[322]

Foulger-Pratt bitterly disputed the claims, but did say, "If there is an issue with safety here it is related to design. That's the county's issue, not ours."[323] On top of that, one of the firm's principles noted, the project was "fraught with mismanagement" by the county.[324]

By the end of April 2013, the cost of the structure had risen to $120 million, though it was still unclear when – or if – the transit center would open.[325] The county and lead contractor attempted to find agreement on a path forward, though the project's inspector had not yet signed off.[326]

26. Red Ink Pays for Red Wine for Red China – (California, Washington and the People's Republic of China) $415,000

Taxpayers are likely to get red in the face when they learn the federal government, awash in red ink, is paying to serve red wine in red China.

The U.S. Department of Agriculture is spending over $415,000 this year to serve up fine wines in China. This handout includes a $369,292 grant from the Emerging Market Program[327] and a $45,984 grant from the Specialty Crop Block Grant Program.[328]

The Emerging Market Program grant is intended to build "a community of 'influentials'" in China to create a demand for fine California wines.[329] The money has been awarded to the Family Winemakers of California (FWC) and Stonebridge Research Group LLC "to develop a roadmap on how to sell California fine wines" in China.[330] The project seeks to "appeal to China's 'aspirational' wine consumers by building the associations between the wines and desirable/prestigious/luxury

Taxpayers are likely to get red in the face when they learn our federal government, awash in red ink, is paying to serve red wine in red China.

experiences."[331] It would do so by "training wine educators who will then deliver the classes across China," according to the president of Stonebridge. "The only way we know how to win a wine customer's heart is to tell them the stories - about handcrafted world class wines, about the people who make them, the places and the history and its intimate connection to the soil, the people and the place. We believe they will realize that these wines are not only great value but highly prestigious."[332] This grant is the first of "an expected three year undertaking."[333]

The Specialty Crop Block Grant Program will bring Chinese wine connoisseurs to Washington state to meet with local wineries.[334] The goal of the project, which is being conducted in partnership with the Washington State Wine Commission and Visit Seattle," is to "build Washington State's reputation as a premier destination for wine tourism."[335]

Because China has a growing market, American wine makers have good reason to promote their products in the Communist country. In 2012, wine sales in China reached 257 billion yuan, about $41 billion.[336] The sale of American wines in the country totaled $74 million, up 18 percent from 2011.[337]

But it makes little sense for the U.S. federal government, which owes China over $1.2 trillion,[338] to be spending some of that borrowed money to pay for wine tours and tastings for Chinese wine connoisseurs, especially when our nation is struggling to implement the budget cuts imposed by sequestration. Real wine connoisseurs know what the best wines are, and don't need government-funded marketing to tell them.

27. Hurricane Sandy "Emergency" Funds Spent on TV Ads – (HUD) $65 million

In January 2013, Congress passed a bill to provide $60.4 billion for the areas devastated by Hurricane Sandy.[339] However, instead of rushing aid to the people who need it most, state-level officials in New York and New Jersey spent the money on tourism-related TV advertisements.

Making this particularly vexing for some local residents, the flow of disaster aid has been both paltry and slow. While many agencies were responsible for administering the aid, the Secretary of Housing and Urban Development (HUD) was appointed to lead the federal recovery effort. As of October 2013, though, only one person on Staten Island has received help, in the form of housing assistance.[340]

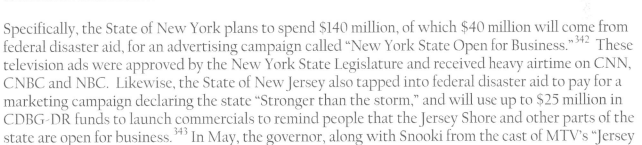

By contrast, funding from HUD for television ads flowed quickly. According to the agency, the federal government approved Community Development Block Grant-Disaster Recovery (CDBG-DR) waivers for the states of New York and New Jersey to allow the states special permission to spend disaster aid funds on tourism advertisements.[341]

Specifically, the State of New York plans to spend $140 million, of which $40 million will come from federal disaster aid, for an advertising campaign called "New York State Open for Business."[342] These television ads were approved by the New York State Legislature and received heavy airtime on CNN, CNBC and NBC. Likewise, the State of New Jersey also tapped into federal disaster aid to pay for a marketing campaign declaring the state "Stronger than the storm," and will use up to $25 million in CDBG-DR funds to launch commercials to remind people that the Jersey Shore and other parts of the state are open for business.[343] In May, the governor, along with Snooki from the cast of MTV's "Jersey Shore," held events on the shore to try and draw people there for the tourism season.[344]

Despite these efforts, though, tourism in the areas hardest hit was way down, calling into question the effectiveness of the ad campaign. Sales for the beach season at some Jersey Shore businesses were down between 20 percent and 40 percent over the year prior.[345]

NEW JERSEY ⚡ STRONGER THAN THE STORM
Plan your trip today

28. We Want a Shrubbery! Gardening and landscaping services at the Brussels home of the NATO Ambassador – (State) $704,198

In Congressional hearings on the terrorist attack on the U.S. Consulate in Benghazi, Libya, State Department officials have testified that "consistent shortfalls have required the department to prioritize funding out of security accounts...the funds provided were inadequate."[346]

So what items are a higher priority than security for embassies and diplomats?

The State Department spent $704,198 on gardening and landscaping services at the 28-acre Brussels home of the U.S. Ambassador to NATO.[347]

Included in the purchase were 960 violas, 960 tulips, 960 begonias, 72 Japanese evergreen shrubs, 504 ivy geraniums, 168 hybrid heath evergreen shrubs, 204 American wintergreens, and 60 English ivy shrubs.[348]

According to a State Department spokesperson, the official residence, named Truman Hall, "regularly hosts visitors from the 28 NATO nations and other Alliance partner countries around the world and is a valuable platform for America's diplomacy."[349]

The spokesperson also stated the contract awarded to Iris Greencare, a Belgian company, was the lowest technically acceptable price.[350] Perhaps the sequestration cuts influenced the State Department to set the maximum amount of solicitation to $500,000 for gardening and landscaping at the U.S. Embassy in Jakarta, Indonesia.[7351] The value remains to be determined for the solicitations for botanical diplomacy at U.S. Embassies in Santiago, Chile; Maseru, Lesotho; and Bangkok, Thailand.[8]

29. Counting Sheep While the Flood Waters Rise – (USGS) $15,000

With flooding anticipated, the counting of the animals began.

Not Noah boarding two of every animal onto his Ark to escape the great Biblical flood, but rather the United States Geological Survey (USGS).

This year, USGS shut down "more than 100 crucial gauges that warn of imminent flooding or lack of needed water" across the country.[352] The move—called an issue of life, property, and safety by the Chief Scientist for Water of the USGS—was blamed on sequestration.[353]

USGS claimed it lacked the $29 million in funding needed to keep the flood gauges operational.

While the budget cuts were blamed, perhaps the decision had more to do with drowsiness from counting sheep as a result of the expansion of the agency's aerial animal census program.

That's right, USGA was spending thousands of dollars counting sheep and other animals at the same time flood gauges were being turned off.

USGA counted pygmy rabbits in Idaho and elk in Washington,[354] eagles and trumpeter swans in Idaho,[355] Sand Hill cranes and sage grouse birds in Colorado,[356] sheep and deer in Nevada,[357] and seals and sea lions in Alaska.[358]

The U.S. Geological Survey utilizes two types of aerial drones, the THawk and the Raven.

The USGA's animal census is more sophisticated than the headcount of the U.S. population taken every ten years as it is conducted via aerial drones. The agency is utilizing "two types of aircraft: a battery-powered, fixed-wing airplane called the Raven and a gas-burning helicopter called the THawk."[359] The Ravens were "designed to monitor enemy positions from afar" and cost approximately $250,000 per system.[360] The USGS "got its first military-surplus drone in 2009 and flew its first real mission in 2011."[361] There are now 36 drones in the U.S. Geological Survey and the Department of the Interior fleet.[362]

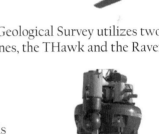

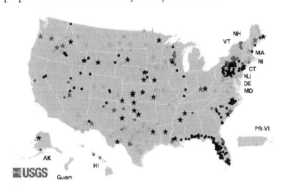

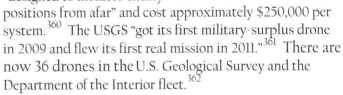

☆ **45 Threatened Stations due to Sequestration, State/local agency has provided temporary funding through September 30, 2013**

★ **10 Endangered Stations Due to Sequestration, Replacement funding has not been secured, Gage in process of being discontinued**

★ **31 Recently-discontinued Stations Due to Sequestration**

86 Total Stations with Funding Issues Due to Sequestration

◎ **86 Threatened stations, Funding unlikely. Station maybe discontinued -or- a gage converted to stage-only**

◉ **101 Endangered stations, Replacement funding has not been secured. Gage in process of being discontinued or converted to stage only**

● **594 Recently-discontinued stations due to funding shortfall**

781 Total Stations with Funding Issues Due to Funding Shortfall

The Department of the Interior acquired the drones, valued at nearly $15 million, from the Department of Defense.[363] Each sheep-counting mission costs $3,000 in labor expenses.[364] By comparison, it costs about $15,500 annually to maintain a flood gauge.[365]

Drone systems are stationed in Alaska, Arizona, Colorado, Idaho and Montana. Each of these states is also home to flood gauges discontinued or threatened by USGS.[366]

While the flood gauges were being shut down, the USGS expanded its National Unmanned Aircraft Systems Project.[367] In fact, there has been a 'groundswell' of Department of Interior drone use in recent years," according to Mike Hutt who manages the Geological Survey's National Unmanned Aircraft Systems Project Office in Denver.[368] "Every week brings more requests from other Interior Department agencies," according to USGS official, and those counts are going beyond just counting wild animals. In Oregon, for example, drones are being used to survey potatoes.[369]

While USGS was counting sheep, other entities tried to fill the safety vacuum left by the agency's decision to shut down flood gauges. The Colorado Water Conservation Board, for example, paid to keep four streamflow gauges running, that "were essential in warning of floods in the state" in September.[370]

Likewise, Washington cannot be caught counting sheep—or acting like sheep—as the rising tide of red ink threatens to submerge the American Dream. This means learning to prioritize true government missions. While counting sheep and other wildlife certainly has scientific value and can reduce the risk to pilots flying missions in hazardous conditions, flood gauges have scientific value as well as the potential to save the lives of thousands of Americans who otherwise would not be alerted to rising flood waters.

The cost of five sheep counting drone missions could pay to restore one closed flood gauge for a whole year.

30. Federally Funded Solar Panels Covered at Manchester-Boston Airport Because the Glare Blinds Pilots and Controllers – (FAA) $3.5 million

When officials at the Manchester-Boston Regional Airport in New Hampshire installed new solar panels, they did not anticipate one quarter of them would not be used 18 months later.[371] In Spring 2012, the panels were placed on top of the airport's parking garage, and 25 percent have remained there, covered with a tarp, rendering them useless.

Problems with the new panels were noticed almost immediately by air traffic controllers who claimed that for 45 minutes each day, glare made it difficult to oversee the airport's runways.[372] However, it is not as though glare was an unforeseen problem. Prior to the solar panel installation, the airport hired consulting firm Harris, Miller, Miller & Hanson to conduct a glare study and provide recommendations to avoid the problem.[373] While the airport followed the firm's recommendations, they were not able to avoid glare in the control tower. The firm received $41,570 for its work, despite the mishap, and has been asked by the airport to help solve the problem.[374]

Federal funds built these solar panels which are now blinding pilots.

The panels were paid for through a $3.5 million grant from the Federal Aviation Administration (FAA), which covered 95 percent of the total cost.[375] According to estimates provided by airport officials, however, the solar panels may never recoup their costs to install. Operating at full capacity, the solar panels might save the airport as much as $100,000 annually in electricity costs, and only $2 million "over the 25 year life of the project."[376]

Moreover, the FAA released its own guidance on solar panel use at airports since mid-2012, after the panels were installed at Manchester Airport.[377] It issued guidance in November 2010, but on June 26, 2012 – based on "new information and field experience" – cautioned airports against relying on it: "All users of this guidance are hereby notified that significant content in [the section on "Reflectivity] may be subject to change, and the FAA cautions users against relying solely on this section at this time."[378] The guidance was produced for the FAA by Harris, Miller, Miller & Hanson – the same contractor hired by the airport to conduct their own glare study.[379]

At the end of August 2012, airport workers were "moving the tarps about every three weeks, depending on the angle of the sun," calling the tarps a "temporary solution." Information on the airport's website noted they hoped the panels would "be repositioned and functioning at 100 percent capacity by next spring," but as of August 2013 tarps remained on a large number of the solar panels.[380]

Government logic: Spend $3.5 million to save $2 million over 25 years. Go figure.

31. State Department "Buys Fans" to Increase Facebook "Likes" – (State) $630,000

Hoping to increase its reach with an international audience, the State Department spent $630,000 "buying fans" for its Facebook and Twitter accounts.[381] The effort was undertaken by the department's Bureau of International Information Programs (IIP), which is responsible for "sustained conversations with foreign audiences to build America's reputation abroad."[382]

The fan-buying effort was an expensive flop. While the money was useful in generating thousands of "likes" on its Facebook pages – even generating 2.5 million fans – few people engaged with the department as a result. On each of its four Facebook pages, fewer than two percent even "liked" its photos and "[m]any postings had fewer than 100 comments or shares."[383] Typical of respondent's remarks for agency photos were comments such as "so nice pic."[384]

Moreover, when Facebook changed the way it displays items in a user's feed, starting in September 2012,[385] the usefulness of the State Department's investment plummeted. Under the changes, news items would no longer appear on a user's page unless it was from a site they frequented. Since many of the State Department's virtual "friends" hardly, if ever, engaged the department online the information it sent out would not be seen by its target audience.[386] The only solution available was to "continually spend money on sponsored story ads."[387]

32. NASA's Little Green Man – (NASA) $390,000

With NASA's manned space flight programs grounded for the foreseeable future, the agency seems to have shifted its focus from making contact with little green men to teaching children about fictional green ninjas.

The Green Ninja is a superhero funded by NASA funding to inspire children to take on climate change. Is this the type of little green men the space agency is focused on now that its mission to the red planet is shelved?

The "Green Ninja" is a cartoon superhero created to motivate "kids to take action on climate change."[388] Eugene Cordero, one of the creators, says "the goal of the project is to make the Green Ninja the new Smokey the Bear."[389]

"Support for the Green Ninja originally came from the National Science Foundation, but now includes funding from NASA."[390] The space agency provided a $390,000 grant for the project "to support professional development for teachers."[391] The 30-month grant from NASA will provide training for teachers "to use Green Ninja media tools in the classroom." These tools include lesson plans, short films and soon an iPhone application.[392]

Green Ninja has his own YouTube channel featuring cartoons,[393] and now episodes of "The Green Ninja Show," which was launched earlier this year.[394]

The animated climate-action superhero has a number of enemies he must defeat, including "a carbon ninja — the Green Ninja's archenemy —, plastic man, coal man and junky corporate man."[395]

While this project may be fun and even educational, NASA would have a much bigger impact inspiring young people to seek out careers in science and technology by focusing its resources on its primary missions. But with

In an episode of *The Green Ninja Show* uploaded to YouTube on November 5, 2013, the Green Ninja teams up with Dr. Burrito to teach kids that vegetarian burritos are more environmentally-friendly than those with beef. The episode had under 500 views one month after it was uploaded.

the manned mission to the red planet shelved, the Green Ninja may be the only little green man the space agency makes contact with for the foreseeable future.

33. Overtime Fraud – (DHS) $9 million

A recent report[396] has alleged "pervasive" overtime fraud and a "gross waste of government funds," at the Department of Homeland Security (DHS).[397] The type of overtime in question is the Administratively Uncontrollable Overtime (AUO), which can only be used by certain DHS employees. For example, border patrol agents frequently respond to situations that require them to work beyond their scheduled hours and AUO is invoked to cover this extra work time. Unfortunately, other DHS employees are abusing the system.

With the assistance of whistleblowers, the Office of Special Counsel (OSC) determined DHS employees routinely abuse AUO and labeled the problem as "pervasive."[398] OSC found nearly $9 million in improper overtime claims in *just* six DHS offices.[399]

One case involved the CBP headquarters in Washington, D.C. The overtime abuses occurred at the Commissioner's Situation Room.[400] One whistleblower, who worked in the Situation Room, described overtime abuses as "employees will sit at their desks for an extra two hours, catching up on Netflix, talking to friends or using it (AUO) for commuting time."[401] According to whistleblowers this overtime abuse was authorized by the Situation Room Director and Assistant Director and included about 27 employees for a total of $696,000 in questionable overtime claims.[402]

DHS has been aware of AUO abuse since 2008 and has done little to stop the problem. The lack of accountability by the Department has allowed this abuse to become an accepted practice.

34. Military Boneyard Boondoggle – (U.S. Air Force) $432 million

The Air Force is clipping the wings of brand new planes before they ever take their maiden flight.

According to its manufacturer, Italian aerospace company Aleniana Aermacchi, the C-27J was designed to provide tactical transport to support combat operations in remote and austere environments. The C-27J, which has supported combat operations in Iraq and Afghanistan, can take off and land from unimproved surfaces and airstrips less than 2,000 feet in length. The C-27J offers "superior and cost-effective performances in any operational condition, extreme mission flexibility, and is uniquely interoperable and interchangeable with heavier military airlifters."[403]

However, in 2012, the Air Force determined that the C-27J did not offer superior capability and capacity to perform general support and direct support airlift missions. The C-27J in fact could only perform the direct support mission and could not match the capability of the C-130 in respect to range, cargo, and passenger transportation.[404]

In August 2012, a former Air Force Chief of Staff testified before Congress that the Air Force did not want to acquire more C-27Js due to fiscal constraints brought by sequestration, the C-27Js limited capabilities, and because the C-130 was more cost effective than the C-27J (the C-27J costing the Air Force $270 million, while the C-130 costs between $204 and $216 million when taking in consideration the current basing construct for the C-27J and C-130[405]).

Contrary to the request by the Air Force to stop production of the planes, and even as it knew the planes would never be used, Congress continued to fund C-27J production in the Fiscal Year 2012

Tucson's Davis-Monthan Air Force Base will soon be home to C-27Js that the Air Force did not want but Congress ordered anyway.

National Defense Authorization Act. After taking its existing C-27Js out of service, the Air Force was then allowed to mothball its brand new C-27Js at Davis-Monthan Air Force Base in Tucson, Arizona -- 16 new C-27Js in September 2013 and an additional five in 2014 -- before these aircraft took a single flight in support of our service members, according to a *Dayton Daily News* investigative report.[406] Making matters worse, the DOD plans to mothball five brand new C-27Js which are expected to be built by April 2014, adding to waste of approximately 4,400 unused aircraft and 13 aerospace vehicles from the DOD and NASA, mothballed, with a total value of more than $35 billion.

35. Surplus MRAP's to Militarize Main Street – ($82.5 Million)

Everyone knows that Ohio State University football games can get wild, but campus cops may have finally taken things too far. Using a Defense Department program, the school along with dozens of other police jurisdictions, are receiving some of the military's surplus armored vehicles.

At a cost of $500,000 each, U.S. taxpayers gifted $82.5 million in surplus Mine Resistant Ambush Protected (MRAP) tactical vehicles to law enforcement agencies in 165 communities, including dozens of rural and sparsely populated regions.[408] Intended for large-scale emergencies, MRAP's are equipped machine gun turrets, bulletproof glass, and armored siding.[409] From Bates County, Missouri[410] to High Springs, Florida,[411] local law enforcement agencies in rural and small-town communities are being equipped with the same military-grade tools that U.S. troops utilized to fight the War on Terror in Iraq and Afghanistan.

Some local residents have objected, noting the weapons of war seem out of place here at home. However, said one recipient county sheriff, "It's intimidating. And it's free."[412] Provided by taxpayers' generosity, the same vehicles strong enough to protect U.S. troops from roadside bombs and machine gun fire and rockets are now being used "to deliver shock and awe while serving warrants" in quiet communities across America[413] through the LESO 1033 Program.[414]

One rural sheriff justified his need for an MRAP by describing, in his view, what a war zone rural America has become.[415] "While this vehicle may be extreme for Bates County to some people, I would call their attention to what is going on in rural areas across the country. Workplace shootings, school shootings, and violence in general are not just big city problems" said[416] the sheriff of Bates County, Missouri (population 16,709).[417]

The Ohio State University MRAP was "built to withstand ballistic arms fire, mine blasts, IEDs, and Nuclear, Biological and Chemical environments that threaten the safety of its crew."

Demand for the free vehicles has been high, though, with the Department of Defense receiving requests for **731 additional** MRAPs, from local law enforcement agencies across the nation.[418] The Warren County (NY) sheriff who was one of the lucky few to land one said he doubts they will even use it that much saying it will probably "spend most of the time in a heated garage."[419]

The Ohio State University police chief reassured students the MRAP will only be utilized for emergencies that occur on the campus, such as officer (not student) rescues, hostage situations, bomb threats, active shooter scenarios, and homeland security purposes.[420] "It's a more special vehicle than the typical armored vehicle. This one can go through water."[421]

36. Duplicative and Wasteful IT Systems – $321 Million

In December 2012, the U.S. Air Force canceled an Information Technology (IT) program that it had been working on since 2005. The Expeditionary Combat Support System (ECSS) was an U.S. Air Force Enterprise Resource Planning (ERP) system that was designed to merge base level and wholesale logistics systems, and to deliver hard net-savings for the USAF.[422] The Air Force scrapped the program after dumping $1 billion into the project, with no identifiable benefit to the military or to the taxpayer. Furthermore, the project would have required an additional $1.1 billion to fix and the system would not have been completed until 2020.[423]

Why settle for one IT system when you can have two that do the same thing? According to the Government Accountability Office (GAO), that is the practice at several federal agencies, which are administering overlapping and duplicative IT systems.

The federal government spends more than $82 billion on IT each year, but according to a recent GAO report three agencies have spent $321 million for overlapping IT purposes over the past several years.[424]

The Department of Homeland Security (DHS) spent over $30 million on two IT programs, both of which supported "immigration enforcement booking management, which includes the processing of apprehended illegal aliens suspected of committing criminal violations of immigration law."[425] The two systems identified by GAO are used by Customs and Border Patrol (CBP) and Immigration and Customs Enforcement (ICE), but both collect nearly identical biographical data on illegal aliens arrested for committing crimes. However, DHS said it has no plans to address the duplicative expenditures.[426]

Four duplicative IT systems were identified at the Department of Defense (DOD) with a price tag of $30.6 million. Two of these systems were in "Health Care Tracking" and two were in "Dental Management." Unlike DHS, DOD agreed to work to eliminate the duplicity, but the results are yet to be seen.[427]

The most costly duplicative IT systems GAO found are maintained by the Department of Health and Human Services (HHS) totaling $260.38 million. Four of HHS's systems related to "Enterprise Information Security," meaning the systems were used to "maintain and secure the operations and assets of HHS and its components." Two other duplicative IT systems were used for Medicare coverage and contained similar information by the same contractor. While HHS was reviewing whether it could consolidate the four systems related to Enterprise Information Security, it stated it was too costly to consolidate two systems related to Medicare coverage.[428]

"We find in many of these reports — and these two current reports are falling into the same boat here — they're well-intentioned initiatives, they're poorly executed and really there's not enough accountability," GAO analyst Dave Powner said.[429]

Powner added, "This is real money and there's lots of duplication."[430]

37. Keeping the Lights on in Empty and Little Used Federal Buildings - $1.5 billion

At 6.6 million square feet the Pentagon is often billed by the military as "the world's largest low-rise office building."[431] The massive amount of square footage in this building alone translates to miles of hallway space alone, but it is dwarfed by the amount of federal property that sits unused every year. If underutilized federal buildings were converted into Pentagons, you could line up 68 of them end-to-end and just barely have enough room.[432]

Many of these buildings, if not severely underutilized, sit empty but still require the normal upkeep that goes along with running a fully functional building. In 2010, GAO found several buildings that were not only empty, but were set for demolition and yet were maintained at taxpayer expense. One such building owned by the Veterans Affairs Administration cost $20,000 a year to operate.[433] A warehouse owned by the General Services sat completely empty from 2008 through 2011, during which time the agency spent nearly $2 million on it.[434]

A radioactive property and a property with a collapsed roof are just two examples of government property in serious disrepair. How does GSA rate these rundown buildings? Excellent condition!

Each year, the government spends *at least* $1.5 billion maintaining properties that it no longer needs.[435]

38. Be All That You Can Be...On Reality TV – (Army) $9 million

In the same month that the Army announced a plan to cut 80,000 troops from its ranks to reflect the country's military needs and budget restraints,[436] it was also testing a new method of advertising to attracting young recruits...at a cost of $9 million of taxpayer funds.[437]

Part reality TV show, part infomercial, "Starting Strong" aired 10 episodes on FOX in 16 large markets from June 2 through August 4.[438] The 23-minute long episodes are also posted on the Army's YouTube channel[439] and promoted on a Facebook page for the series.[440] The Army tapped both its media agency and advertising agency to purchase commercial time for the series and to promote the TV show on social media.[441]

In describing the role of advertising for recruiting, a spokesperson said that "joining the Army is kind of like dating somebody; you don't marry them on the first date.[442] Unfortunately for the Army and for the American taxpayer, "Starting Strong" was a first date flop.

Airing on Sunday mornings, "the real audience for ['Starting Strong'] is either asleep or on their way to church" and "are more likely to watch them on the GoArmy.com YouTube channel."[443] But as of September 30, 2013, the Starting Strong episodes on YouTube only averaged 35, 473 views.[444] These viewers only watched an average of 5 minutes and 35 seconds of the 23-minute long episodes.[445]

One review of the TV series best summarized how the American taxpayer should feel about the Army's infomercial. "[T]he Army brass should hope that budget-slashing, pro-sequestration members of Congress don't see our tax dollars at work."[446]

39. Camp Leatherneck Headquarters Facility – (U.S. Department of Defense) $34 million

As troops in Afghanistan were closing bases and sending military equipment back home, DOD was finalizing construction of a state-of-the-art, 64,000-square-foot command HQ facility on Camp Leatherneck that has never been occupied, and will likely be torn down, or turned over to the Afghan government as the facility will likely fall outside the camp's new security perimeter. [447]

[448]

No mere victim of changing battlefield conditions, the Marine Corps requested the project be canceled months after it was initiated in 2010. Nonetheless, the Air Force's 772nd Enterprise Sourcing Squadron issued a task order to AMEC Earth and Environmental Inc. to build the facility in February 2011, and the U.S. government took control of it in November 2012. Work has continued on the facility in 2013 to address deficiencies in construction noted in a Department of Defense Inspector General report.

Even transferring the facility to the Afghan Security Forces will necessitate additional costs for U.S. taxpayers. The building will require a "major overhaul" in heating, ventilation and air-conditioning systems because the building was constructed based on U.S. construction standards, not Afghan standards, and as a result, the power runs at a different voltage, complicating the transfer.

40. Bridge to Nowhere Still Going Nowhere – (AK) $2.9 million

An Alaska state agency is pushing forward to clear an expensive right-of-way for a controversial billion dollar bridge project that will likely never be finished.

The result is that thirteen homes and businesses that are squarely in the current right-of-way of the Knik Arm Bridge will be demolished.[449] The Knik Arm Bridge and Toll Authority (KABATA) has already spent $2.9 million to buy properties including several homes and an apartment building.[450]

Recently a Subway and a Tesoro Alaska franchise were scheduled to be shutdown because of the bridge, but they received a temporary "reprieve."[451]

The controversial Knik Arm Bridge, sometimes called a "bridge to nowhere" has long been the dream of developers seeking access to more undeveloped land. The first phase of Knik Arm is expected to cost around $750 million for a two-lane project. The second phase of the project which would expand the bridge to four lanes with more access roads will bring the costs to more than $1.1 billion.[452] However, a state audit of the project, which relied on KABATA's own data, put the cost at $1.6 billion.[453]

The seizing of property and land has some local Government Hill community officials up in arms. "We think this is a travesty," said Stephanie Kesler, president of the local community council. Despite the financial roadblocks for the project, "we strongly believe they are doing this to create the appearance of momentum and inevitability."[454] Kesler's group has called for all right-of-way work to be halted because the bridge to nowhere is going nowhere.

According to federal figures, more than $239 million had been allocated to the Knik Arm project in four federal laws. As of October 31, 2013, $67 million had been spent on a bridge to nowhere that is unlikely to ever be built.[455]

41. Pairing Prime Cuts with Wine – (Oklahoma) $200,000

This year, more than 637,000 Oklahomans saw a decrease in food assistance provided by the USDA.[456] While these Oklahoma families adjusted to a smaller budget to put food on their tables, USDA was simultaneously spending hundreds of thousands of dollars to serve up more Oklahoma wine.

Whispering Meadow Vineyards and Winery, located in McAlester, Oklahoma, received $200,000 from USDA to purchase new equipment including "11 new tanks and a new automated bottling machine" to increase wine production. With this new equipment, the winery is now "the most state-of-the-art winemaking facility in the state of Oklahoma."[457] As a result, the winery hopes to double the number of cases of wine produced every year and is undergoing some "major" renovations. "We are finishing the final phases of our barrel room that we call our "Wine Cave," said the owner of Whispering Meadow.[458]

What wines pair best with prime cuts? USDA funds effort to double the wine production of an Oklahoma winery while cutting food assistance to thousands of Oklahoma families.

While Congress is toasting to spending taxpayer's money, they've served up a glass of what has become their most popular, aged beverage: misplaced priorities and out of touch bureaucracy. The contrast below is sure to leave a bitter taste in anyone's mouth.

The winery is a genuine Oklahoma success story, and its need to expand to meet the demand for its products demonstrates both its success and why Congress must prioritize federal spending.

With a $17 trillion national debt, *everyone* needs to be part of the solution.

Danielle Morse, who receives food assistance, says she is prepared to "stretch her already lean budget to account" for the cuts. "As long as they're helping me feed my children then I'm not going to worry about how much is dropped, unless it was dropped a considerable amount," she said.[459]

Washington should demonstrate the same attitude. The wine will be fine without a government dime.

42. Paterson Great Falls National Historic Site – (NPS) $350,000

To the dismay of many Americans, national parks throughout the country were closed to the public during the 16-day government shutdown in October. Except for one Federal park in New Jersey the National Park Service determined should not have been a national park in the first place. Hundreds of thousands of dollars in annual appropriations are directed towards the site. Despite the federal funds pouring into the park, Paterson Great Falls is not official federal property and was therefore able to remain open to the public during the October government shutdown.

Graffiti can be found throughout the Paterson Great Falls NHP

Congress established the Paterson Great Falls National Historic Park as part of the Omnibus Public Land Management Act of 2009, a mega bill comprised of more than 160 individual public lands bills.[460] Local leaders hoped restoring the "historically significant landmark" that has "fallen into a state of neglect" will help provide an economic boost to the "postindustrial city struggling with drugs, crime and unemployment."[461]

The inclusion of Paterson Great Falls NHP into the Park System by Congress overcame objections from the National Park Service, which determined after a three-year study of the area "that the resources of the Great Falls Historic District are not suitable for inclusion in the national park system."[462] The NPS study further concluded" the estimated costs associated with the Great Falls Historic District are not feasible when considering the impact that such costs would have on existing units of the national park system in the Northeast Region."[463]

In 2013, $350,000 from the NPS budget was allotted to Paterson Great Falls National Historic Site—with little to show for it. A local newspaper reported, "in the past two years since the park was created, there's been minimal change at the Great Falls. The park does not yet have a fully-operating visitor's center, refreshment stand, historic exhibits or amenities available at other national parks."[464] Instead, visitors to the falls will find trash littered throughout the site, overgrown grass, and a significant level of graffiti, including on the statue of Alexander Hamilton.[465]

Disregarding the concerns of the National Park Service, Congress established the Paterson Great Falls National Historic Park in 2009.

Only a few years after Congress established the historic site, "the area is still littered with trash, graffiti and a run-down, forlorn feeling of neglect."[466]

43. You're Invited to a Hollywood Party at Paramount Studios...Sponsored by U.S. Taxpayers – (HHS) $195,000

Just days before the government shutdown, the Department of Health and Human Services instructed the Substance Abuse and Mental Health Services Administration (SAMHSA) to use its available grant balances to continue operating vital services.[467]

But instead of pooling together resources to provide critical mental health services during the shutdown, SAMHSA spent taxpayer dollars to throw a Hollywood party![468]

Five days before the government shutdown, SAMHSA rolled out its own red carpet at Paramount Studios in Hollywood.[469] In true Hollywood fashion, actors, directors, publicists, and stylists posed for plenty of pictures before letting loose at the federally-funded bash.[470]

This is not the first eyebrow-raising expense on SAMHSA's taxpayer-backed tab. Members of Congress from both political parties have questioned the agency's wasteful spending on frivolous and professionally-questionable conferences,[471] as well as the use of its federal grants to lobby against duly enacted laws by the grantees.[472]

With $168 million in sequestration cuts to SAMHSA preventing 330,000 people from receiving mental health services in 2013,[473] the House Subcommittee on Oversight and Investigations cautioned SAMHSA's administrator, Pamela Hyde, to "be certain that your number one mission needs to be fulfilled and everything else comes secondary."[474] After a lawmaker expressed her desire that "[wasteful] expenditures aren't being made...with the sequester and other cuts looming,"[475] Hyde stated that she "had no choice as public administrator but to focus [SAMHSA's] dollars and we do that every day."[476]

It seems that the mental health needs of Americans became a secondary mission of SAMHSA when it spent scarce resources on a taxpayer-funded Hollywood party.

44. Excessive fees for Justice Department Employees to Speak With Live Travel Agents Instead of Booking Online – (DOJ) $626,250

The Department of Justice is wasting money on air travel costs through a poorly designed travel website and by failing to discourage the overuse of travel agents, according to the agency's inspector general.

A September 2013 inspector general report on travel spending by DOJ employees found they too often turned to live travel agents instead of using the agency's e-travel website, GetThere.[477] DOJ travel was administered by a contractor, CWTSatoTravel (CWT), which provided both the online website as well as live booking services over the phone. Each time an employee booked airline travel on the website, the contractor would receive a fee of $6.49, while the cost of each booking completed over the phone would cost DOJ nearly five times more, or $31.[478]

In 2010, the agency began to reach out more aggressively to employees in the hope of ensuring flights were booked online 75 percent of the time.[479] However, by June 2013, DOJ employees were using the online portal for only 60 percent of their flights.[480] Since the agency purchases an average of 167,000 airline tickets annually, the cost of using live agents instead of the website amounted to $626,250.

Even if employees used the website it would have resulted in any savings for the agency, and in fact may have cost more. Design flaws in how flights were displayed often failed to show employees the cheapest flights, or if they did provided confusing information to suggest they were not allowed to choose them. The problem stemmed from the execution of a government-wide program called "City Pairs," which negotiates the price of any flight purchased by the federal government between 500 cities. While employees are encouraged to look for the City Pair flight, which does not change over the course of a year, they are required also to look for cheaper flights should they come available. DOJ's website, GetThere, would display non-"City Pair" flights as "out of policy" even though it was, in fact, agency policy to look at *all* flights. As a result, employees would often choose the higher-priced flight.

This is not the first time DOJ was called out for excessive air travel costs. A February 2013 report by the Government Accountability Office showed that a culture of excessive travel spending started at the top. The report found that from 2007 through 2011, the three individuals who served as Attorney General took 659 "nonmission flights using DOJ aircraft at a total cost of $11.4 million."[481]

45. Intergalactic Planetary Pizza Tasting – (NASA) $124,955

Pizza so good it'll send your taste buds out of this world! NASA may not be able to get astronauts to Mars, or even the Space Station, but the "space" agency is investing in pizza. This year, NASA gave a $124,955 grant to Arjun Contractor, a mechanical engineer with a small company hoping to build a 3-D pizza printer.[482,483]

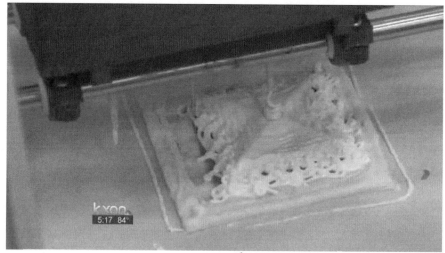

"Cheese topping" extruded onto dough.

Sprayed by a device that works like a typical, household inkjet printer, the 3-D victuals could be composed of dry powders that mix with water or oil. "This mixture is blended and extruded into the desired shape," says the grant description.[484] Pizza may be the optimal food because "it can be printed in distinct layers, so it only requires the print head to extrude one substance at a time."[485] Key components of the creation could include "international flavors and fragrances to ensure the production of nutritious and flavorful mission supplies."[486]

One of the reasons Contractor sees the project as revolutionary is "we eventually have to change our perception of what we see as food."[487]

Mmm. Just like Mom's.

Unfortunately, in being tantalized by the idea of such scrumptious delights, NASA may have forgotten about its other contracts for pizza delivery. In FY2012, NASA paid almost $1 million to one of the biggest government contractors, Lockheed Martin, to develop food for a journey to Mars. Every year, the average budget for Martian food development is $1 million.[488]

A NASA scientist involved in food research has noted that the research will take time. For ideas like this one, "[I]t could be years until it becomes feasible," she said.[489] Other foods NASA has sought to develop for a Mars mission – which will not take place for at least 20 years, if that – are "tofu bacon, scrambled eggs, caramel cake, lemon cake, French fries and peanut butter cookies."[490]

Uncle Sam is left wondering if he needs to leave a tip for his slice of multidimensional pizza pie.

46. Race to the Bottom – (Army) $29 million

Dale Earnhardt Jr. has a need for speed. The National Guard has a need for the best and brightest that America has to offer. At first glance, a sponsorship with a member of NASCAR royalty and one of the sport's most popular franchises would be a lucrative opportunity for the National Guard's recruiting efforts. But five years and over $136 million later, the Guard might consider putting this partnership in reverse.[491] Out of the 24,800 individuals who contacted the military branch directly because of the sponsorship, only 20 were qualified for military service and none of them joined.[492] Earnhardt may be able to go from zero to sixty in a few seconds, but when it comes to recruiting efforts his sponsorship is still in the pits.

But the National Guard just keeps doubling down on its bet. They've signed on to be a sponsor for Earnhardt's 2014 season.[493] With a shrinking defense budget, this is one case of spending that might be ready for the caution flag.

Not a single person has joined the Army National Guard as a result of the $136 million spent sponsoring race legend Dale Earnhardt Jr. over the past five years to recruit new members.

47. Postal Service pays "Futurist" Faith Popcorn for advice on stamps – (USPS) $566,000

Hoping to divine the future for stamps and how to keep "relevant, interesting and integral," the Postal Service contracted with "Faith Popcorn's Brain Reserve."[494]

Faith Popcorn is a futurist perhaps best known for her outlandish business predictions in her 1992 book, "The Popcorn Report." The *Library Journal* panned the novel in 1991, "While at times she exhibits a woeful ignorance of business history (e.g. Popcorn anchors the roots of consumerism belatedly in the 1970s), her thoughtful book is guaranteed to stimulate creative thinking."[495]

Futurist and USPS contractor Faith Popcorn

In 2006, she predicted "[m]echanized 'hugging' booths will take the place of pay-phones in many cities."[496] "[C]uddle parties" marked the beginning of this trend, she noted.[497] She also said genetic "engineering services will be able to create pets from scratch and pepper your future companion's DNA with your own. The result will be a unique representation of you: a pet that looks and acts like you."[498]

To assess the future of stamps, Faith Popcorn's Brain Reserve planned to hold several internal "BrainJams" as well as call in outside experts.[499] Ms. Popcorn herself, the "Creative Director," expected to bill 62.5 hours of work at the rate of $836/hour.[500]

Her firm is also doing other work for the Postal Service: "Innovation: A daily in-home visitation service for the elderly and ill."[501] In this service, mail carriers would offer to ensure people are taking their prescriptions or need any help.[502] Ms. Popcorn's firm is also studying whether the mail carriers should offer a "daily personal visit and brief chat" for a fee.[503] Apparently, she has predicted the future of the USPS to be a health care provider.

Given its extensive in-house resources, the Postal Service should focus on its core competencies rather than paying for interstellar predictions. The Postal Service does not currently use taxpayer dollars for its operations, but Congress continues to bail out its many losing operations.

A futurist might say that this doesn't portend well for the taxpayer.

48. Professional Golfers Get a Hole in One With Government Giveaways – (IRS) $10 million

While most avid golf fans would pay thousands of dollars to caddy for their favorite professional golfer, few realize they are already subsidizing the golfing industry and even the multi-million dollar athletes themselves. In a grand slam conglomeration of federal benefits, the Professional Golfer's Association (PGA), the PGA Tour, and the players, are putting for greenbacks when it comes to government benefits. Golf pros are in little need of government assistance, as evidenced by Forbes' recent list of the world's 100 highest paid athletes. Professional golfers hold five of the top 100 post, include the coveted number one slot, which went to Tiger Woods, who made more than $78 million last year.[504]

Highlighted in last year's Wastebook was the PGA Tour's tax-exempt status.[505] Despite generating over $900 million in revenue,[506] the PGA Tour classifies itself exempt from federal income taxes on earnings. Eliminating the ability for the PGA to claim tax-exempt status could result in nearly $10 million in increases federal revenue annually. Taxpayers should not be asked to subsidize sports organizations already benefiting widely from willing fans and turning a profit, while claiming to be non-profit organizations.

The PGA rakes in millions but pays no taxes due to their status.

Pretending to be a non-profit organization isn't the only mulligan claimed by the professional golfing industry. In fact, the golf pros are scooping up tax breaks for all their time spent on the links. Enacted as part of tax reform in 1986, the resident alien exemption for foreign professional golfers exempts foreign athletes participating in certain charitable events in the United States from being required to count this time in the States toward their permanent resident alien status (183 days).[507] In other words, taxpayers are providing a tax break to foreign professional golfers, allowing them to live in the United States and avoid paying taxes on their world-wide earned income.

The carve-out was targeted to the PGA, and at the time, The Philadelphia Inquirer reported, "The PGA's decision to seek Quayle's help may have been influenced by the fact that one of the senator's staff members - Greg Zoeller - is the cousin of 1984 U.S. Open champion Fuzzy Zoeller, Juday [a Quayle aide] said."[508] Twenty-seven years later the provision remains.

The 1986 tax reform effort not only banked this break for foreign golfers, but handed businesses a special tax break for purchasing tickets for PGA Tour events over other sporting events. Businesses are not allowed more than 50 percent of the cost for any entertainment event. Through obscure wording in law, Congress gave an exception for PGA Tour tickets, which can run over $1,000 per day for some tournaments.[509]

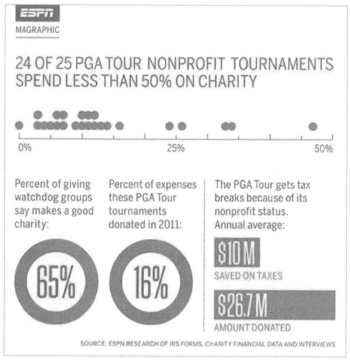

Businesses can deduct the full purchase price for PGA Tour tickets, reducing their federal tax liability by more than they might otherwise be able to do. This bonus for businesses is a bogey for taxpayers.

Digging taxpayers further into the golf subsidy sand trap, in 2004 Congress created yet another tax loophole for golfing superstars, who bring home millions of dollars in tournament winnings every year. With passage of the 2004 American Jobs Creation Act,[510] Congress granted the PGA an exemption for its unique deferred compensation structure, which allows a portion of player winnings to be put into a tax-free account based on their performance. The 2004 American Jobs Creation Act limited the use of certain types of compensation packages used to avoid taxes, but exempted the professional golfers receiving compensation packages from the PGA, further reducing their immediate tax liability.[511]

The full cost of these handouts to the professional golfing industry are unknown because of the clever and cryptic nature of the tax loopholes. Yet, it is clear taxpayers lose more than $10 million every year, likely more, subsidizing some of the highest paid athletes in the world.

49. IRS Employees Get Union Training at Vegas Conference – (IRS) $437,000

While Internal Revenue Service (IRS) employees sacrificed work hours and associated pay during government-wide furloughs, some IRS employees are being paid to spend hundreds of thousands of hours conducting union work, including union training in desirable offsite locations like Las Vegas.

In the first six months of 2013, and the busiest part of the calendar year for tax filings, IRS employees already spent 399,772 hours of taxpayer-funded work time on union activity.[512] In a practice authorized under law known as "Official Time,"[513] federal employees may get paid by taxpayers to carry out union duties instead of the jobs they were hired to perform.

This and other information unearthed by the House Ways and Means Committee shows that the IRS' cost of Official Time was $21.6 million in fiscal year 2012, and estimated costs for fiscal year 2013 are $15.3 million – including amounting to $437,548 on some but not all travel costs through June 2013.[514]

In 2013, the IRS allowed some employees to attend training conferences sponsored by the National Treasury Employees Union (NTEU) occurring in Las Vegas, New Orleans, Saratoga Springs, San Antonio, Boston, and the Washington, D.C. metro area.

One such training convention took place at the Flamingo Casino on the Vegas Strip, known for its "Margaritaville Casino."[515]

While the union said it would pay travel costs, IRS documents show that staffers were told to charge the "Citibank Government Travel Charge Card," and salary would still be covered by taxpayers under Official Time arrangements.[516]

While some authorized use of Official Time may be appropriate, lawmakers have also questioned the extent to which agencies like the IRS are employing this practice. According to a Freedom of Information Request secured by Americans for Limited Government, [517] over 200 IRS employees *spend 100 percent of their work time performing union work.*

In a June 27, 2013 letter to the IRS, U.S. Senator Tom Coburn and Representative Phil Gingrey also questioned the agency's choice to protect Official Time over other national priorities. The lawmakers wrote, "While the IRS continues to request more funding to further close the more than 14.5 percent tax gap, especially under the current budget crunch and sequestration, it makes little sense to use taxpayer resources to pay for union work."[518]

50. Playing Games with Taxpayer Money – (IMLS) $225,000

The federal government is literally playing games with taxpayer money continuing financial support for exhibits showcasing "the history of play in America."

The Institute of Museum and Library Services (IMLS) awarded a $149,903 Museums for America grant to The Strong, a Rochester

The National Museum of Play has received hundreds of thousands of dollars in federal funds to tell the story of how play in America has changed and remained the same with fun activities and a huge collection of games and toys.

museum, to assist with the expansion of its "artifact-dense, interactive, interpretive exhibit" *America at Play*.[519] It is the third consecutive year the museum has received funding from the federal agency.

"The Strong's collection of dolls, stuffed animals, toy soldiers, action figures, and other figural playthings is the largest diversified collection of such artifacts in a public institution in the United States, showcasing not only how toys have changed over time, but also how these changes have reflected and influenced American culture."[520]

There will be a number of play zones within the museum that "will illuminate changes and continuities in American play over three centuries."[521]

The IMLS grant to the museum is being "applied toward the fabrication and installation of a 4,000-square-foot figurative play zone that focuses on the history and evolution of play through pretend figures that represent living creatures" (sic).[522] This "figurative play" zone is "expected to open in November 2014 and will focus on dolls, stuffed animals, toy soldiers, and action figures. The final phase of America at Play will focus on toy vehicles and construction toys."[523]

The National Museum of Play spent part of several federal grants this year to finance the "America at Play" project.

Last year, the Museum was awarded $150,000 by IMLS the installation of an "exhibit on games and puzzles titled *Game Time!*,"[524] which invites guests to move like a piece on a giant game board through 300 years of games, puzzles, and public amusements."[525]

The National Museum of Play also received a $113,277 two-year grant from the IMLS in 2011 "for activities of its International Center for the History of Electronic Games" to "conduct a detailed conservation survey of approximately 7,000 video games" and for other activities intended to "save our video game heritage." Visitors can play *Pac-Man*, an arcade version of *Guitar Hero*, the latest PlayStation 3, Xbox 360, and Wii games as well as "discover how video games changed the way people play, learn, and relate to each other."[526] The museum provides a virtual tour of its International Center for the History of Electronic Games.[527]

With toys old and new and fun events like the recently held Star Wars themed "In Another Galaxy Weekend,"[528] the National Museum of Play offers fun and entertainment for kids of all ages. But our

$17 trillion national debt is not play money, so it is time to say "game over" to playing the taxpayers to pay for the museum's doll and video game fun zones.

51. Custom Crystal Wine Glasses and Barware – (U.S. Department of State) $5 million

Hours before the federal government was shut down and 800,000 federal employees were furloughed over the budget impasse, the State Department awarded a $5 million, multi-year contract to Simon Pearce, a Vermont-based specialty glassmaker, for the production of custom, hand-blown crystal stemware and barware for its embassies.

The State Department's solicitation for its fancy new glasses claims that the "United States international relations, national interest and success are, in part, built upon the ability of our ambassadors to entertain host country nationals in our embassies and residences abroad."[529]

Former Secretary of State Hilary Clinton furthers U.S. diplomatic interests over dinner/Photo: State Department.

And so the State Department is very particular about its glassware standards—in addition to glassware that is "free of imperfections" and sold in "high end retail department stores" like "Neiman Marcus, Bloomingdales, Saks Fifth Avenue, Bergdorf Goldman," the winning glassware was required to produce "a sharp high-pitched resonant sound when tapped with a metal object, such as a fork or spoon" and be emblazoned with the Department of State seal.[530]

If only the State Department was as particular about the performance of its programs as it is about entertaining dignitaries and diplomats.

52. Tinkling Away Tax Dollars; Human urine used to fertilize farm crops – (USDA) $15,000

The Rich Earth Institute (REI), a nonprofit organization in Vermont, received a $15,000 grant from the USDA Agriculture Research and Education (SARE) program for a project in which a hay field is fertilized with human urine.[531]

As part of the project, REI is hoping to collect 3,000 gallons of urine from volunteers.[532] The urine is then sanitized and "applied as a stream" to the fields to "encourage it to soak into the soil."[533] The soil will be analyzed for nutrients after the crop is harvested.[534]

Abe Noe-Hays, REI co-founder, says ideally "the urine you produce in a year can be enough to produce the food you would need for most of that year."[535] He said "we got 60 volunteers right away who said, 'Sure, I'd love to collect my urine and give it to your project," noting

"with this, every time people go to the bathroom, they feel good about themselves."[536]

Urinating the hay field.

Kim Nace, co-founder and administrative director, says "once you get through the 'ick' factor, people are really excited about contributing. Whatever the reason, people have strong feelings about human waste."[537]

RICH EARTH INSTITUTE **FERTILIZER FROM URINE** Clean Rivers. Sustainable Farms.

Home   Food Nutrient Cycle   The Problem   The Solution   Urine Project   Get Involved »   Media   About Us/Contact »   FAQ

Donate Urine

We are now collecting urine for the 2013 growing season!

Will you help us reach our goal of 3,000 gallons by July 15th?

We are looking for at least 150 people who live in or near Brattleboro, VT to collect urine for our second test project.

To sign up to donate, please fill out the form below with "urine donor" in the subject line. We can set you up with containers and suggestions to make urine collection easy.

The study, which is part of REI's mission "to advance and promote human manure as a resource,"[538] is the "first state approved and publicly documented use of urine as a fertilizer in the United States."[539] The study concept is not new. "Urine has been used as fertilizer since ancient times."[540] And over the past decade similar studies have been conducted worldwide in Europe, Asia, and South America.[541] A 2007 study conducted in Finland, for example, found cabbage fertilized with urine grew faster and larger[542] but that sauerkraut produced from the cabbage grown in urine tasted different. About two-thirds of the taste testers preferred sauerkraut made from cabbage not grown with human urine.[543] Furthermore, there was also no difference in nutritional value of the cabbage fertilized with urine.[544]

Whatever the outcome of the current study, the farmer who owns the hayfields being used notes "urine by itself isn't a complete fertilizer for food crops. The ratio of nitrogen to other key plant nutrients is too high."[545] For many consumers, the "ick" factor may be even higher.

53. Stuck in Neutral: Earmark for Transportation Center still Behind Schedule after 15 years – (DOT) $8 million

In 1998, the epic love story *Titanic* was at the top of the box office and people were able to "Google" something for the very first time. Congress was hard at work in 1998, too, earmarking millions for a state-of-the-art transportation research center. Fifteen years, multiple audits and investigations, and at least $8 million in wasted taxpayer funds, the research center isn't producing research, has lost its federal designation, and is openly referred to as a "boondoggle."[546] The project is so far off track, even its namesake patron has distanced himself from it.[547]

South Carolina State was designated by the Department of Transportation as a "Tier 1 University Transportation Center in 1998," which paved the way for additional federal funding to support transportation-related research and development.[548] With growth in transportation-related programs planned, South Carolina State University decided to build a new center, that was to include 6 new buildings and a 720 space parking deck with an ultimate completion date of 2020.[549] The project included a mix of funds from federal agencies, including the Department of Transportation Federal Highway Administration, the Department of Housing and Urban Development, the state of South Carolina, and other sources.[550] As of June 2011, total federal funding obligated for the Center was $24.3 million, with $8 million of that amount fully spent.[551]

As the project got underway, however, it quickly ran into problems, many of which pointed to a lack of management on the University's part. In a 2010 article, then Vice President of Finance for the University said "Everything that could possibly have gone wrong went wrong on this project."[552] The University held a groundbreaking ceremony in October 2005, but couldn't actually start construction. Why? Seven years into the project, the University didn't own all of the land needed to construct the center. After purchasing property in 2005, the University had what it thought it needed, until 2007, when the construction company figured out that additional land still needed to be purchased, and the University learned that it didn't own the streets.[553] It wasn't until April 2008 that the University resolved all of those issues.[554]

By that point, however, planning for the project had gone so poorly that the Department of Transportation revoked the University's designation as a Tier 1 center in 2006, meaning that additional federal funding under the grant program ceased.[555] According to a March 2009 letter from

Congressman Clyburn to University President Dr. George Cooper, the Federal Highway Administration was not pleased with operations at the Center, which led to the loss of designation.[556]

In 2008, the Federal Highway Administration wrote to President Cooper, stating that construction documents for the first phase contained "an inordinate amount of errors and omissions" and that acceptable contract documents had "not yet been submitted, resulting in over ten months of corrective work."[557] That same letter showed that, of the $22 million in federal funding made available to build the center, only $3.5 million had actually been expended.[558]

The history of problems associated with the Center was detailed in a 2010 article in the *Charleston Post and Courier*, including the additional strange twist that the chief architect hired, at a cost of $2.5 million, to design the center, died in April 2010, leading to additional setbacks.[559] Broader concerns prompted the General Assembly in South Carolina to request that the Legislative Audit Council conduct a review of the center, which was completed in June 2011, and which documented further problems:

> The total cost to complete the center grew from its original estimate of $70 million, to $107 million.[560]
> The project incurred $1 million in cost increases because companies who had lower bids for construction contracts did not sufficiently meet federal requirements and University-established goals for participation by "Disadvantaged Business Enterprises."
> Documents prepared by the architect included plans for "an executive office suite" in the Center "designated as being for the use of a Congressman" and for which the $455,000 cost was more than twice the cost on a square foot basis for other, similar office space.
> As a requirement of receiving transportation research grant funding, recipients are required to publish final research reports. The Audit Council tried to find public versions of the reports, but was unable to do so.
> University staff used grant funds to cover travel expenses, and received reimbursement for hotel stays that exceeded GSA limits. In one case, an employee stayed at a hotel with a rate of $199 per night in Clemson, South Carolina, when GSA's lodging limit was $70.
> University employees were paid twice in some cases, using grant funds to cover their full-time salaries, then getting paid with additional grant funds to work on individual projects.[561]

The report concluded by saying that South Carolina State University "has no viable plan" to secure the remaining funding necessary to complete the Center, and that management of the project has been so poor that the University is at risk of having to repay significant amount of federal grant funds.[562] So far, a research team of two people are the only ones to move into the single, scaled-back building that has been constructed thus far.[563]

When asked for comment in January, Congressman Clyburn had "no comment on the building that bears his name."[564]

54. Globetrotting Postal Regulator – (PRC) $19,000

Ruth Goldway, the Chair of the Postal Regulatory Commissioner (PRC), has been flying high on the taxpayer dime.

Since 1970, the PRC has overseen important facets of the U.S. Postal Service's operations. The 2013 calendar year has been a particularly busy for the regulator given the complex challenges facing the Postal Service as mail volume declines.

Despite these responsibilities, Goldway took six trips totaling $19,000 this year.

Compared to 2012, her travel costs have *increased* by $4,000.

Goldway's travel costs are rising despite coming under fire for excessive international travel in the past. In February 2012, Senator Tom Carper, requested detailed justifications and itineraries for all official trips taken by Goldway and those of her past two predecessors.[565]

Senator Carper stated that, "A significant increase in the amount of travel by the commission chair — or any member of the commission — raises legitimate questions. This is a time when the leadership of the Congress, the Postal Service and the Commission should be focused like a laser on the Postal Service's financial problems."[566]

At the time, Goldway was urged to limit trips to what was only truly necessary.

Goldway has pushed back on critics, stating: "I know that travel is an easy mark for people, but I really think that what we do is well within the bonds of responsibility and I make a special effort to make sure that any travel I take is extremely frugal. I'm a small person, I can get on a plane easily, but I think it's important to travel."[567]

Nevertheless, Goldway's travel costs increased this year, despite such pleas, and the majority of costs were incurred from international trips. The other reason this raises concerns is that, under law, the State Department is the *de facto* lead of international postal matters.[568]

Despite this, Goldway's international travel persisted and outpaced that of other PRC commissioners. In 2013, only one commissioner reported any travel - a solitary trip, totaling $3,100, to San Francisco for the National Postal Forum.[569]

Documentation of Goldway's travels also reveals a habit of adding personal days to PRC trips. While personal days are paid for with her private funds, documentation detailing Goldway's trips raise questions about the business importance of the trips.

For example, during Chairman Goldway's April 2013 trip to Bern, Switzerland, she was gone for 11 days to attend a technical meeting of the Universal Postal Union (UPU) for which two PRC staff would also be in attendance. However, for this trip, more time was spent on personal days and travel then in an official capacity. What's more, the UPU was conducting business on the 17, 18 and 19th when Goldway was on travel and personal time.

April 17	Travel to Zurich, No Meetings
April 18	Personal Day
April 19	Personal Day
April 20	Personal Day
April 21	Travel to Bern, No Meetings
April 22	PRC Staff Meeting, meeting from 3-6
April 23	Conference Meetings and Diplomatic Dinner
April 24	Conference Meetings and Diplomatic Dinner
April 25	Plenary
April 26	"prepared notes on plenary," Diplomatic Dinner
April 27	Travel home, No meetings

Goldway's questionable use of PRC funds extends beyond travel and to conference sponsorships. Under Goldway's leadership as Chair, the PRC has sponsored $30,000 worth of international postal conferences since June of 2010.

55. The Denver Museum of Miniatures, Dolls and Toys – (CO) $40,810

The federal government is adding to its monstrous debt by funding a miniature museum.

The Institute of Museum and Library Services (IMLS) awarded $40,810 to the Denver Museum of Miniatures, Dolls and Toys (DMMDT) to "create a digital inventory of its collection of 2,180 historic, iconic, and artisan toys."[570]

The "relatively small museum"[571] has a number of permanent exhibits, including "dolls; fully furnished miniature houses; miniature trains, planes and cars; giant teddy bears; a miniature circus; antique dolls."[572] "It is a great place to come think about the toys you loved as a kid, but may have forgotten. The museum's director describes the museum as "a place you can see what toys your grandparents may have played with."[573]

Rock 'Em Sock 'Em Robots and a variety of dolls of all sizes are among the toys exhibited at the Denver Museum of Miniatures, Dolls and Toys.

The museum was founded in 1981 "through the support of a grass-roots community coalition of miniature doll artists, business owners, and civic leaders" and managed by volunteers "with no paid staff."[574] But with this grant, "the museum will hire a full-time, temporary inventory manager to work with staff and volunteers to inventory and photograph the collection and update information in the collections database. The project will produce manuals, standardized procedures, and reports on the inventory."[575]

According to a job announcement posted by the museum, the Inventory Manager to be hired with this grant would be responsible for conducting a "physical inventory" and digital photographs of the museum's toy collection. The "essential qualifications and skills" required include "excellent problem solving, critical thinking and decision making skills" and the "ability to lift up to 50 lbs."[576]

The doll museum already has photographs of many of its toys posted on the museum's Facebook page.[577] There are also other doll and miniature museums in the United States, including the Great American Dollhouse Museum in Kentucky and the Doll and Toy Museum of New York City.[578]

This miniature tea cup, the size of a fingertip, can be seen at the Denver Museum of Miniatures, Dolls and Toys.

While it may seem important for the Denver Museum of Miniatures, Dolls and Toys to photograph its collection of doll houses and toys, it is difficult to justify the federal government funding the effort while at the same time trimming tens of millions of dollars from the annual

budget of the nation's premier museum institution, the Smithsonian, which may result in staff layoffs and even the closing of some Smithsonian museums in 2014.[579]

56. Studying Little Red Crabs Instead of Little Red Men – (NASA) $237,205

One NASA-funded venture may be enough to make taxpayers a little crabby. Our nation's space agency cannot fly people to the moon or even the International Space Station, but it is still studying little red creatures. Not Martians, but Christmas Island red crabs.

This year, a researcher at the University of Washington (UW) used part of a $1.1 million space agency grant to help analyze what triggered the sanguine critters to begin their annual migration from "their inland burrows to drop their eggs in the ocean."[580,581] In the salty seawater, the eggs develop, and the next generation of red crabs emerges.

Historical weather and migration data revealed red crabs generally begin their yearly journeys when rainfall reaches 22 millimeters in a certain timeframe.[582]

This knowledge about red crabs will likely be useful is very few places in the universe. The crabs certainly will not be found in Mars, or even any other earthly location. The Christmas Island red crab studied is only found on the namesake island.[583]

While not all of the researcher's NASA grant went toward this study, no NASA funds should be used to study ecological problems (on Earth, at least) already being addressed by our nation's premier scientific research agency, the National Science Foundation (NSF). In fact, NSF also funded a graduate research fellowship of another researcher on the project.[584]

57. Federal Government Paying Salaries to Hundreds of Thousands of Tax Cheats – $3.6 billion

While millions of Americans continue to send back portions of their hard earned wages to Washington, many federal employees are tax cheats.

During the year of sweeping budget cuts, millions of federal employees faced layoffs, furloughs, and other cutbacks as a result of Congress' failure to replace sequestration with responsible, targeted cuts. Most of these federal employees are responsible citizens who pay their taxes. Some, however, don't feel they have to live by the rules like other Americans.

In 2011, the IRS found nearly 312,000 federal employees and retirees were delinquent on their federal income taxes, owing a total of $3.5 billion in unpaid federal income taxes. This represented an 11.5 percent increase in the number of federal employees failing to pay their taxes, and a 2.9 percent increase in the total taxes owed the Treasury by these public servants. [585]

The 2011 figures, the most recent year for which data are available, include 107,658 civilian federal employees owing more than $1 billion in unpaid taxes; 141,980 were military and civilian retirees $2.1 billion in delinquent taxes; and 61,928 were current military with $329 million in outstanding taxes. [586]

It is inappropriate for any individual in violation of the law, including tax law, to retain full time employment with the federal government. And yet, nearly every federal agency and office, starting with the White House, Congress, and even the Treasury Department, continue to employ individuals who are failing to pay their taxes.

Congress, the Courts, and the White House have failed to lead by example, with the three entities employing a total of 1,622 individuals owing a combined $23.8 million in taxes as of 2011.

Federal employees have a clear obligation, just as the rest of American citizens do, to pay their federal income taxes.

58. Mo' Money Mo' Problems: Millions of $100 bills ruined – (Bureau of Engraving and Printing) › $4 million

The Bureau of Engraving and Printing has been reckless at the wheel with its license to print money.

Dubbed the nation's "money factory," the Bureau produces tens of billions of dollars of paper money each month.[587] Along with the U.S. Mint, which produces all of the nation's coinage, the Bureau is one of two—legal—manufacturers of U.S. currency and the sole printer of paper money.

One of the major initiatives of the agency in recent years has been to design a new $100 bill. Christened the "NextGen" $100 note, it is designed primarily to combat counterfeiting with state-of-the-art design features incapable of duplication by even the most sophisticated criminals. It will feature a Liberty Bell that changes color, a hidden message on Ben Franklin's collar, and tiny 3-D images that move when one tilts the bill.[588]

The Bureau has witnessed setback after setback in the rollout of the NextGen note, which was originally scheduled to be released in early 2011. [589] The redesigned note was released on October 8, 2013.[590]

According to a Bureau spokeswoman, the cause of the latest incident in 2013 is something known as "mashing," a defect that occurs when too much ink is applied to the paper and the lines of the artwork are not as crisp as they should be.[591] As a result of the mashing error, the Federal Reserve to date has returned over 30 million NextGen bills—worth over $3 billion—to the Bureau, demanding a refund.[592] The Fed has also refused to purchase any more NextGens from the Washington, D.C., plant in which they were printed, ordering instead the Bureau's other money factory in Fort Worth, Texas, to accelerate their production. A July 2013 memo from the Fed blamed inadequate internal control measures for the defective bills. [593]

What is the cost for this mashing defect? The new NextGen bills cost about 12.6 cents each to print.[594] Multiply that 30 million times over for each defective bill to get a total price tag of just under $4 million for printing the bad bills.[595] Additionally, the Bureau must dispose of the bad bills and spend additional hours making up for the mistakes made by employees of the agency.[596]

In its latest currency budget, the Fed reported that it would order 2.5 billion new $100 bills this year.[597] With NextGens costing 4.8 cents more per bill to manufacture than current $100 bills,[598] the Fed's request alone for the new $100 bills will put the taxpayer out approximately $120 million more than if the old bill design were to be retained.

These mishaps are on top of the additional $9.5 million in 2013 set aside for a questionable education program that includes global outreach efforts about the new $100 bill.[599] The $100 NextGen note, once heralded as a necessary cutting edge piece of technology, is turning out to be little more than a wooden nickel.

59. Brewery gets one on the house – (USDA) $450,000

How much money would you expect the federal government to provide to one of the more popular, financially successful craft breweries? Uncle Sam gave $450,000 this year to Alaskan Brewing Company to help them install a new environmentally friendly boiler.[600]

Alaskan Brewing Company, known across the country for its famous Alaskan Amber, is the 12th best-selling craft brewery in the nation.[601] The company sold 130,000 barrels of beer in 2011, an 11.2 percent increase from 2010. In 2012, sales continued to climb to 140,000 barrels of beer.

Alaskan Brewing Company will continue to make tasty beer for the masses, with a big profit boost courtesy of the federal government.

60. Scam Scholarships – (ED) $1.2 billion

Taxpayers are seeing their dollars thrown away to scam artists, and students struggling to pay for college may find higher tuition costs as some community colleges try to recover the millions of dollars they're losing each year from federal Pell Grant fraud and abuse.[602]

Out of the $33.5 billion in Pell Grants the federal government doled out last year, individuals posing as students - called "Pell Runners"[603] - took off with $1.2 billion.[604]

Given how easy it is receive the funds, it's no wonder there is significant fraud. When students register for classes at a participating college, they can fill out a financial aid form. If they qualify for a Pell Grant – based only on financial need – the federal government will issue the grant to the school.[605] The school then takes out the cost of tuition for the semester and sends the remaining funds directly to the student.[606] The student can use the leftovers to pay for a variety of purposes, such as food and living expenses.[607] Because community colleges are generally low-cost, Pell Grant recipients can have one or two thousand dollars sent to them for their personal use. [608] Once the money is received, however, scamming recipients disappear, leaving the school to try to find them to pay back the funds, and oftentimes moving on to do the same at another school.[609] Tracking down these scammers is nearly impossible, and the college usually ends up paying back the fraudulently received grant out of their own monies.[610]

At Henry Ford Community College this year alone, over $4 million of taxpayer money went to individuals who claimed they were full-time students, only to take the money and run, never actually setting foot inside a classroom.[611]

The federal government has not done enough to curb the abuse. Some schools have been taking matters into their own hands, implementing measures to try to reduce the incidents of fraud. Some impose a longer waiting period before distributing the funds to the student performing more stringent checks, one school waiting until 10 percent of the way into the semester, while other schools are increasing tuition, in part to cover the costs of Pell Grant abuse.[612]

In either situation, it's the honest students that suffer: longer waiting periods means it will take longer to get the money they need, and higher tuition costs means they will have to get by with less next semester when the college sends them a reduced check.

61. Extreme Makeover – (NJ) $141,886

Paterson, New Jersey, doesn't seem like a town that would be wasting money. With more than half its citizens living below the poverty line, it can't raise enough revenue to support the costs of running the city. [613, 614] Major infusions of cash from outside sources, particularly the state government, keep the city from bankruptcy. "Without it [state aid], our City will sink," Paterson's Mayor Jeffery Jones said in November.[615]

So it was a surprise for some Paterson residents to learn the city council decided to spend over $140,000 in federal housing aid to fix up an vacant property that had already received $260,000 in

Before

work by the city. Council members who opposed the spending pointed out that the city officials had spent more on the property than the house was actually worth.[616] (The house's estimated value is $171,000, according to Zillow.com.[617])

"I shudder to think what could have been done with the money," said Paterson councilman William McKoy.[618]

After

62. If You Build It, Airlines Will Come? – (FAA) $3,125,000

The St. Cloud Regional Airport is Minnesota's "Airport of Dreams," receiving over $24 million since 2000 for improvements and to attract commercial airlines.[619] But unlike Kevin Costner's baseball diamond in a cornfield, the millions of federal investments in the St. Cloud Regional Airport haven't lured the all-stars of the airline industry.

Despite $3,125,000 in federal aviation grants for its 9,000 square foot terminal and $750,000 in federal stimulus funds for a passenger boarding bridge, there is no daily commercial service at the airport.[620] To date, the only commercial airline carrier flying in and out of St. Cloud is Allegiant Air's bi-weekly round-trip service to Phoenix.[621]

It's not because the airport hasn't been trying to lure commercial airline service. The Greater St. Cloud Development Corporation launched a public-private partnership campaign called "Let's Go" to raise money to resume daily commercial flights.[622] The Let's Go campaign has raised over $6.1 million.[623]

With almost $10 million in public-private partnerships and federal grants, why is the St. Cloud Regional Airport *still* dependent on the American taxpayer? Perhaps the airport director, Bill Towle, best sums it up.

"We still move at the speed of public government, we just move slower."[624] Not only is this a huge waste of tax dollars, it also duplicates the work of the Essential Air Service program at the FAA, which spent $192 million in subsidies to lure big airlines to small airports.

63. Need Brains! Fighting Zombies with Pluses and Minuses – (NC) $150,000

Somehow zombies have gnawed their way onto Uncle Sam's payroll.

This year, the National Science Foundation (NSF) paid an interactive media firm to create a "Web-based, action-adventure, narrative-based, role-playing game where the player defends against zombies in an effort to save the human race."[625] While zombies are hardly something most people will ever encounter, the goal of the game is to teach middle school students how to apply math skills in "real-world tasks."[626]

NSF awarded the game designer $150,000 to craft the zombie experience.[627] Even with enough money to buy thousands of textbooks, the grant designer will not be building a full game. Instead, three "mini-games" will be designed and tested with just 80 middle school students.[628] Ironically, the same amount of funding could have paid the annual salaries of almost 5 teachers in North Carolina.[629]

Zombies are certainly not new to video games and have been used to teach math as well.   Uncle Sam must have been so stunned by the mongrels that he didn't realize other zombie-themed math games and apps already exist, such "Man Vs. Zombies" and "Maths of the Dead." In addition, a simple search for other math games and apps available for iPhones or Android turns up thousands of results. Free learning apps are widely available.

The Department of Education has previously awarded the company almost $1 million in grants to design other games as well.[630] One game, Math Monster Mystery, is "a compelling narrative, presented in motion comic format" and intended for elementary school.[631] Another, called "PlatinuMath," is designed to help elementary school teachers before they start their careers.[632]

Zombies can self-perpetuate, but taxpayers' scarce resources cannot. Perhaps the federal government should focus on groundbreaking research rather than low-priority videogames.

64. The FBI Investigates Hollywood Movie Plots – (FBI) $1.5 million

While FBI special agents courageously protect the Unites States against foreign spies, terrorists, gangs, and serial killers, a special unit at the bureau is collaborating with Hollywood movie producers to nab fictional mobsters and other imaginary bad guys.

Although the FBI has a sordid history with Hollywood, such as when it "conducted a sweeping and sustained investigation of the motion picture industry to expose Hollywood's alleged subversion of "the American Way" during the reign of J. Edgar Hoover,[633] the agency is now trying to new approach to influence movie makers.

The bureau's Investigative Publicity and Public Affairs Unit, which has an annual budget of $1.5 million,[634] provides screenwriters, movie and TV producers, and authors advice on costumes, props, scenery, and weapons as well as b-roll footage and fact checking.[635] The FBI requests copies of the film script and plot to review and a "description how the FBI fits into the project and its relative importance."[636] The agency "helped lend authenticity to 649 projects, usually films, TV shows and books" in just one year.[637]

The FBI provided assistance for the motion pictures "The Kingdom," "Shooter," and "Breach" as well as television shows including "Without A Trace," "CSI," "Numb3rs," "Criminal Minds," and "The Closer."[638]

The movie "Shooter" earned over $95.6 million worldwide.[639] The movie tells the tale of an assassination attempt on the President of the United States. "The Kingdom" grossed over $86.6 million[640] while "Breach" brought in over $40.9 million.[641]

The FBI lent its support with the production of "Shooter," a movie about a presidential assassination attempt.

While these box office bonanzas were bringing in millions, the FBI was having its own budget shaved by sequestration. Over the past year, the FBI reduced hiring, training and equipment purchases to comply with sequestration and is threatening to shut down its offices and furlough employees for as many as ten days in the near future, which would have an impact of real investigations and intelligence gathering.[642] The Attorney General claims sequestration is "materially reducing FBI's investigative capacity to address mortgage fraud, cybercrime, human trafficking, terrorism, financial fraud, organized crime, to just name just a few of its critical mission areas."[643]

Hollywood is not without its own experts who can provide much of the same expertise and advice as the FBI. Scott Nelson, a retired agent who worked for the FBI for 25 years, for example, "is part of a now-sprawling community of expert 'consultants' who help Hollywood film-makers to realistically portray everything from fight scenes to the intricacies of real- life police investigations." He has been described as "the star who's always just out of shot" and the "go to person when "Hollywood actors need to walk and talk like secret agents or villains."[644]

So perhaps the real unsolved mystery is why is the FBI spending taxpayer money to assist with the production of Hollywood blockbusters at a time when budget cuts are reducing the agency's ability to combat real crimes and threats?

Working with the FBI:
A Guide for Writers, Authors, and Producers

We can help: if you are a writer, author, or producer who wants to feature the FBI, we may be able to work with you to create an accurate portrayal of the Bureau. We've been doing it since the 1930s.

Specifically, the **Investigative Publicity and Public Affairs Unit** (IPPAU) in our Office of Public Affairs is a small staff that spends a portion of its time working with domestic and international screenwriters, producers, authors, and other industry personnel associated with TV programs, documentaries, made-for-TV movies, books, and motion pictures. In addition, the unit is the same one that manages national and international publicity for wanted fugitives (including the "Ten Most Wanted Fugitives"), Most Wanted Terrorists, and missing children, and it also coordinates other proactive initiatives.

What we need from you:

- Your name, any pertinent company name, point of contact, address, e-mail, and phone number;
- Acknowledgement whether the project is "sold," "green lit," commissioned, or speculative;
- A description how the FBI fits into the project and its relative importance;
- An explanation of FBI characters and actions (what they will be doing);
- Film script, plot, or treatment;
- Project status/timeline/production schedule (if known);
- Specificity regarding cases, procedures, or information needed; and
- A list of FBI personnel desired (if known) for interviews or backgrounders (note: please allow ample time for the approval process.)

What we can provide you:

- Guidance on content regarding FBI investigations, procedures, structure, and history;
- Information on costumes, props, scenery, and weapons;
- Fact checks;
- Liaison and coordination with local FBI field offices;
- Coordination of location shots; and
- Access to FBI facilities for filming scenes, interviews, or b-roll footage.

Contact information:

- Call FBI Headquarters at (202) 324-3000 and ask for the Investigative Publicity and Public Affairs Unit.

The FBI Investigative Publicity and Public Affairs Unit provides screenwriters, movie and TV producers, and authors advice on costumes, props, scenery, and weapons as well as b-roll footage and fact checking.[645]

65. Cash Cows – (USDA) $19.5 million

Researchers from Kansas State University are worried that cattle and bison may shrink in size over the next 50 years due to global warming. Rising temperatures *could* cause grass to grow more slowly, in turn resulting in smaller cattle and bison that eat the grass.[646]

Never fear. Some of their colleagues at Kansas State are looking into it, funded by a $9.6 million, five-year grant from the U.S. Department of Agriculture (USDA). Scientists from Oklahoma State University, the University of Oklahoma, the USDA, and Tarleton State University will join forces with Kansas State in combating climate-induced bovine weight loss.[647]

This diverse coalition will be just one of many research teams around the country funded by the USDA's National Institute of Food and Agriculture. In total, the USDA will be awarding $19.5 million nationwide to support the development of "climate solutions for beef and dairy cattle."[648]

Although primarily composed of scientists, the Kansas State research team will be joined by non-scientists as well in its research. Leading the team will be three Kansas State professors, one of whom is an associate professor of sociology.[649]

Why sociology? It seems this research project is not completely devoted to scientific inquiry. In addition to improving soil and water quality and developing diversified forage sources, the research team will focus its efforts on developing "marketing options" and "ways to provide more stable farm household income."[650]

Taxpayer cash to find out how skinny cows will get with less grass.

66. Federal frat: man caves, pin ups, and filth – (EPA) $479,000

The EPA is well known for its fervent efforts in protecting animals' habitats. Perhaps not as widely documented is its very own "animal house," a sanctuary for anyone looking to party away his days on the taxpayer dollar.

EPA? More like Epsilon Pi Alpha.

The 70,000-square foot "Epsilon House" is one of the agency's largest storage facilities, located in Landover, Maryland. Officially titled the "Main EPA Headquarters Warehouse," housed within are the excess inventories for the agency's nearby Washington, D.C. hub. Although the EPA is in charge of the warehouse, Apex Logistics LLC, a federal contractor, was tasked with the day-to-day operations at the facility from 2007 to 2013.[651]

However, a May 2013 investigation by the EPA's Office of Inspector General would forever expel Apex from Epsilon House.

Instead of an unassuming storage facility, the OIG found a vermin-ridden, testosterone-infused party house cordoned off into multiple "man caves" for the Apex Logistics contractors. Spelunking into the

caves revealed that the contractors had pilfered numerous pieces of equipment from the EPA for their own leisure, including televisions, refrigerators, radios, microwaves, chairs, and couches. Additionally found were photos, pin ups, calendars, clothing, books, magazines, and videos.[652]

The guys even had the opportunity to start their own band. Inspectors found three pianos and various wind band instruments— apparently all EPA property—within the warehouse.[653]

Perhaps the most grandiose amenity of Epsilon House was its exercise facility,

Photos showing examples of unauthorized personal spaces. (EPA OIG photos)

complete with borrowed workout equipment from the EPA "that could rival a gym's."[654]

This is all in addition to "a locked office inside the facility for which we could not determine a purpose," according to investigators.[655]

To hide their illicit leisure activities, contractors arranged the unauthorized personal spaces so that they were out of sight of security cameras through the use of screens, partitions, and piled-up boxes.[656]

According to investigators, "EPA management confirmed they had not visited the warehouse before the Office of Inspector General briefed the agency over concerns with poor oversight of the storage facility."[657]

The party is now over, and the taxpayers are left feeling the hangover. Since the initial award of its contract in 2007, Apex had been paid by the EPA over $5.3 million for labor costs and management of Epsilon House.[658]

67. The Gopher Protection Program – (DoD) $5.25 Million

Even as furloughs sent tens of thousands of Defense Department (DoD) employees home without pay, the agency spent millions to protecting the pocket gopher, gopher tortoise, Florida pine snake and others.

Two military bases, one in Florida and one in Washington, received a total of $5.25 million as part of DoD's Readiness and Environmental Protection Integration (REPI) Program.[659] The program works to offset the environmental impact of military training near bases by investing in local conservation efforts.

The biggest award, amounting to $3.5 million, went to Joint Base Lewis-McChord (JBLM) near Tacoma, Washington, to "preserve, restore and manage critical prairie habitat."[660]

While the Environmental Protection Agency is already dedicated to environmental issue, one military ecologist, Jeffrey Foster, noted that it's a defense mission as well: "Although our primary mission is fighting wars and military training, like other federal agencies, we have a requirement to support the recovery of listed species."[661]

An additional $1.75 million was sent to Eglin Air Force Base in Florida to help purchase 20,800 acres of land.[662] State officials noted the purchased land would provide a home for the "Florida black bear, gopher tortoise, Florida pine snake, Pine Barrens treefrog and eastern diamondback rattlesnake."[663]

68. A federally funded "Moosical" – (NEA) $10,000

Move over, Rudolph. There's a new antlered holiday character in town, and he's got the financial backing of U.S. taxpayers.

Funded by a $10,000 federal grant from the National Endowment of the Arts, "Mooseltoe: A New Moosical" will be touring the nation this holiday season.[664]

Taxpayer dollars pay for "Mooseltoe" to feature voices from celebrities from Broadway, television, and movies, as well as costumes from the costume designer of Broadway's "The Lion King."[665]

In addition to its original songs, parents will appreciate the 16 characters in "Mooseltoe" that are entertaining their children on the taxpayers' dime, including three snobby penguins, a mobster snowman, and a fat walrus.[666]

69. Nothing says "Indianapolis Urban Waterway System" like Interpretive Dance – (NSF) $2.9 million

An "outdoor museum" featuring dance, poetry and sculpture will soon be able to help residents of Indianapolis learn more about the city's urban waterways.

The National Science Foundation (NSF) provided Butler University's Center for Urban Ecology with $2.9 million to create the "City as a Living Laboratory" initiative throughout Indianapolis.[667] Project officials hope to use the money "to create sites along six Indianapolis waterways where arts and science will be used to educate the public about Indianapolis's water system."[668]

Project planners intend to use the artwork to "interpret scientific content," which would be available not only to those traversing the city's bike paths, but also on a smartphone app.[669] Butler University will be joined by the Center for Urban Health at Indiana University-Purdue University Indianapolis, which will conduct the research needed to support the project. Gabriel Fillipelli, the center's director, noted the project's goal was to raise awareness that waterways were more than just commerce and transportation, but that they "want people in urban areas to learn more about their connection to the environment."[670]

Indianapolis Mayor Greg Ballard said that "this unique combination of art, science and trails will provide great new places for families, walkers, runners and cyclists to see our beautiful city and perhaps even learn a thing or two in the process."[671]

70. $158,500 Pile of Rubble

Americans undoubtedly value the preservation of landmarks, buildings, and other areas that are of historical significance and value, and New Orleans is a U.S. city full of historical properties worth preserving. But a new federal program intended to be a "national model of how to succeed in preservation" instead used taxpayers' money to demolish instead of to preserve historical homes in New Orleans.[672]

In an effort to spare 81 historical homes from the wrecking ball, the City of New Orleans in 2010 redirected millions of dollars in federal block grants to hire an experienced contractor to move these homes from the site of two new hospitals.[673] The contractor would then deliver the homes to local non-profits which would renovate these homes, and then sell them to low-income families.[674]

But this preservation plan fell apart upon implementation, resulting in $158,500 from taxpayers being spent on one home which was ultimately demolished in October 2013.[675,676]

When the contractor, Builders of Hope, moved the homes, it removed the roofs from the homes to fit under city's power lines and sawed off the backs of those houses which were determined to be too long for tight street turns.[677] So the non-profits often received homes without roofs, walls, back halves, and nothing to protect the homes from rotting under New Orleans' notorious heat, humidity, rain, and wind.[678]

At this point, taxpayers spent $38,500 to move one home to 1601 Dumaine Street without a roof and back wall.[679] After months of deteriorating under the elements, the Historic Landmarks District Commission (HDLC) in charge of overseeing the home's new neighborhood wanted to demolish the house.[680] Instead of acknowledging the home's impossible disrepair, the non-profit which now owned the home, Providence Community Housing, insisted that the home could be renovated and obtained $120,000 in additional federal funding from the Department of Housing and Urban Development to renovate the house.[681]

By October 2013, the house was a $158,500 pile of rubble.

The legally required permits to demolish the moved house were never applied for, and, when first asked about the house's fate, a Vice President of Providence Community Housing ("Providence") denied that the house had been demolished.[682]

The blame game between the City of New Orleans, Providence, Builders of Hope, and New Orleans residents reveals how taxpayers paid $158,500 to move and then destroy a historical home.

The City of New Orleans alleged that Builders of Hope, the contractor paid to move the house, mismanaged its funds and failed to pay its subcontractors, which resulted in the homes not being protected from weather damage.[683] Builders of Hope alleged that the City of New Orleans were months behind in sending payments for legitimate invoices that it submitted, preventing payments to its subcontractors, thus leaving the homes in disrepair.[684] A contractor for Providence told an inspector from the City's Department of Safety and Permits that the home at 1601 Dumaine could not be salvaged because of its dilapidated condition upon its receipt from Builders of Hope.[685]

A spokesman for Mayor Landrieu stated that Providence's demolition of the home was "outside the scope of what the City had originally permitted" when it granted funds for renovations.[686]

A board member with the Foundation for Historical Louisiana blames the City of New Orleans which "was responsible to make sure the money was spent wisely and that the houses were restored."[687]

While all the parties involved are busy pointing fingers at each other for the home's demolition, they all concur that taxpayers' money was wasted. A Vice President of Providence stated, "I do feel like it was a waste of taxpayer dollars."[688] An executive of Builders of Hope declared the preservation project to be "so messed up. It's a disaster."[689]

71. Government Funding Gets Spicy with Salsa and Bloody Marys – (USDA) $16,792,508

The United States Department of Agriculture awarded over $16 million to 110 businesses to fund the development of new products.[690] The grants were made through the USDA's "Value-Added Producer Grants" program, which "help[s] agricultural producers increase their income by expanding marketing opportunities, creating new products or developing new uses for existing products."[691]

Examples of "new products" included salsa and Bloody Mary mix. Fish Hawk Acres, LLC in Rock Cave, West Virginia was awarded $45,000 in taxpayer funds to market their brand salsa and Bloody Mary mix. Justifying the need for more types of salsa and Bloody Mary mix is challenging. Recent reports note Salsa outsells ketchup in the United States.[692]

Glenmary Gardens in Bristol, Virginia received a $213,000 grant "to expand the processing and marketing of locally grown fruits and vegetable into jellies, ice cream and flavored syrups."[693]

A USDA press release noted that in dealing with sequestration, it "has already undertaken historic efforts" to save taxpayer funds "through targeted, common-sense reductions."[694]

72. The Case of the Old Vacant Grist Mill – (VA) $2 million

The Department of Veterans Affairs is planning a $2 million renovation of an over 250 year old building known as the Old Grist Mill. While the building was nominated to the National Register of Historic Places in 1974,[695] it is rarely visited and has not been shuttered since the Civil War.[696]

The federal government is considering turning the Old Grist Mill into office space. An architecture firm reviewed the building and prepared an extensive renovation plan for the building, both inside and out. That firm determined it would cost $2 million to renovate the 3,600 square foot space for use as office space.[697] In March 2013, the VA began looking for a construction firm to renovate the Old Grist Mill and another building close by with an estimated renovation cost of between $2 million and $5 million.[698] The project specified it would require "a new water wheel will be installed on the exterior to mimic, as closely as possible, the original Mill."[699]

Photo Credit: GAO

A recent report by the Government Accountability Office (GAO) singled out the renovations to the Old Grist Mill and questioned the merit of the expense. The agency noted "installing modern building systems and making building code improvements – such as adding a bathroom and a stairwell – will be challenging."[700]

That said, a local historian noted the Old Grist Mill was "probably in pretty good shape considering its age and the fact that it's not necessarily useful."[701]

73. Footing the Bill for a Bestseller – (NSF) $1,750,000

Facing $356 million in sequestration cuts, researchers and scientists at the National Science Foundation (NSF) faced lay-offs and reduced resources for projects.[702] But instead of allocating funds to critical scientific research being, the NSF awarded a $1.75 million grant to create a PBS documentary that promotes the title and topic of a *New York Times* best-selling book.[703]

"In Defense of Food" will be a two-hour documentary based on the same-titled book by Michael Pollan and will broadcast on PBS in 2014.[704] Michael Pollan has written five books, all *New York Times* bestsellers, on the relationships between food, agriculture, and culinary science.[705]

However, Kikim Media, the company paid to produce the taxpayer-funded documentary, describes the film as showing "how a combination of uncertain and incomplete science, weak-kneed politicians, and clever marketing campaigns have shaped America's eating habits in a way that have made us less and less healthy."[706] Critics in the science industry have panned Pollan's "food science" books as lacking "the scientific principles that should define a premier research university or guide what faculty pass on to their students in the classroom."[707]

NSF explains that the goal of the documentary is to engage its audience about the scientific research of food and how food science is utilized in media and marketing.[708] According to the NSF, the ultimate value of the documentary is "to enhance public understanding of the crucial importance of science in people's everyday lives and in shaping dozens of daily decisions."[709]

74. Education Grant Funds Used to Settle Lawsuit – (FL DOE) $1.25 million

Federal taxpayer money designated to improve children's schools in Florida were instead spent to settle a lawsuit between the state and a former contractor.

The Florida Department of Education[710] is forking over $1.25 million to settle a lawsuit with Infinity Software Development, a company that was contracted by the state to build an education website.[711]

The legal fracas leaves in limbo the fate of an educational website which "was intended to provide practice lessons," to "help students, parents and teachers master new academic standards."[712] The resulting controversy has left "Florida educators without a preparation resource officials expected would be in use."[713]

Several months after the contract was signed in December 2011, state officials started to become concerned that Infinity "had turned in unacceptable lessons and tests,"[714] and that the company was "six month behind schedule."[715] In one example, state officials raised concerns that the term "the pursuit of happiness," according to one Infinity website lesson, was used in the preamble of the Constitution, when the phrase is found in the Declaration of Independence.[716] The company contends that the problem was state officials didn't "review the work in a timely fashion or failed to sign off on work completed by the company."[717] Either way, Floridian children and taxpayers lose in this deal.

The $1.25 million settlement was paid from the $700 million "Race to the Top" federal grants from the Department of Education the state received to "improve student achievement in the state."[718] Earlier this year, the state determined that using federal grant funds to settle this lawsuit was an appropriate use of federal taxpayer funds. Meanwhile, the Khan Academy, an online classroom which receives no federal funding, reaches ten million students each month and charges nothing.[719] The federal government is trying to duplicate what the private sector already does exceptionally well.

75. Old Fashioned Portraits of Administration Officials – (NASA, DHS, HUD) $300,000

Everyone knows a picture is worth a thousand words. Little may people know taxpayers are paying for bureaucrats' oil portraits worth tens of thousands of dollars each.

Over the last decade, federal agencies have commissioned dozens of oil paintings to immortalize their upper-level management for the cost of hundreds of thousands of dollars, enough to raise dozens families over the poverty level.[720] This year alone, federal agencies bought or took delivery of nearly $300,000 in official oil portraits of senior officials, according to government contracting data.[721] Taxpayer dollars eternalized leaders such as former Energy Secretary Steven Chu ($20,000),[722] and Lori B. Garver, former NASA Deputy Administrator ($23,000).[723] Both resigned their positions earlier this year.

Portraits are not restricted to those sitting in office. Agencies have ordered pieces to commemorate former officials who left years prior. This May, the Department of Homeland Security unveiled a $30,000 portrait of Gov. Tom Ridge, first Secretary of the Department of Homeland Security who left in 2005.[724] A second portrait – of Michael Chertoff, the Department's second Secretary – has also been painted, though not yet unveiled. That portrait also cost $30,000.[725] Similarly, the Department of Housing and Urban Development (HUD) ordered a $20,000 portrait of former Secretary Steve Preston, who served for just seven months.[726]

While the average portrait cost has been about $22,000, several have cost more than some families will earn in years.[727] In 2007, HUD paid $100,000 for a 30" x 40" oil painting and required it to be "framed in gold."[728] The Commerce Department paid $40,000 for a life-size portrait of former Secretary Gutierrez in 2008.[729] In the last decade, the Defense Department has ordered at least six oil paintings that cost between $40,000 and $50,000.[730] Altogether, the Pentagon has ordered more portraits than any other agency – 25 of at least 69 ordered in the last decade.[731]

While agencies have said the commissioned artwork simply keeps in step with tradition, some critics have questioned whether it must continue. Says one taxpayer advocate, "It's not like people are going to be lining up for an exhibit, 'HUD Secretaries Through the Years.' And just because it's a Washington tradition doesn't mean they have to keep doing it." [732] HUD portraits, in fact, are only displayed near the secretary's office in its headquarters. [733]

Several bipartisan bills have been introduced to cap and limit spending on federal portraits. While commemorating leaders with portraits may be reasonable, limitless and unnecessary spending on them is not.

76. Environmentally Friendly Coffee Drying Study – (USDA) $25,000

According to the National Coffee Association, Americans have been consuming coffee since at least the mid 1600's.[734] While modern machinery allows for the rapid "drying" of coffee beans, farmers across the world have used the sun to dry coffee for centuries.

In comes the U.S. Department of Agriculture, which is funding groundbreaking research into the coffee drying process, giving $25,000 to one Hawaii coffee plantation to study more environmentally friendly means for getting water out of their beans.[735]

The study will include such methods as "passive solar-heated air" (the sun and wind), "photovoltaic-generated electricity" (solar panels powering drying machinery), and "solar-heated water systems" (the sun again).[736]

This critical research into the use of the sun to dry coffee will verify what farmers across the globe have been doing for centuries.

Rows of sunbathing coffee beans.

77. Taxpayers Shell Out Half-a-Million for Street Block in Town of 1,150 – (DOT) $532,000

Outgoing U.S. Secretary of Transportation Ray LaHood ended his tenure describing the state of America's roads as "one big pothole."[737] LaHood blamed a lack of transportation funding for the deteriorating condition of U.S. roads and highways and unsafe bridges.[738] The outgoing Secretary emphasized that the U.S. Department of Transportation needed a bold plan to fund transportation infrastructure.[739]

So when a tiny Kansas town wanted to spruce up one block on its Main Street, one would naturally assume that this town would use local funds, not federal dollars, for improvements that would be an exclusive benefit to the town.

Instead, the Kansas town of Rossville received $532,000 from the U.S. Department of Transportation in Washington, D.C. because there "hasn't been much done to [the] main street in years."[740]

U.S. taxpayers shelled out over half a million dollars for improvements to one-tenth of a mile[741] on the Main Street of a town with a population of only 1,150.[742] Taxpayers in New York, Louisiana, Oklahoma, and California paid to make Rossville's one-block downtown area "more decorative and colorful."[743]

These decorative and colorful improvements to one street block in Rossville, Kansas cost U.S. taxpayers $462 per resident of Rossville or $38,000 for each of the 14 businesses located on this block of Main Street.[744]

78. Yale University Spends Federal Research Grant Studying the Oddity of the Duck Penis – (NSF) $384,989

While bipartisanship has been in short supply around Washington these days, at least one scientific venture has received support during both the current administration and the former: duck genitalia research.

Yale University launched a project in 2005 with funding from the National Science Foundation (NSF), to study the oddities of the duck penis. In 2009, the school received an additional $384,989 to continue its work, which will expire in 2013.[745] The project found its way into the limelight when it was discovered the funding came from the 2009 stimulus bill, which among other things was intended, "To provide investments needed to increase economic efficiency by spurring technological advances in science and health."[746]

According to the NSF website, the project – titled "Conflict, Social Behavior and Evolution" – was intended to better understand duck reproductive activity, with the goal of also better understanding human relationships.[747] It also notes the project will, "incorporate high school students from under-represented minorities."[748]

The key finding of the study was the corkscrew-like shape of a duck's penis, which can be resisted by female ducks through their own biological design. "This is literally anti-screw anatomy," quipped lead researcher Richard Prum.[749]

When asked by one news outlet why NSF decided to support an inquiry into the length of duck penises, its spokesperson noted that it was basic research, adding, "Government funded grants for research have assisted in creating the barcode and Google."[750]

79. Thomson Prison Blues – (DOJ) $2 million

In October 2012, the Administration circumvented Congress and purchased the Illinois state-owned Thomson Correctional Facility for $165 million. For over a decade, the prison sat empty under Illinois ownership, and the state did not have the budget to open and operate the prison.[751]

The Department of Justice has been trying to bail out the State of Illinois and had been requesting authorization to purchase Thompson Prison for years, but the House Appropriations Committee has opposed funding for the purchase of the prison.[752,753]

However, in clear contradiction to the will of Congress,[754] Attorney General Eric Holder purchased the prison for $165 million by using funds in various DOJ accounts, including $151 million from the DOJ Assets Forfeiture Fund.[755] The Fund is supposed to be used to offset the costs of criminal forfeiture cases, such as law enforcement activities, storing and maintain forfeited assets and payments to victims and lienholders, not to purchase prisons.[756]

Stuck in Thomson Prison. The federal government went around Congress to buy the empty prison with no plan to fill it. Now the taxpayer is footing the $2 million maintenance bill.

Yet, after its unapproved purchase, in FY 2013, the Administration failed to produce a budget that provides for the funds necessary to activate Thomson or to fund the ongoing maintenance needs of the facility until it opens.[757,758] According to the Department of Justice, the agency spent approximately $2 million in FY 2013 to maintain the empty facility.

In its FY 2014 budget request, the Obama Administration finally requested approximately $166 million to activate three prisons, including Thomson.[759] The President's FY 2014 Budget includes $43.7 million in salaries and expenses to begin activating Thomson,[760] and $15 million to renovate and convert Thomson to federal prison use.[761]

In July 2013, the Senate Appropriations Committee approved $166.3 million to activate three prisons, including Thomson.[762] It will take at least two years to activate Thomson, and by the time of its estimated 2015 opening, "projected costs include $25 million for upgrades and $168 million for equipment and staffing."

An empty prison purchased for no reason that costs $2 million to operate.

This bad investment has taxpayers singing the Thompson Prison Blues.

80. Can You Hear Me Now? Millions Wasted on Untested, Malfunctioning IT – (USDA) $20 million

As the workplace becomes increasingly mobile, the federal government is opting for devices other than BlackBerrys. The Obama Administration announced a Digital Government Strategy for federal employees to access workplace networks from mobile devices without compromising privacy and security concerns. [763] In accordance with this strategy, the Department of Homeland Security, Department of Defense, and National Institute of Standards and Technology developed a baseline of standard security requirements for mobile computing and a framework design to reference in designing security and privacy protections. [764] This would allow federal employees to use a range of popular brand devices without compromising government networks and leaking information, and even allow some offices to implement a bring-your-own-device policy instead of on government-issued devices. [765]

Technology insiders applauded the government's decision to develop the mobile technology to permit federal employees to work remotely. [766] A survey of federal managers and federal workers found that each employee would add an additional seven hours each week in productivity, amounting to $14,000 in productivity gains. [767] Of those federal workers who already have mobile device access, they spend a weekly average of nine additional hours on top of their full-time work schedules checking in to their workplace networks. [768] Almost half of these workers report working more efficiently outside the office. [769]

The Department of Agriculture forked over $20 million to several companies for MDM integration which is now one year behind schedule and malfunctioning. [770] Perhaps if the USDA hired one of the companies approved by the GSA for mobile management solutions, then the USDA would not be having these rollout problems. [771] Or maybe if the USDA required a demonstration of the bidding companies' capabilities for MDM integration in the USDA's network, then USDA employees would now be using their own iPhones and Android to access their workplace servers. [772]

Instead, the USDA paid three contractors $20 million. [773]

Testing before handing over taxpayers' money would have shown that one contractor's software is not compatible with part of the USDA's network security infrastructure. [774] Eight months after the MDM system was supposed to have completed a 30-day, 3,000 phone test phase, this test phase has been pushed back, and the USDA is still just testing one component of the contractor's incompatible software to determine whether the software will be used or abandoned. [775]

According to the USDA's Request for Proposal, the agency already supported more than 3,000 mobile devices before the $20 million project and hoped to expand the number of mobile devices to more than 100,000 over the next few years. [776] As of late July, only 1,370 devices were on the USDA's MDM system [777]

Surely, given the failure of the MDM integration at the USDA, other federal agencies would restrain themselves from awarding millions in taxpayer dollars to these contractors without first testing their product?

Think again. One of these three contractors was awarded $212.1 million in government contracts just in 2013. [778] The contractor with the incompatible software has several multi-million dollar government contracts with the CIA, NSA, FBI, DHS, and the Air Force. [779]

Instead of pouring millions of dollars to fix "glitches," taxpayers would prefer their money go towards testing new technologies first to prevent such rollout problems.

81. Government Pays $500 per gallon in Afghanistan – (USAID) $507,000

The U.S. Agency for International Development (USAID) operates a program to help increase access to healthcare for Afghan citizens through the construction of hospitals and mid-wife training centers throughout Afghanistan.[780]

One particular hospital project that has received specific attention from the Special Inspector General for Afghanistan Reconstruction (SIGAR) is the Gardez Hospital. An organization that funnels money from USAID the recipients in Afghanistan awarded a contract to Sayed Bilal Sadath Construction Company (SBSCC),[781] an Afghan company, for $13.5 million to build the new hospital.[782] This new 100-bed hospital in Gardez, Afghanistan is currently about 23 months behind its original schedule,[783] because it has been seriously hampered by the facility's remote location and by an active insurgency.

USAID, through the middle man, paid $300,000 to SBSCC for 600 gallons of diesel fuel that made the purchase price $500 per gallon.[784] The market price for diesel fuel in Afghanistan is approximately $5.00 per gallon, making this purchase worth $3,000 and therefore, an overpayment of $297,000.[785]

The U.S. Agency for International Development paid $500 per gallon for diesel fuel in Afghanistan, where the market price is $5 a gallon.

SIGAR noted in an April 2013 audit report that the Afghan government may not be able to sustain the new Gardez hospital once it is completed and that the new hospital's annual operation and maintenance costs could exceed five times the annual operating costs for the hospital it is replacing.[786] Nearly $60 million has been spent on a hospital that is doomed to fail.

82. Cash for Gas – (USDA) $403,627

The U.S. Department of Agriculture is trying their hand at alchemy.[787] The department's $403,627 federal grant to the Woodcrest Dairy Farm won't help the farm turn trash into gold, however. Instead, the farm is hoping that the grant serves as a philosopher's stone for somewhat cruder sort of transformation – the creation of a bio-digester to turn the methane gas from cow manure into electricity.

Neighbors of the farm appreciate it less for any environmental impact and more for the impact on their nostrils. "It will be better on the neighbors because the manure comes out of the digester without the terrible odor," Mr. Braun said.[788] The grant might make the manure less stinky, but wasting taxpayer money stinks to high heaven.

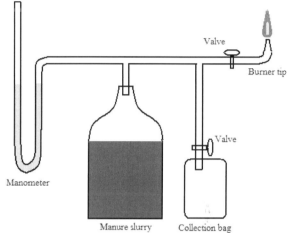

Yes, that says "manure slurry."

The USDA is convinced that these cows hold the secret to renewable energy – you just have to pay the tab – Allbreedsblog.com.

83. It's A Round-Up...of Taxpayer Money!

Animal activists call it a waste of taxpayer money.[789] The National Academy of Science (NAS) calls it "expensive and unproductive."[790] Government auditors have been warning of its unsustainability for years.[791] Yet, the Wild Horse Program, implemented by the Department of the Interior's Bureau of Land Management (BLM), continues to operate at the cost to taxpayers of $76 million a year.[792]

The Wild Horse Program began in 1970 to protect the wild horse population from slaughter and to sustain natural resources and vegetation for both wild horses and cattle and other wildlife.[793] At the expense of $1,000 each, wild horses are rounded up and removed from the wild.[794] Two-thirds of them are corralled in a "holding system" of taxpayer-funded corrals, feed lots, and pastures.[795] Each year, the BLM rounds up 9,400 horses, and today, the holding population of over 50,000 horses exceeds the wild population of 35,000 horses.[796] The cost of holding these wild horses in long-term corrals is the main expense in the program's $76 million annual price tag.[797]

The NAS argues that the BLM's remedy of corralling wild horses is actually worsening the wild horse problem. The report issued by the NAS explains that the more wild horses the government corrals, then there is more vegetation available in the wild, which may actually contribute to an increase in the wild horse population.[798]

The BLM's solution to reduce the holding population does little to offset the costs of the Wild Horse Program. For $10 a horse, almost anyone can purchase a horse from the BLM, which is a $1000 loss for the costs rounding up and holding the horse.[799]

Once a wild horse is purchased from the BLM, it often does not spend the rest of its life galloping around green pastures. Instead, these horses are illegally being sold across state and national lines to slaughterhouses, where the market price for the horses is much higher. A USDA spokesperson confirmed that USDA vets at U.S.-Mexico border crossings sometimes see BLM-branded horses in slaughter export pens.[800]

84. East Coast Hurricane Aid Spent on West Coast Research – $1.1 million

When Hurricane Sandy came slamming into the East Coast last fall, Congress immediately did exactly what everyone expected they would do: spent money on the West Coast.

Untold millions of lives were upended by Hurricane Sandy, causing billions of dollars in damage and dozens of lives lost. To assist those in need, Congress responded to the disaster by passing $60 billion in emergency disaster relief.[801] While some questioned whether such a large amount could be spent quickly, lawmakers in the affected areas said "The need for emergency disaster relief is beyond urgent."[802]

While the aid dollars are trickling out slowly, $8 million have been awarded to well-funded academic institutions and organizations for research projects, through a grant funded by the U.S. Health and Human Services Department (HHS).[803] Researchers on the west coast are getting $1.1 million from HHS to study the effect of the storm.

In California, the RAND Corporation received approximately $657,000 to "explore how partnerships between local health departments and community-based organizations contribute to the public health system's ability to respond to and recover from emergencies and contribute to resilience."[804]

A grant of $444,000 went to the American College of Emergency Physicians in Irving, Texas to study how "health care systems were impacted negatively before, during, and after Hurricane Sandy and to develop comprehensive recommendations on how to strengthen health care systems going forward to treat patients effectively during disaster events."[805]

However, even as research money was spread around the nation, many victims of Hurricane Sandy remain displaced from their homes, some never to return. That is the case of Kathryn Fitzgerald in Long Beach, New York, whose home was badly damaged in the storm, causing her and her daughter to flee.[806] Despite having a paid-up policy with the National Flood Insurance Program, she was awarded only a fraction of the amount in damages.[807] She was left with no choice but to pay $11,000 out of pocket to tear her house down, and now lives in an apartment with no hope of getting back her old life.[808]

85. Fishy grants for cronies – (U.S. Fish and Wildlife Services) $30 million

Traveling along the Mississippi's Gulf Coast, one can find numerous yacht clubs, art museums, and even the John C. Stennis Space Center, one of NASA's field test facilities. Many of these sites have received funding through federal coastal conservation grants.

According to a June 2013 study by the Department of Interior Office of Inspector General, out of approximately $40 million (of a total $100 million) in Coastal Impact Assistance Program (CIAP) grants throughout Mississippi, investigators concluded that about $30 million were "ineligible" and "unsupported" and could be "put to better use." [809]

The investigation found numerous examples of grants originally intended for coastal preservation that were being siphoned off for glitzy pet projects to draw in tourists. One such recipient was the Ohr-O'Keefe Museum of Art, which received $500,000. Investigators concluded that less than 4 percent of the original amount of grant money intended for conservation could actually have been used for those purposes. The rest was used to invest in new skylights and flooring at the museum. [810]

Other projects only tangentially related to conservation included $211,700 for a 6-foot-wide asphalt trail in a landlocked Mississippi county and $500,000 for a general-purpose classroom at NASA's Stennis Space Center. Proponents of the asphalt trail argued that the benefits of the trail would "flow to the coastal zone," while supporters of the NASA classroom argued that visitors could theoretically be informed about "space, marine and environmental sciences."[811] Seriously!

Perhaps even worse than these "conservation" projects were instances of cronyism uncovered by investigators.

Strikingly, conflicts of interest between a Mississippi DMR CIAP official, the Mississippi Gulf Coast National Heritage Area, and their family and friends were some of the benefactors of 23 grants totaling roughly $16 million.[812] For example, Mississippi DMR acquired Harbor Landing, a yacht club and boat storage facility in Ocean Springs, from a friend of Bill Walker, DMR director at the time of acquisition.[813]

Even more concerning were findings that Walker's wife was employed by the University of Southern Mississippi and the Institute for Marine Mammal Studies, two entities that received millions in CIAP grants. In fact, when Walker's wife joined the Institute for Marine Mammal Studies in 2010, the press release heralding her new job stated she would "bring millions in grant funding and many marine programs to IMMS."[814]

86. Federal Dollars For Some Yam Fine Vodka in a Dry County – (USDA) $100,000

The United States Department of Agriculture (USDA) has expressed serious concern over recent sequestration efforts and how across-the-board budget cuts will have a damaging effect on the agency's programs and workforce.[815] In the face of today's challenging budget environment, the agency should be channeling resources into critical government functions. No one ever said achieving this balance would be easy, but the USDA appears to have muddled their priorities when it comes to cutting costs. For example, the Department has threatened that underprivileged women and children may cease to receive agency-funded nutrition and health care assistance[816] – but seems to have no problem handing out funds to sustain America's drinking habits.

USDA's recent support of a domestic distillery in rural Greene County, North Carolina illustrates this striking disconnect. In a somewhat precarious business venture, farmers established Covington Spirits to craft and sell vodka made from leftover yams – products of sweet potato farming operations that were unsuitable for market sale due to size and shape issues. The Snow Hill-based operation aimed to convert those spuds to a premium grade beverage with the goal of "ending America's dependence on foreign vodka," as its slogan goes.[817]

"The best yam vodka on earth!"

Covington Spirits set up shop in early 2013 with assistance from none other than the USDA. The company received money from the federal government in the form of a Value-Added Producer Grant (VAPG) "to help explore the feasibility" of the yam-infused vodka. However, this particular grant award is startlingly ironic. While Greene County has ABC stores, it is essentially a "dry" community, banning any "liquor-by-drink" (also known as "mixed drinks" to common consumers) sales.[818] How feasible can a vodka business venture be in a place that partially prohibits its very existence?

Liquor stores in North Carolina are state-run, but local rules allow counties and towns to institute their own regulations. Greene County's mixed drink ban creates economic challenges for Covington Spirits and their ability to sell their product locally – a crucial fact that was overlooked when the USDA decided to fund the distillery.

Spending on sweet potato liquor in a place subject to stringent liquor laws is a questionable federal investment. If the USDA is as concerned as it says it is regarding sequestration reductions, the agency needs to rethink spending money on yam vodka.

87. Don't Share this Story: the FDA is Monitoring What People Say About it Online (FDA) – ($180,000)

From reddit, the self-declared front page of the internet, to Facebook and Twitter – no cat video that mentions the FDA will be safe from its wary eyes.

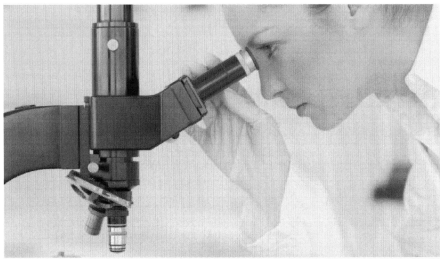

The FDA has awarded a contract of up to $180,000 dollars to IB5k to set up a social networking watchdog for the agency.[819] The goal of the service is to monitor what the public thinks and says about the FDA, answer questions posted on a variety of sites relating to the agency, and observe public sentiment through likes, follows, and mentions on Facebook and Twitter.[820]

IB5K's contract includes the use of two data-mining internet tools. Correllate allows companies to analyze the general mood of posts and determine the audience demographics for a particular post.[821] The second, called Aware, will allow the FDA to determine how effective its own posts on social media are at reaching the public.

Being liked is important, but maybe federal agencies should take some time away from figuring out what people think about them and more time just doing their job?

FDA spent $180,000 to examine what people are saying about the agency online—money that should have been spent examining the safety of our food and drugs.

88. Four Score and Seven Clicks From Now: historical multi-player computer games – (NEH) $300,000

A professor at Hope College has received almost $300,000 from the National Endowment of the Humanities (NEH) for his multi-player computer game that finally brings Civil War reenactors onlin.[822] The game is "Valley Sim" and it allows students to "take on the identity of one of 25 real-life citizens of two communities that were on opposite sides of the Civil War."[823]

Unlike Everquest or League of Legends, however, this multiplayer game is short on the swords and sorcery. The game is an interactive experience where students take on the identity of their character and interact through an internet chat system.[824]

The NEH grant will be used to expand the basic framework of the game into a tool that can be applied to other areas of the humanities. Perhaps we'll see Battlefield or Call of Duty replacing WWII lectures? Or maybe the money can prop up something less wasteful in the realm of higher education.

As cool as it might be to introduce games into the classroom, it might be a better idea to convince students to put the controller down and get back to the basics instead.

It's the Social Network for Civil War re-enactors.

89. Is Urine Behind Increased Goat-Human Contact? (NPS) -- $150,000

Seasoned hiker and hunters in Montana know how to attract mountain goats to their camps.

Yet, goat-human relations will be the subject of intense study at Glacier National Park in Montana over the next three years. Researchers hope to document why goats keep hanging out in areas popular with humans, such as the park's Logan Pass.

Annual visitors to Glacier National Park now number almost 3 million,[825] and according to Glacier National Park's spokesperson, Barb Maynes, goat incidents at the park have been "extremely unusual and to our knowledge unprecedented."[826] Nevertheless, researchers will spend $150,000 in National Park Service (NPS) to capture 20-25 goats, collar them with GPS devices and track their movements over a three-year period.[827]

"We have had 'semi-aggressive' goats, particularly in the Logan Pass parking lot," noted Jack Potter, the park's chief science and resource manager.[828] After attempts to shoo the goats away with pepper spray were unsuccessful, Potter entreated visitors, "Avoid urinating on the trail or near the trail."[829]

In 2010, NPS first attempted to study the mountain goats in Logan Pass, but it was scrapped after NPS researchers injected lethal doses of tranquilizer to the first two goats they tried to capture.[830]

Not the actual goats that were killed.

On June 24, 2013, the NPS announced that it was giving the study another shot.[831] Using students from the University of Montana, the park has launched its study, set to wrap up after three years.[832] Until it is concluded, the NPS goat-management protocol remains in effect, park officials noted: "If goats approach closer, encourage them to leave the area with loud noises, arm waving, snapping plastic bags, and rock throwing."[833]

Granite Creek Avalanche Glacier National Park

The main webpage describing the critical maintenance backlog at our nation's prized national parks uses this photo of damage to a road in Glacier National Park at the top of the page.[834] Yet the Park Service is spending $150,000 to study something outdoor enthusiasts have long known: goats like urine.[835]

90. Puppets Take Long Island – (NEH) $150,000

While the Muppets may have taken Manhattan, the federal government spent $150,000 to support the Puppets Take Long Island festival in Sag Harbor, New York.[836]

The eight-week long promotion of puppets was the answer for the Long Island Regional Economic Development Council to attract tourism to Long Island.[837]

Another purpose of the puppet festival is to "raise awareness of Long Island as a destination offering high-quality performing arts for families," but, unfortunately, less than half of the festival's puppet artists are actually located in New York.[838]

The federally-funded festival also provides workshops for children to learn skills in puppet design and presentation.[839]

91. NSF Spending Millions on Ineffective Educational Games – (NSF) $4.4 million

The National Science Foundation (NSF) is spending over $4.4 million of taxpayer dollars into its solution for educating young minds: Alternate Reality Games (ARG).[840,841,842,843]

Part-flash mob, part-World of Warcraft, ARGs are social gaming experiences in which players participate both in the real world and online to collaborate with other players to find clues and solve puzzles to eventually complete a narrative storyline.[844] Developed as a marketing tool to promote television shows, movies, and commercial products.

The goal of the NSF's games are to attract teenage girls and underrepresented groups to Science, Technology, Engineering, and Math (STEM) careers, as well as educate these students in deep-time sciences, astrobiology, astrophysics, interplanetary space travel, and Earth sciences.[845,846,847,848] However, an analysis of an earlier ARG theorized that girls stopped participating in the ARG due to its science-fiction genre storyline.[849]

The NSF award stated that "the research [of educational ARGs] is well grounded in the literature."[850] Unfortunately, this statement is not accurate. Game experts have lamented the very limited literature on educational ARGs,[851] adding that ARGs "lack an in-depth critical and statistical academic analysis,"[852] and that "the promise of games in general, and ARGs in particular, as rich learning and informing experiences has been poorly documented."[853] For those ARGs that have been executed, there is a "lack of empirical data to support if educational ARGs work" and a lack of understanding how to effectively utilize the games in education.[854]

The few critical analyses of ARGs have revealed several reasons that these games do not actually engage students nor contribute to learning methods. Known among ARG insiders as the inverted pyramid modal, the majority of engagement in the ARGs is done by a very small minority of "obsessed" players.[855] Most players in the ARGs are not motivated to participate and instead casually observe the work of the obsessed players.[13] In addition, assessing whether a student is actually learning from an ARG is virtually impossible to determine. Studies have noted that "players will sometime define other learning goals for themselves" even when the ARG has specific learning goals and objectives.[856] The teamwork focus and collaborative nature of ARGs make it difficult for teachers to assess individual performance, and there is no way for students to "show their work" to give teachers insight into their thought-process and cognitive development.[857,858]

Despite $356 million in sequestration cuts, the NSF could still fork over $4.4 million to create games for students that provide no educational value.[859]

92. Penny for Your Thoughts and $800,000 in Taxpayer Money for One Idea – (NV) $800,000

In 2012, Las Vegas was economically bouncing back. Gambling and entertainment brought in $15.3 billion in revenues from its record number 39.7 million visitors that year.[1] Home prices had jumped, and jobs grew at a higher rate than the national average.[860]

But to the Administration, Las Vegas is in such great need of a long-term economic vision, that they would give out an $800,000 grant to pay for it.[2] This prize for an idea is funded by Economic Development Administration's Department of Commerce.[861]

To the dismay of Las Vegas City Councilman Stavros Anthony, who opposed accepting the federal grant, "the 800,000 that we give to somebody, they could go down to San Diego and buy a beach house with it." Councilman Bob Beers called the Strong Communities, Strong Cities grant program "vague and amorphous."[862]

It's not just Las Vegas Councilmen who are baffled by the no-strings-attached-taxpayer-funded prize. Andrew Brod, a senior research fellow at UNC-Greensboro's Bryan School of Business and Economics, described the grant program's $800,0001 million prize in Greensboro as unnecessary bait.[863]

"It still implies the concept behind the program is you have to dangle $1 million in front of people in order to get the best economic development idea...This program believes that economic development isn't about doing the hard work in investing in infrastructure and education, but instead it's about getting that magical idea."[864]

93. Confusing Earned Income Tax Credit Results in Billions in Improper Payments – (IRS) $11 billion

In an audit conducted by the Treasury Department Inspector General for Tax Administration, the IRS paid up to $13.6 billion in false claims for EITC in 2012. [865] The Inspector General found it "disturbing" that the IRS continues to give out more than $11 billion in improper EITC payments each year. [866]

The EITC is a refundable tax credit available to the working poor in order to offset automatic Social Security withdrawals from their paychecks. [867]

But due to the complexity of the law underlying the EITC, fraud, and the high turnover rate of those eligible for payments, the IRS is projected to make improper payments for up to 28 percent of the more than $55 billion in EITC payments. [868]

Although Executive Order 13520 requires the IRS to establish annual targets for reducing improper payments and to report to auditors each quarter of any EITC payments over $5,000, the IRS has yet to be in compliance with the Executive Order. [869]

Therefore, the IRS will continue to violate the President's order and erroneously dish out more money in improper payments than the entire budgets of the Environmental Protection Agency, Department of the Interior, and the Department of Labor. [870]

94. Small Business Administration Uses Taxpayer Dollars to Study Weak Legislation Imposing More Taxes (SBA)

Due to $92 million in sequestration cuts, the U.S. Small Business Administration (SBA) eliminated $69 million from its disaster loan and business loan programs.[871] The SBA chief lamented that every dollar from the SBA's loan subsidy programs guarantee $51 in lending to small business owners.[872] The budget cuts to the loan subsidy programs would result in preventing struggling small business owners from obtaining more than $900 million in capital.[873]

But instead of reallocating as much of its financial resources possible to things such as loan subsidy programs, the SBA awarded researchers $80,000 in taxpayers' money for a study on legislation proposed in Congress.[874]

The SBA used taxpayers' dollars to conduct a study on whether or not Congress should levy even more taxes on consumers.[875]

Did this study at least influence this legislation to pass through Congress this year?

Not at all. The study was released during one of the final weeks of the Congressional Session while the bill lingered in the House since June 2013.[876]

95. Taxpayers Spend Almost $200 Million for a not-so-green Renovation – (GSA) $200 million

In 2009, everyone could agree that the Bishop Henry Whipple Federal Building in Fort Snelling, Minnesota needed an upgrade. The 617,000 square foot building contained asbestos throughout, and it needed to upgrade its mechanical, plumbing, and electrical systems.[877] To keep operating costs down, the original plan for the building's renovation was to reduce energy costs by 23.6 percent.[878] The estimated cost of these upgrades to the B.H. Whipple Federal Building was calculated by the General Services Administration (GSA) to be $115 million, or about $186 per square foot.[879]

Then came Executive Order 13514 from President Obama which required federal buildings to "go green" by increasing sustainability and reducing energy and water usage.[880] The stimulus finding from the 2009 American Recovery Act provided additional funds to implement this green initiative in 247 federal buildings.[881] The plans for the Whipple Federal Building turned from a partial renovation to a full-scale "modernization."[882]
So the GSA planned this modernization of the Whipple Federal Building with a goal of realizing 30 percent in energy savings in the building and receiving a Silver LEED certification.[883]

But four years later, the budget for making the Whipple Federal Building "green" is now *70 percent* higher than the initial construction budget.[884]

96. The National Science Foundation Puts Tea Party Members' Cognitive Abilities Under the Microscope... with Surprising Results – (CT) $398,990

No, Tea Partiers are not worse at science, according to the conclusions of one law professor who studied political identification and cognitive abilities using a National Science Foundation (NSF) grant. In fact, identification with the Tea Party correlated slightly with better scientific comprehension, a result the investigator found "surprising."[885]

A broader study of political parties and cognitive reasoning yielded similar conclusions for the Yale University law professor.

Identification with the Republican Party correlates with a better performance on a cognitive reasoning test, a conclusion which even stunned the study's author. "[Cognitive] scores *increased* with the strength of subjects' identification with the Republican Party" (emphasis original).[886] The author described this result as "puzzling" and had predicted the "cognitive scores would be negatively correlated with right-wing ideology."[887]

His taxpayer-funded survey also revealed, "Liberals and conservatives were uniformly prone to ideologically motivated reasoning."[888]

To carry out this study, 1,750 adults took an online survey that asked about political party identification and ideology and put participants through a three-question cognitive reasoning test.[889] Then, participants also answered questions about how they perceived the three-question test as a measure of their ability.[890]

NSF funds for the study came from a $398,990 grant intended for much different biology-related purpose: to analyze how the public perceives the risks of synthetic biology, "an emerging technology that permits scientists to design living organisms unlike any found in nature."[891]

A National Science Foundation funded researcher said his finding that identification with the Tea Party correlated with better scientific comprehension was "surprising." What is more surprising is that a politically motivated study liked received federal funding when hundreds of other science based grants were being denied financial assistance by NSF.

NSF announced earlier this year that a result of sequestration "the total number of new research grants will be reduced."[892] Approximately 600 new NSF grants were not funded.[893] It is difficult to justify funding this politically motivated project while cutting off federal support for hundreds of scientific proposals.

97. NPS Route 66 Corridor Preservation Program – (NPS) $81,224

Every year, the National Park Service's Route 66 Corridor Preservation Program provides federal funding for the "restoration of restaurants, motels, gas stations and neon signs, as well as for planning, research and educational initiatives."[894] Federal support for the Route 66 program was originally scheduled to terminate in 2009 and transition to a non-federal entity. However, Congress extended the federal commitment an additional 10 years, protecting the low-priority program and its associated frivolous spending through 2019.

In 2013, $81,224 was awarded by the NPS for six projects, including heating and air equipment rehabilitation, roof repairs, and neon sign restoration for businesses along Route 66.[895] One such grant went to the privately owned Hill Top Motel in Kingman, Arizona motel, which received $20,000 in federal funds to "assist with rehabilitation of the heating and air conditioning systems, along with minor roof repairs."[896] Another $10,055 federal grant was awarded to DeCamp Junction, self-described as "a bar that happens to serve awesome food."[897] The privately owned "lively road house and community center" in Staunton, Illinois will utilize the federal funds to replace an extensively damaged roof.[898]

Federal funds will be used for repairs at an Illinois bar.

Federal resources will also be used to restore an "orphaned" neon sign in Litchfield, Illinois. The Vic Suhling Gas for Less Filling Station was opened from 1957 until 1973, and the building was finally razed in 1990. Yet, the sign for the station remained, towering over an empty lot for the subsequent 20 years. The sign was intended to be torn down in the early 2000's, but was "was saved due to the forsight[sic] of visionary community members."[899] In 2013, with the help of $11,275 in federal funds, this long abandoned neon sign will be restored to operating condition in conjunction with Litchfield Museum and Route 66 Welcome Center Association. Another $7,715 grant awarded in 2013 will restore signs at the Whiting Bros Gas Station #72, an automotive services station in New Mexico.

Over the last decade, the program has spent more than $217,000 to restore 29 neon signs along Route 66.[900]

Nearly $20,000 in federal funds will be used to restore signs along route 66.

98. Golf Car Manufacturer Gets New Factory – (MT) $368,000

Golfers may soon be zipping up and down fairways faster than ever if a Montana company develops what they hope will be the next big thing in "golf cars."

Using $368,000 in Community Development Block Grant (CDBG) funding, Lincoln County, Montana will refurbish a building for LiV Golf Cars, Inc. which it will use for manufacturing.[901] Local officials plan to convert an old maintenance facility into a car assembly plant for the company, which would specialize in cars powered by lithium-ion batteries.[902]

According to company owners, what makes golf cars by this company special is it would be the the first-of-its-kind to run without a lead-acid battery.[903] When asked whether any of the major golf car manufacturers use lithium-ion batteries, owner Jon Hoster said, "no one."[904] He is hoping to bring as many as 45 jobs to the area after three years,[905] though whether that is achievable is still unknown.

"We have zero percent of the market right now, so the potential for us to grow can only go up," he said.[906]

Efforts to use federal funding to promote manufacturing jobs in the town, however, have not gone well in recent years. In 2011, Stinger Welding was given $17 million in federal financing to "complete its fabrication plant" with promise to bring "200-plus good-paying jobs."[907] By the end of 2012, the company fell on hard times and the plant was closed, with nearly 70 people losing their jobs.[908]

99. Budget-busting meals on wheels – (Amtrak) $60 million

It looks like Amtrak has been railroading the American people.

According to Amtrak's inspector general, the publicly funded passenger rail service chalked up $72 million in food-service losses alone in FY 2012.[909] As bad as that number may seem, it's an improvement from previous years' losses from food service: in 2006, the railroad lost $105.2 million from its dining operations.[910]

Almost all of the losses stemmed from providing meals on long-distance trains.[911] While some shorter rail routes in the heavily trafficked Northeast Corridor actually netted Amtrak a tiny bit of money in the form of food service revenue, 99 percent of its $72 million losses in the food service area occurred on long-distance passenger routes.[912]

Amtrak's food services losses have cost taxpayers nearly $1 billion, including approximately $60 million in 2013.

After examining the cuisine served on these long-distance routes, it becomes clear why the company is hemorrhaging cash. On Amtrak's Auto Train, which runs from Virginia to Florida, passengers are offered complimentary wine and cheese. The Auto Train is not unique: three other long-distance routes provide free wine and champagne to sleeper-car passengers, which all together cost Amtrak $428,000 in 2012.[913]

After complimentary cocktails, passengers on long distance routes can find the following dishes awaiting them in the dining car. On the 43-hour Chicago-Los Angeles Southwest Chief, travelers can enjoy a $23.25 Mahi-Mahi dinner accompanied by a vegetable medley and three-grain rice pilaf.[914]

Aren't things are getting better if the food service losses dropped from $105.2 million in 2006 to $72 million in 2012?

No. Apparently, Amtrak has not just been cooking up expensive meals. It has also been cooking the books.

It turns out Amtrak's boost in food and beverage finances are the result of transferring revenue from ticket sales into food service accounts.[915]

According to House Oversight and Government Reform Committee member John Mica, without accounting gimmicks taken into account, Amtrak's food service losses "now approach $1 billion."[916]

100. Audit Finds United States Marshals Service Spent Big on Swag – (USMS) $6,000

In November 2013, the Department of Justice Office of the Inspector General (DOJ OIG) released a report which reviewed the United States Marshals Service's (USMS) use of appropriated funds for promotional items, or "swag." In total, the DOJ OIG found the USMS Investigative Operations Division (IOD) "spent at least $793,118 on promotional items over a 6 year period and that these expenditures were excessive and, in some instances, in contravention of Department Policies and Government Accountability Office (GAO) decisions and guidance."[917]

Over a six-year period, the USMS IOD spent almost $800,000 on swag ranging from challenge coins, drinkware, pens as well as "USMS-themed Christmas ornaments, blankets, ties and other non-essential items is poor stewardship of our citizens' hard-earned tax dollars."[918]

In 2005, USMS IOD had 112 full-time employees and spent $29,138 on promotional items, or $260 per employee.[919] By 2010, the number of employees and spending on swag increased the spending per employee to $1,069.

The DOJ IG found this "growth in spending on promotional items was the result of the absence of internal controls and accountability within the USMS, and the failure of USMS personnel who were given purchasing responsibilities to exercise good judgment."[920] At least one USMS IOD witness stated the agency was relying on employees to use good judgment in making purchases, but other witnesses' statements prove no such judgment was exercised as many of the items ended up in desk drawers and locked closets, and were distributed to employees as needed "without identifying or tracking who took the promotional items, the number of promotional items taken, the purpose for which the promotional items would be used, or to whom they would be given."[921]

For example, while items such as Christmas ornaments were not purchased in the first three years of the evaluation period, when the economy took a dive in 2008, spending on Christmas ornaments began and actually increased every year for three years.[922] In fiscal year 2008, the USMS IOD spent $2875; in 2009, it spent $4622; and in 2010, it spent $6108.[923] Over 3 years, the

A USMS beer mug, worn from years of use, displays the agency's logo. The agency should spend scarce resources making sure no guilty man escapes, not buying beer mugs for their buddies.

USMS IOD purchased 1,679 ornaments, totaling $13,605 or $8.10 per ornament.[924] 453 of those ornaments were purchased in 2010 alone, but ultimately none were distributed. Upon a certain employee's interview with the DOJ OIG in June 2012, the ornaments still sat in his office due to "a USMS directive banning the purchase and distribution of promotional items."[925]

The ornaments were generally used as gifts for USMS IOD staff and guests at the annual Christmas party and for those operating the America's Most Wanted tipline.[926] One assistant chief stated the ornaments were a "word of encouragement" to employees, a "recognition of their work done throughout the year," and "improved morale." However, in general, rules state appropriated funds may not be used for personal gifts to government employees, unless "there is a direct link between the items and the agency's purposes for which Congress has appropriated funding."[927] The DOJ IG explicitly stated none of these reasons established the expenses as necessary.[928]

Yet, the USMS employee who approved the purchase of 285 ornaments, "didn't think much" of buying them and that they were "cute."[929]

In response to concerns raised about the agencies affinity for swag, the agency finally is cutting back, and the administration budget is now only $6,000 to stuff their swag bag.[930] Good thing they stocked up.

[1] Barnes, Julian E. "U.S. Military Eyes Cut to Pay, Benefits; Joint Chiefs Grapple with Less to Spend.," *wsj.com*. Wall Street Journal. 17 November 2013. ‹ttp://online.wsj.com/news/articles/SB10001424052702303755045792041411223865178›.

[2] NBC 5 Dallas-Fort Worth. "Cost of Jailing Hassan: About $548,000 So Far." *NBCDFW.com*. NBC 5, Dallas-Fort Worth. Web. ‹http://www.nbcdfw.com/investigations/Cost-of-Jailing-Hasan-About-548000-So-Far-211316621.html›.

[3] Phares, Walid. "Ft. Hood: The Largest 'Terror Act' Since 9/11?" *foxnews.com*. FOX News Network. 9 November 2009. ‹http://www.foxnews.com/opinion/2009/11/06/walid-phares-ft-hood-murder-terror-attack/›.

[4] Martinez, Luis. "Thunderbirds and Blue Angels to Resume Air Shows, But No More Flyovers," *abcnews.com*. ABC News, 22 October 2013. ‹http://abcnews.go.com/blogs/politics/2013/10/thunderbirds-and-blue-angels-to-resume-air-shows-but-no-more-flyovers/›.

[5] According to information provided by the Air Force.

[6] O'Neal Parker, Lonnae. "Smithsonian to Close Some Exhibit Areas Because of Sequestration." *Washingtonpost.com*. The Washington Post. 29 April 2013. ‹http://articles.washingtonpost.com/2013-04-29/entertainment/38900027_1_sequester-closures-board-budget-cuts›.

[7] "USGS UAS Missions: Planned," U.S. Department of the Interior, Geological Survey website, accessed April 26, 2013; http://rmgsc.cr.usgs.gov/UAS/missions.shtml?current=3.

[8] The Washington Post. "Impact of a Government Shutdown." *Washingtonpost.com*. The Washington Post. Published 25 September 2013; Updated 2 October 2013. Web. ‹http://www.washingtonpost.com/wp-srv/special/politics/2013-shutdown-federal-department-impact/?hpid=zl›.

[9] Hlavaty, Craig . "NASA Needs Volunteers To Stay In Bed for 15 Weeks Straight." *Chron.com*. Houston Chronicle. 18 September 2013. Web. ‹http://www.chron.com/news/article/NASA-needs-volunteers-to-stay-in-bed-for-15-weeks-4821188.php?cmpid=hpfc#photo-5202164›.

[10] Easley, Jonathan. "HealthCare.gov Costs Total $677M." Web log post. *HealtWatch*. Capitol Hill Publishing Corp., 11 Dec. 2013. Web. ‹http://thehill.com/blogs/healthwatch/health-reform-implementation/192761-healthcaregov-costs-at-677m-through-october›.

[11] The White House, Office of Management and Budget. *Impacts and Costs of the October 2013 Federal Government Shutdown*. Executive Office of the President of the United States. November 2013. Web. ‹http://www.whitehouse.gov/sites/default/files/omb/reports/impacts-and-costs-of-october-2013-federal-government-shutdown-report.pdf›. (4).

[12] OPM. "Guidance for Shutdown Furloughs." *Opm.gov*. U.S. US Office of Personnel Management. 11 October 2013. Web ‹http://www.opm.gov/policy-data-oversight/pay-leave/furlough-guidance/guidance-for-shutdown-furloughs.pdf›.

[13] Carmen DeNavas-Walt, Carmen, Bernadette D. Proctor, and Jessica C. Smith. *Income, Poverty, and Health Insurance Coverage in the United States: 2012*. Report No. P60-245, U.S. Department of Commerce Economics and Statistics Administration, U.S. Census Bureau, September 2013. Web. ‹http://www.census.gov/prod/2013pubs/p60-245.pdf›.

[14] Information provided to the Congressional Research Service by the Department of the Treasury Assistant Secretary, Legislative Affairs, December 11, 2013.

[15] The White House, Office of Management and Budget. *Impacts and Costs of the October 2013 Federal Government Shutdown.* Executive Office of the President of the United States. November 2013. Web. <http://www.whitehouse.gov/sites/default/files/omb/reports/impacts-and-costs-of-october-2013-federal-government-shutdown-report.pdf>. (20).

[16] The White House, Office of Management and Budget. *Impacts and Costs of the October 2013 Federal Government Shutdown.* Executive Office of the President of the United States. November 2013. Web. <http://www.whitehouse.gov/sites/default/files/omb/reports/impacts-and-costs-of-october-2013-federal-government-shutdown-report.pdf>. (21).

[17] Information provided to the Congressional Research Service by the Department of Veterans Affairs Office of Congressional & Legislative Affairs, December 4, 2013.

[18] The White House, Office of Management and Budget. *Impacts and Costs of the October 2013 Federal Government Shutdown.* Executive Office of the President of the United States. November 2013. Web. <http://www.whitehouse.gov/sites/default/files/omb/reports/impacts-and-costs-of-october-2013-federal-government-shutdown-report.pdf>. (4).

[19] Information provided to the Congressional Research Service by the *National Aeronautics and Space Administration* Office of Legislative and Intergovernmental Affairs, December 4, 2013.

[20] National Center for Education Statistics. "Fast Facts: Elementary and Secondary – Teacher Trends." U.S. Department of Education Institute of Education Sciences National Center for Education Statistics. Web. <http://nces.ed.gov/fastfacts/display.asp?id=28>.

[21] Bureau of Labor Statistics. "Occupational Employment and Wages, May 2012; 29-1141 Registered Nurses." *Bls.gov.* Web.<http://www.bls.gov/oes/current/oes291141.htm>.

[22] Bureau of Labor Statistics. "Occupational Employment and Wages, May 2012; 33-3051 Police and Sheriff's Patrol Officers." *Bls.gov.* Web. < http://www.bls.gov/oes/current/oes333051.htm>.

[23] Wall, Audrey S. "Table 4.11 Selected States Administrative Officials: Annual Salaries." *The Book of the States.* 2013 ed. Washington, DC: Council of State Government, 2013. 177-82. *Knowledgecenter.csg.com.* Council of State Government. Web. <http://knowledgecenter.csg.org/kc/system/files/4.11_2013.pdf>.

[24] Statement by the Honorable John M. McHugh, Secretary of the Army, and General Raymond T. Odierno, Chief of Staff, United States Army, before the U.S. Senate Committee on Armed Services, on the Posture of the United States Army, April 23, 2013. Web. <http://www.armed-services.senate.gov/hearings/oversight-department-of-the-army>.

[25] "Congressional Inquiry about Soldier of Steel Campaign," Army National Guard-Guard Strength Division (ARNG-GSS) information paper, September 30, 2013.

[26] "Congressional Inquiry about Soldier of Steel Campaign," Army National Guard-Guard Strength Division (ARNG-GSS) information paper, September 30, 2013.

[27] "Congressional Inquiry about Soldier of Steel Campaign," Army National Guard-Guard Strength Division (ARNG-GSS) information paper, September 30, 2013.

[28] "Congressional Inquiry about Soldier of Steel Campaign," Army National Guard-Guard Strength Division (ARNG-GSS) information paper, September 30, 2013.

[29] "Soldier of Steel," Neo-Pangea website, accessed October 22, 2013. Web. <http://www.neo-pangea.com/portfolio/lm-and-o/soldier-of-steel.html>.

[30] National Guard. "The Soldier of Steel Training Plan," Online Video Clip. *YouTube.* YouTube, 16 June 2013. Web. <http://www.youtube.com/watch?v=-uJylK2o6ng&feature=c4-overview-vl&list=PLBMP1mGfH08ohGQoFMBWTPsuqlbnaBmxr>.

[31] Hendrick Motorsports website, accessed October 22, 2013. Web. <http://www.hendrickmotorsports.com/news/photos/2013/06/10/Earnhardt-to-drive-Man-of-Steel-Chevy-at-Michigan#1>.

[32] Panther Racing, Inc. "Man of Steel: Panther's National Guard IndyCar Gets Superman Makeover for Indy 500," *Pantherracing.com.* 11 May 2013 Web <http://www.pantherracing.com/news/index.cfm?cid=56430 >.

[33] "Congressional Inquiry about Soldier of Steel Campaign," Army National Guard-Guard Strength Division (ARNG-GSS) information paper, September 30, 2013.

[34] Information provided by the Army National Guard Advertising Branch Chief to the Congressional Research Service, October 21, 2013.

[35] Morrison, Maureen, "Superman Reboot 'Man of Steel' Snares $160M in Promotions; Summer Blockbuster Boasts More Than 100 Global Marketing Partners," Advertising Age, 3 June 2013. Web. <http://adage.com/article/news/superman-reboot-man-steel-snares-160m-promotions/241822/>.

[36] BoxOffice.com accessed 22 Oct 2013 <http://www.boxoffice.com/statistics/movies/superman-man-of-steel-2012>.

[37] Statement by the Honorable John M. McHugh, Secretary of the Army, and General Raymond T. Odierno, Chief of Staff, United States Army, before the U.S. Senate Committee on Armed Services, on the Posture of the United States Army, April 23, 2013. Web. ‹http://www.armed-services.senate.gov/hearings/oversight-department-of-the-army›.

[38] Popular Romance Editors. "About the Project." *Popularromanceproject.org.* The Roy Rosenzweig Center for History and New Media. Web.‹ http://popularromanceproject.org/about›.

[39] The Roy Rosenzweig Center for History and New Media. "Popular Romance Project Receives NEH Funding." *Chnm.gmu.edu.* The Roy Rosenzweig Center for History and New Media. 11 April 2013. Web. ‹http://chnm.gmu.edu/news/popular-romance-project-receives-neh-funding/›.

[40] The Roy Rosenzweig Center for History and New Media. "Popular Romance Project Receives NEH Funding." *Chnm.gmu.edu.* The Roy Rosenzweig Center for History and New Media. 11 April 2013. Web. ‹http://chnm.gmu.edu/news/popular-romance-project-receives-neh-funding/›

[41] The Roy Rosenzweig Center for History and New Media. "Popular Romance Project Receives NEH Funding." *Chnm.gmu.edu.* The Roy Rosenzweig Center for History and New Media. 11 April 2013. Web. ‹http://chnm.gmu.edu/news/popular-romance-project-receives-neh-funding/›

[42] The Roy Rosenzweig Center for History and New Media. "Popular Romance Project Receives NEH Funding." *Chnm.gmu.edu.* The Roy Rosenzweig Center for History and New Media. 11 April 2013. Web. ‹http://chnm.gmu.edu/news/popular-romance-project-receives-neh-funding/›.

[43] Kaplan, Deborah. "Hero or Stalker?" *popularromanceproject.com.* The Roy Rosenzweig Center for History and New Media. 8 March 2012. Web. ‹http://popularromanceproject.org/talking-about-romance/1365/›.

[44] Gleason, William. "Call me?" *popularromanceproject.com.* The Roy Rosenzweig Center for History and New Media. 6 September 2012. Web. ‹http://popularromanceproject.org/talking-about-romance/3082/›.

[45] Kamble, Jayashree. "Bond in Love." *popularromanceproject.com.* The Roy Rosenzweig Center for History and New Media. 3 September 2013. Web ‹http://popularromanceproject.org/talking-about-romance/5327/#more-5327›.

[46] Chant, Ian. "Popular Romance Project Connects Readers, Writers, Scholars, and Libraries." *Lj.libraryjournal.com.* Library Journal. 26 September 2013. ‹http://lj.libraryjournal.com/2013/09/publishing/popular-romance-project-connects-readers-writers-scholars-and-libraries/#_›.

[47] Chant, Ian. "Popular Romance Project Connects Readers, Writers, Scholars, and Libraries." *Lj.libraryjournal.com.* Library Journal. 26 September 2013. Web. ‹http://lj.libraryjournal.com/2013/09/publishing/popular-romance-project-connects-readers-writers-scholars-and-libraries/#_›.

[48] National Endowment for the Humanities. "Popular Romance Project Website." *Securegrants.neh.gov.* National Endowment for the Humanities, Grant number TR5040913, 1 September 2013 – 31 March 2015. Web. ‹https://securegrants.neh.gov/publicquery/main.aspx?f=1&gn=TR5040913›.

[49] National Endowment for the Humanities . "The Popular Romance Project Film and Website: Creating Community in a Mass Cultural World." *Securegrants.neh.gov.* National Endowment for the Humanities, Grant No. TR-50389-12, 1 October 2012 – 30 September 2015.Web. ‹ https://securegrants.neh.gov/publicquery/main.aspx?f=1&gn=TR-50389-12›.

[50] National Endowment for the Humanities. "The Popular Romance Project: Exploring the Romance Novel from Multiple Perspectives Across Time an Culture." *Securegrants.neh.gov.* National Endowment for the Humanities, Grant No. TD-50256-10, 1 September 2010 – 29 February 2012.Web. ‹https://securegrants.neh.gov/publicquery/main.aspx?f=1&gn=TD-50256-10›.

[51] Kahn, Laurie. "More Details about the Popular Romance Project and its Funding." *Kickstarter.com.* 6 August 2012. Web. ‹http://www.kickstarter.com/projects/1162698421/love-between-the-covers/posts/282731›.

[52] Romance Writers of America. "Romance Industry Statistics." *Rwa.org.* Romance Writers of America. Web. ‹http://www.rwa.org/p/cm/ld/fid=580›.

[53] Grim, Ryan, Jennifer Bendery, and Shahien Nasiripour. "Nuclear Fallout: The Real-World Consequences of Senate Filibuster Reform." *HuffingtonPost.com.* TheHufffingtonPost.com Inc. 21 November 2013. Web. ‹http://www.huffingtonpost.com/2013/11/21/senate-filibuster_n_4319665.html›.

[54] Lesniewski, Niels. "Uncertain 'Nuclear' Fallout in Senate." Weblog post.*Rollcall.com/wgdb.* CQ-Roll Call Inc., 25 Nov. 2013. Web. ‹http://blogs.rollcall.com/wgdb/uncertain-nuclear-fallout-in-senate/›.

[55] Quinnipiac University Polling Institute. Newsroom.*Obama Gets Small Bounce From Health Care Win, Quinnipiac University National Poll Finds; Net Disapproval Of Health Reform Drops 9 Points. Quinnipiac.edu.* Quinnipiac University. 25 Mar. 2010. Web. ‹http://www.quinnipiac.edu/institutes-and-centers/polling-institute/polling-institute-contacts-and-information/›.

[56] Quinnipiac University Polling Institute. Newsroom.Obama's Approval Bounces Back, Quinnipiac University National Poll Finds; Health Care s Best and Worst Thing He's Done. *Quinnipiac.edu.* Quinnipiac University.13 January 2011. Web. ‹http://www.quinnipiac.edu/institutes-and-centers/polling-institute/national/release-detail?ReleaseID=›.

[57] Cohen, Jon. "Poll: Few Americans Focused on Filibuster Issue," *abcnew.com*. ABC News Internet Ventures. Yahoo! 23 May 2005. Web. <http://abcnews.go.com/Politics/PollVault/story?id=783806>.

[58] Quinnipiac University Polling Institute. Newsroom. Obama's Approval Bounces Back, Quinnipiac University National Poll Finds; Health Care s Best and Worst Thing He's Done. *Quinnipiac.edu*. Quinnipiac University. 13 January 2011. Web. <http://www.quinnipiac.edu/institutes-and-centers/polling-institute/national/release-detail?ReleaseID=>.

[59] Jackson, David. "Obama Applauds Filibuster Rule Change." *Usatoday.com*. Gannett. 21 November 2013. Web. <http://www.usatoday.com/story/news/2013/11/21/obama-senate-nuclear-option-statement/3664905/>.

[60] National Science Foundation. "Majority Rule and Minority Rights: A Panel Study of Democratic Values and Attitudes toward the Senate Filibuster Among the American Public." Award Abstract #0960991. National Science Foundation. 2 December 2013. Web. < http://www.nsf.gov/awardsearch/showAward?AWD_ID=0960991>.

[61] National Science Foundation. "Majority Rule and Minority Rights: A Panel Study of Democratic Values and Attitudes toward the Senate Filibuster Among the American Public." Award Abstract #0960991. National Science Foundation. 2 December 2013. Web. < http://www.nsf.gov/awardsearch/showAward?AWD_ID=0960991>.

[62] National Science Foundation. "Majority Rule and Minority Rights: A Panel Study of Democratic Values and Attitudes toward the Senate Filibuster Among the American Public." Award Abstract #0960991. National Science Foundation. 2 December 2013. Web. < http://www.nsf.gov/awardsearch/showAward?AWD_ID=0960991>.

[63] Mellman, Mark. "Mark Mellman: Public Opinion and the Filibuster." *Thehill.com*. Capitol Hill Publishing Corp. 19 November 2013. Web. <http://thehill.com/opinion/mark-mellman/190836-mark-mellman-public-opinion-and-the-filibuster>.

[64] Blumenthal, Mark, and Ariel Edwards-Levy. "HUFFPOLLSTER: Few Outside Washington Have Strong Opinions On Filibuster." *Huffingtonpost.com*. TheHuffingtonPost.com, Inc. 21 November 2013. Web. <http://www.huffingtonpost.com/2013/11/21/huffpollster-filibuster-a_n_4319565.html>.

[65] National Science Foundation. "Majority Rule and Minority Rights: A Panel Study of Democratic Values and Attitudes toward the Senate Filibuster Among the American Public." Award Abstract #0960991. National Science Foundation. 2 December 2013. Web. < http://www.nsf.gov/awardsearch/showAward?AWD_ID=0960991>.

[66] Jackson, David. "Obama Applauds Filibuster Rule Change." *Usatoday.com*. USA Today. 21 November 2013. Web. <http://www.usatoday.com/story/news/2013/11/21/obama-senate-nuclear-option-statement/3664905/>.

[67] Suresh, Subra. "Impact of FY 2013 Sequestration Order on NSF Awards." Letter to NSF Grant Awardee Organizations. 27 Feb. 2013. *Nsf.gov*. Web. <http://www.nsf.gov/pubs/2013/in133/in133.pdf>.

[68] Darla Cameron, David A. Fahrenthold and Lisa Rein, "Tracking the Predicted Sequester Impacts." *Washingtonpost.com*. The Washington Post. 30 June 2013. Web. <http://www.washingtonpost.com/wp-srv/special/politics/sequestration-federal-agency-update/>.

[69] USDA. "Guaranteed Loans Offer Affordable Financing to Rural Homebuyers,." USDA Rural Development Single Family Housing Guaranteed Loan Program. 8 Nov. 2013. Web. <http://www.rurdev.usda.gov/HSF-About_Guaranteed_Loans.html>.

[70] Conlin, Michelle, and Janet Roberts. "Special Report: A Rural Housing Program City Slickers Just Love." *Reuters.com*. Reuters. 28 March 2013. Web. <http://www.reuters.com/article/2013/03/28/us-usa-mortgages-usda-special-report-idUSBRE92R0QC20130328>.

[71] Congressional Research Service. "USDA Rural Housing Service Mortgages and Rural Business Services Loans," Memorandum to Senator Tom Coburn, M.D. 2 November 2013.

[72] USDA Office of Inspector General. *Loss Claims Related to Single Family Housing Guaranteed Loans*. Rep. no. 04703-0003-HY. Washington, D.C.: 2013. Print.

[73] Congressional Research Service. "USDA Rural Housing Service Mortgages and Rural Business Services Loans," Memorandum to Senator Tom Coburn, M.D. 2 November 2013

[74] Cowan, Tadlock. "An Overview of USDA Rural Development Programs," *CRS.gov*. Congressional Research Service. Report No. 7-5700. 3 May 2013.

[75] USDA. "Guaranteed Loans Offer Affordable Financing to Rural Homebuyers,." USDA Rural Development Single Family Housing Guaranteed Loan Program. 8 Nov. 2013. Web. <http://www.rurdev.usda.gov/HSF-About_Guaranteed_Loans.html>.

[76] Treviño, Tammye. "USDA Housing Programs Administered in Accordance with Federal Law." *Rurdev.USDA.gov*. USDA Rural Development. Press Release No. STELPRD4019835. 18 March 2013. Web. <http://www.rurdev.usda.gov/STELPRD4019835.html>.

[77] Conlin, Michelle, and Janet Roberts. "Special Report: A Rural Housing Program City Slickers Just Love." *Reuters.com.* Reuters. 28 March 2013. Web. ‹http://www.reuters.com/article/2013/03/28/us-usa-mortgages-usda-special-report-idUSBRE92R0QC20130328›.

[78] Congressional Research Service. "USDA Rural Housing Service Mortgages and Rural Business Services Loans," Memorandum to Senator Tom Coburn, M.D. 2 November 2013.

[79] Aoun, Gabriela. "Maui Voted Best Island In The World... And Has Been for the Last 20 Years." *HuffingtonPost.com.* Huffington Post. 15 Oct. 2013. Web. ‹http://www.huffingtonpost.com/2013/10/15/maui-best-island_n_4102707.html›.

[80] Condé Nast Traveler. "Top 25 Islands in the World – Readers' Choice Awards.," *cntraveler.com.* Condé Nast. Nov. 2013. Web. ‹http://www.cntraveler.com/readers-choice-awards/best-islands-world_slideshow_item24_25›.

[81] Condé Nast Traveler. "Top 25 Islands in the World – Readers' Choice Awards.," *cntraveler.com.* Condé Nast. Nov. 2013. Web. ‹http://www.cntraveler.com/readers-choice-awards/best-islands-world_slideshow_2-Kauai_24›.

[82] Gerber, Sharon. "USDA/Rural Housing Loans Offer 100% Financing on Hawaii Homes," *HawaiiReporter.com.* Hawaii Life/Hawaii Reporter. 13 February 2012. Web. ‹http://www.hawaiireporter.com/usdarural-housing-loans-offer-100-financing-on-hawaii-homes/123›.

[83] Gerber, Sharon. "USDA/Rural Housing Loans Offer 100% Financing on Hawaii Homes," *HawaiiReporter.com.* Hawaii Life/Hawaii Reporter. 13 February 2012. Web. ‹http://www.hawaiireporter.com/usdarural-housing-loans-offer-100-financing-on-hawaii-homes/123›.

[84] USDA OIG. *Loss Claims Related to Single Family Housing Guaranteed Loans.* Rep. no. 04703-0003-HY. Washington, D.C.: n.p., 2013. Print.

[85] USDA OIG. *Loss Claims Related to Single Family Housing Guaranteed Loans.* Rep. no. 04703-0003-HY. Washington, D.C.: n.p., 2013. Print.

[86] Treviño, Tammye. "USDA Housing Programs Administered in Accordance with Federal Law." *Rurdev.USDA.gov.* USDA Rural Development. Press Release No. STELPRD4019835. 18 March 2013. Web. ‹http://www.rurdev.usda.gov/STELPRD4019835.html›.

[87] Conlin, Michelle, and Janet Roberts. "Special Report: A Rural Housing Program City Slickers Just Love." *Reuters.com.* Reuters. 28 March 2013. Web. ‹http://www.reuters.com/article/2013/03/28/us-usa-mortgages-usda-special-report-idUSBRE92R0QC20130328›.

[88] Conlin, Michelle, and Janet Roberts. "Special Report: A Rural Housing Program City Slickers Just Love." *Reuters.com.* Reuters. 28 March 2013. Web. ‹http://www.reuters.com/article/2013/03/28/us-usa-mortgages-usda-special-report-idUSBRE92R0QC20130328›.

[89] Vilsack, Thomas J. USDA Secretary. Letter to Chairwoman Barbara Mikulski, Senate Committee on Appropriations. 5 February 2013. Washington, D.C.

[90] USDA. "Rental Assistance Sequestration." *Rurdev.USDA.gov.* USDA Rural Development. September 2013. Web. ‹http://www.rurdev.usda.gov/HMF_RA_Information.html›.

[91] USDA. "List of MFH Properties - Receiving Borrower Letter," *Rurdev.USDA.gov.* USDA Rural Development. September 2013. Web. ‹http://www.rurdev.usda.gov/supportdocuments/RA_Projects_Affected.pdf›.

[92] USDA OIG. *Loss Claims Related to Single Family Housing Guaranteed Loans.* Rep. no. 04703-0003-HY. Washington, D.C.: 2013. Print.

[93] Information confirmed by the Congressional Research Service. Section 162 of the Internal Revenue Code or any other statute does not disallow deductions for expenses related to operating a brothel.

[94] Friess, Steve. "Nevada Brothels Want to Pay Tax, But State Says No," *nytimes.com.* The New York Times Company. 26 January 2009. Web. ‹http://www.nytimes.com/2009/01/26/world/americas/26iht-brothel.1.19671349.html?pagewanted=all&_r=0›.

[95] Information provided by the Congressional Research Service, 29 August 2013.

[96] Doan, Michael. "Prostitutes Called Legitimate Expense For Nevada Brothel," *Associated Press.* The Dispatch. July 27, 1978.

[97] Duryee, Tricia, and Mark Rahner. "Brilliant Deductions: Some Taxpayers Try Anything Once," *seattletimes.com.* The Seattle Times Company. 15 April 2002. Web. ‹http://community.seattletimes.nwsource.com/archive/?date=20020415&slug=taxfun15›.

[98] Randazzo, Ryan. "Wacky Writeoffs," *Reno Gazette-Journal*, April 15, 2001.

[99] Vekshin, Alison. "Brothels in Nevada Suffer as Web Disrupts Oldest Trade," *Bloomberg.com.* Bloomberg L.P. 28 August 2013. Web. ‹http://www.bloomberg.com/news/2013-08-28/brothels-in-nevada-shrivel-as-web-disrupts-oldest-trade.html›.

[100] Vekshin, Alison. "Brothels in Nevada Suffer as Web Disrupts Oldest Trade," *Bloomberg.com.* Bloomberg L.P. 28 August 2013. Web. ‹http://www.bloomberg.com/news/2013-08-28/brothels-in-nevada-shrivel-as-web-disrupts-oldest-trade.html›.

[101] Vekshin, Alison. "Brothels in Nevada Suffer as Web Disrupts Oldest Trade," *Bloomberg.com*. Bloomberg L.P. 28 August 2013. Web. ‹http://www.bloomberg.com/news/2013-08-28/brothels-in-nevada-shrivel-as-web-disrupts-oldest-trade.html›.

[102] Whitcomb, Dan, and Ellen Wulfhorst. "Harry Reid's Prostitution Remarks Ignite Debate in Nevada," *huffingtonpost.com*. Thomson Reuters. 6 March 2011. Web. ‹http://www.huffingtonpost.com/2011/03/06/harry-reids-prostitution-_n_832064.html›.

[103] Londoño, Ernesto, "Scrapping equipment key to Afghan drawdown," *WashingtonPost.com*. The Washington Post. 19 June 2013. Web. ‹http://www.washingtonpost.com/world/asia_pacific/scrapping-equipment-key-to-afghan-drawdown/2013/06/19/9d435258-d83f-11e2-b418-9dfa095e125d_story.html›.

[104] AFP. "US Scraps Tons Of Gear s It Leaves Afghanistan."*DefenseNews.com*. Agence France-Presse. 20 June 2013. Web. http://www.defensenews.com/article/20130620/DEFREG04/306200012/US-Scraps-Tons-Gear-Leaves-Afghanistan›.

[105] Londoño, Ernesto, "Scrapping equipment key to Afghan drawdown," *WashingtonPost.com*. The Washington Post. 19 June 2013. Web. ‹http://www.washingtonpost.com/world/asia_pacific/scrapping-equipment-key-to-afghan-drawdown/2013/06/19/9d435258-d83f-11e2-b418-9dfa095e125d_story.html›.

[106] Londoño, Ernesto, "Scrapping equipment key to Afghan drawdown," *WashingtonPost.com*. The Washington Post. 19 June 2013. Web. ‹http://www.washingtonpost.com/world/asia_pacific/scrapping-equipment-key-to-afghan-drawdown/2013/06/19/9d435258-d83f-11e2-b418-9dfa095e125d_story.html›.

[107] Vanden Brook, Tom. "Tab for Bringing Gear Home From Afghanistan: $3 Billion." *USAToday.com*. USA Today. 20 September 2013. Web. ‹http://www.usatoday.com/story/news/world/2013/09/20/afghanistan-war-gear-cost/2843351/›.

[108] Londoño, Ernesto, "Scrapping equipment key to Afghan drawdown," *WashingtonPost.com*. The Washington Post. 19 June 2013. Web. ‹http://www.washingtonpost.com/world/asia_pacific/scrapping-equipment-key-to-afghan-drawdown/2013/06/19/9d435258-d83f-11e2-b418-9dfa095e125d_story.html›.

[109] Londoño, Ernesto, "Scrapping equipment key to Afghan drawdown," *WashingtonPost.com*. The Washington Post. 19 June 2013. Web. ‹http://www.washingtonpost.com/world/asia_pacific/scrapping-equipment-key-to-afghan-drawdown/2013/06/19/9d435258-d83f-11e2-b418-9dfa095e125d_story.html›.

[110] Londoño, Ernesto, "Scrapping equipment key to Afghan drawdown," *WashingtonPost.com*. The Washington Post. 19 June 2013. Web. ‹http://www.washingtonpost.com/world/asia_pacific/scrapping-equipment-key-to-afghan-drawdown/2013/06/19/9d435258-d83f-11e2-b418-9dfa095e125d_story.html›.

[111] Londoño, Ernesto, "Scrapping equipment key to Afghan drawdown," *WashingtonPost.com*. The Washington Post. 19 June 2013. Web. ‹http://www.washingtonpost.com/world/asia_pacific/scrapping-equipment-key-to-afghan-drawdown/2013/06/19/9d435258-d83f-11e2-b418-9dfa095e125d_story.html›.

[112] Merle, Renae. "Racing to Defeat the Roadside Bomb," *WashingtonPost,com*. The Washington Post. 3 July 2007. Web. ‹http://www.washingtonpost.com/wp-dyn/content/article/2007/07/02/AR2007070201708.html›.

[113] Bridge, Robert. "Operation Junkyard: US scrapping 'tons' of equipment as Afghan exit looms," *RT.com*. RT News Network. 20 June 2013. Web. ‹http://rt.com/news/afghanistan-us-withdrawal-war-003/›.

[114] Ferris-Rotman, Amie, "Afghan scrap yards eye unwanted U.S. gear for steel industry," *Reuters.com*. Reuters. 15 May 2013. ‹http://www.reuters.com/article/2013/05/15/us-afghanistan-scrap-idUSBRE94E09920130515›.

[115] Maass, Harold. "The Military is Literally Throwing Away $7 Billion in Afghanistan," *TheWeek.com*. The Week. 20 June 2013. Web. ‹http://theweek.com/article/index/245927/the-military-is-literally-throwing-away-7-billion-in-afghanistan›.

[116] Erwin, Sandra, "Debate Continues Over Fate of U.S. Military Gear in Afghanistan," *NationalDefenseMagazine.com*. National Defense Magazine. 13 June 2013. ‹http://www.nationaldefensemagazine.org/blog/Lists/Posts/Post.aspx?ID=1175›.

[117] National Technical Information Service Website. "About NTIS." *Ntis.gov*. US Department of Commerce. Web. ‹http://www.ntis.gov/about/index.aspx›.

[118] National Technical Information Service Website. "About NTIS." *Ntis.gov*. US Department of Commerce. Web. ‹http://www.ntis.gov/about/index.aspx›.

[119] Melvin, Valerie. *Information Management: National Technical Information Service's Dissemination of Technical Reports Needs Congressional Attention*. Rep. no. GAO-13-99. Report to Congressional Committees Washington, D.C.: Government Accountability Office, 2012. Web. ‹http://www.gao.gov/products/GAO-13-99›.

[120] Melvin, Valerie. *Information Management: National Technical Information Service's Dissemination of Technical Reports Needs Congressional Attention*. Rep. no. GAO-13-99. Report to Congressional Committees Washington, D.C.: Government Accountability Office, 2012. Web. ‹http://www.gao.gov/products/GAO-13-99›.

[121] Melvin, Valerie. *Information Management: National Technical Information Service's Dissemination of Technical Reports Needs Congressional Attention*. Rep. no. GAO-13-99. Report to Congressional Committees. Washington, D.C.: Government Accountability Office, 2012. Web. ‹http://www.gao.gov/products/GAO-13-99›. p3

[122] GAO. *Information Management: Dissemination of Technical Reports*. Rep. no. GAO-01-490. Report to Congressional Requesters. 18 May 2001. Web. ‹ http://www.gao.gov/products/GAO-01-490›. p14

[123] National Technical Information Service Website. "About NTIS." *Ntis.gov*. US Department of Commerce. Web. ‹http://www.ntis.gov/products/publications.aspx›.

[124] U.S Army QuarterMaster Corps Website. "Food Service Publications and Links." *Quartermaster.army.mil*. Joint Culinary Center of Excellence, Publications, Armed Forces Recipe Service-V2003. Updated 11 August 2013. Web. ‹http://www.quartermaster.army.mil/jccoe/publications/food_links.html›.

[125] U.S Army QuarterMaster Corps Website. "Food Service Publications and Links." *Quartermaster.army.mil*. Joint Culinary Center of Excellence, Publications, Armed Forces Recipe Service-V2003. Updated 11 August 2013. Web. ‹http://www.quartermaster.army.mil/jccoe/publications/food_links.html›.

[126] National Technical Information Service Website. "Food Code 2009." *Ntis.gov*. US Department of Commerce. 2009. Web. ‹http://www.ntis.gov/products/food-code.aspx›.

[127] Food and Drug Administration Website. "Food Code 2009." *Fda.gov*. US Department of Health & Human Services. Updated 8 November 20013. Web. ‹http://www.fda.gov/Food/GuidanceRegulation/RetailFoodProtection/FoodCode/UCM2019396.htm›.

[128] Melvin, Valerie. *Information Management: National Technical Information Service's Dissemination of Technical Reports Needs Congressional Attention*. Rep. no. GAO-13-99. Report to Congressional Committees Washington, D.C.: Government Accountability Office, 2012. Web. ‹http://www.gao.gov/products/GAO-13-99›. p23

[129] Melvin, Valerie. *Information Management: National Technical Information Service's Dissemination of Technical Reports Needs Congressional Attention*. Rep. no. GAO-13-99. Report to Congressional Committees Washington, D.C.: Government Accountability Office, 2012. Web. ‹http://www.gao.gov/products/GAO-13-99›. p24.

[130] GAO. *Information Policy: NTIS' Financial Position Provides an Opportunity to Reassess Its Mission*. US Rep. no. GAO/GGD-00-147. Report to Congressional Committees. Washington, D.C.: Government Accountability Office. 30 June 2000. Web. ‹http://www.gao.gov/products/GGD-00-147›.

[131] GAO. *Information Management: Dissemination of Technical Reports*. Rep. no. GAO-01-490. Report to Congressional Requesters. 18 May 2001. Web. ‹ http://www.gao.gov/products/GAO-01-490›. p2.

GAO. *Information Policy: NTIS' Financial Position Provides an Opportunity to Reassess Its Mission*. US Rep. no. GAO/GGD-00-147. Report to Congressional Committees. Washington, D.C.: Government Accountability Office. 30 June 2000. Web. ‹http://www.gao.gov/products/GGD-00-147›. p1.

[133] GAO. *Information Management: Dissemination of Technical Reports*. Rep. no. GAO-01-490. Report to Congressional Requesters. 18 May 2001. Web. ‹ http://www.gao.gov/products/GAO-01-490›. p5.

[134] Easley, Jonathan. "HealthCare.gov Costs Total $677M." Web log post. *HealthWatch*. Capitol Hill Publishing Corp., 11 Dec. 2013. Web. ‹http://thehill.com/blogs/healthwatch/health-reform-implementation/192761-healthcaregov-costs-at-677m-through-october›.

[135] Johnson, Carla K. "'Obamacare' National Marketing Campaign to Cost Nearly $700 Million," *washiongton.cbslocal.com*. Associated Press. 24 July 2013. Web. ‹http://washington.cbslocal.com/2013/07/24/obamacare-national-marketing-campaign-to-cost-nearly-700-million/›.

[136] Sun, Lena H., and Scott Wilson. "Health Insurance Exchange Launched despite Signs of Serious Problems." *Washington Post*. The Washington Post, 22 Oct. 2013. Web. ‹http://www.washingtonpost.com/national/health-science/health-insurance-exchange-launched-despite-signs-of-serious-problems/2013/10/21/161a3500-3a85-11e3-b6a9-da62c264f40e_story.html?hpid=z1›.

[137] Condon, Stephanie. "HHS: At least 106,185 enrolled in Obamacare so far," *CBSnews.com*. CBS News. 13 November 2013. Web. ‹http://www.cbsnews.com/8301-250_162-57612226/hhs-at-least-106185-enrolled-in-obamacare-so-far/›.

[138] Roy, Avik. "The Obamacare Exchange Scorecard: Around 100,000 Enrollees And Five Million Cancellations," *forbes.com*. Forbes. 12 November 2013. Web. ‹http://www.forbes.com/sites/theapothecary/2013/11/12/the-obamacare-exchange-scorecard-around-100000-enrollees-and-five-million-cancellations/›.

[139] Website of Senator Tom Coburn, M.D. "CODE RED: Obamacare After One-Month of Enrollment." 13 November 2013. Web. ‹http://newsok.com/oklahoma-sen.-tom-coburn-talks-cancer-health-care-leaving-congress/article/3907870›.

[140] Kaplan, Rebecca. "Disapproval of Obamacare Spikes In New Poll," *cbsnews.com*. CBS News. 19 November 2013. Web. ‹http://www.cbsnews.com/8301-250_162-57612963/disapproval-of-obamacare-spikes-in-new-poll/›.

[141] The White House. Office of the Press Secretary. *Statement by the President on the Affordable Care Act*. www.whitehouse.gov. 14 Nov. 2013. Web. ‹http://www.whitehouse.gov/the-press-office/2013/11/14/statement-president-affordable-care-act›.

[142] Johnson, Carla K. "'Obamacare' National Marketing Campaign To Cost Nearly $700 Million," *washiongton.cbslocal.com.* Associated Press. 24 July 2013. Web. ‹http://washington.cbslocal.com/2013/07/24/obamacare-national-marketing-campaign-to-cost-nearly-700-million/›.

[143] Palmer, Anna, and Allen, Jonathan. "Obamacare Marketing Push On Hold," *Politico.com* Politico. 31 October 2013. Web. ‹http://www.politico.com/story/2013/10/obamacare-marketing-push-on-hold-99201.html#ixzz2kkomYeLQ›.

[144] Wayne, Alex, and Anna Edney. "Obamacare Consultants Warned of Health Website Failure." *Bloomberg.com.* Bloomberg News. 19 November 2013. Web. ‹http://www.bloomberg.com/news/2013-11-19/obamacare-consultants-warned-of-health-website-failure.html›.

[145] Palmer, Anna, and Jonathan Allen. "Obamacare Marketing Push On Hold," *Politico.com* Politico. 31 October 2013. Web. ‹http://www.politico.com/story/2013/10/obamacare-marketing-push-on-hold-99201.html#ixzz2kkomYeLQ›.

[146] Palmer, Anna, and Jonathan Allen. "Obamacare Marketing Push On Hold," *Politico.com* Politico. 31 October 2013. Web. ‹http://www.politico.com/story/2013/10/obamacare-marketing-push-on-hold-99201.html#ixzz2kkomYeLQ›.

[147] Johnson, Carla K. "'Obamacare' National Marketing Campaign To Cost Nearly $700 Million," *washiongton.cbslocal.com.* Associated Press. 24 July 2013. Web. ‹http://washington.cbslocal.com/2013/07/24/obamacare-national-marketing-campaign-to-cost-nearly-700-million/›.

[148] Johnson, Carla K. "'Obamacare' National Marketing Campaign To Cost Nearly $700 Million," *washiongton.cbslocal.com.* Associated Press. 24 July 2013. Web. ‹http://washington.cbslocal.com/2013/07/24/obamacare-national-marketing-campaign-to-cost-nearly-700-million/›.

[149] Moheny, Gillian. "The Strangest Ads to Promote Obamacare Sign-Ups." *Abcnews.go.com.* ABC News 14 November 2013. Web. ‹http://abcnews.go.com/Health/strangest-obamacare-ads/story?id=20876057›.

[150] MNsure YouTube channel. Web. ‹http://www.youtube.com/user/MNsure?feature=watch›. Accessed 18 November 2013.

[151] Moheny, Gillian. "The Strangest Ads to Promote Obamacare Sign-Ups." *Abcnews.go.com.* ABC News 14 November 2013. Web. ‹http://abcnews.go.com/Health/strangest-obamacare-ads/story?id=20876057›.

[152] Johnson, Carla K. "'Obamacare' National Marketing Campaign To Cost Nearly $700 Million," *washiongton.cbslocal.com.* Associated Press. 24 July 2013. Web.

[153] Waplanfinder. "No More Surprises | WA Healthplanfinder." Online video clip. *YouTube.* YouTube, 17 September 2013. Web. ‹http://www.youtube.com/watch?v=s0YzmwrszPY›.

[154] Werner, Anna. "Oregon Spends Big to Pitch Youth on Obamacare Benefits," *cbsnews.com.* CBS Interactive Inc. 28 July 2013. Web. ‹http://www.cbsnews.com/8301-18563_162-57595869/›.

[155] Cover Oregon. "Cover Oregon: 'Fly With Your Own Wings' – Dave Depper." Online video clip. *YouTube.* YouTube. 6 September 2013. Web. ‹http://www.youtube.com/watch?v=SLpKDNVU9dA›.

[156] Chebium, Raju. "Oregon Ranks Last in Health Insurance Sign-ups." *Usatoday.com.* Gannett. 11 December 2013. Web. ‹ http://www.usatoday.com/story/news/politics/2013/12/11/oregon-last-insurance-signups/3992583/›.

[157] Newman, Andrew Adam. "Songs and Sunscreen Spread the Health Insurance Message." *Nytimes.com.* The New York Times Company. 31 July 2013. ‹http://www.nytimes.com/2013/08/01/business/media/songs-and-sunscreen-spread-the-health-insurance-message.html›.

[158] Associated Press. "Obama Administration Posts Low Health Care Signups; 3,700 In Colorado," *gazette.com.* Associated Press. 13 November 2013. Web. ‹http://gazette.com/obama-administration-posts-low-health-care-signups-3700-in-colorado/article/1509293›.

[159] Associated Press. "Obama Administration Posts Low Health Care Signups; 3,700 In Colorado," *gazette.com.* Associated Press. 13 November 2013. Web. ‹http://gazette.com/obama-administration-posts-low-health-care-signups-3700-in-colorado/article/1509293›..

[160] Erdahl, Kent. "Colo. Man Signs Up For His Insurance, His Dog Gets Covered Instead," *kdvr.com.* FOX 31 Denver. 15 November 2013. Web. ‹http://kdvr.com/2013/11/15/colo-man-signs-up-for-his-insurance-his-dog-gets-covered-instead/›.

[161] ConnectForHealthCO. "Vegas Television Commercial." Online video clip. *YouTube.* YouTube. 14 May 2013. Web. ‹http://www.youtube.com/watch?v=yJ7DYjykk8g›.

[162] Kliff, Sarah. "Will Bourbon Help Kentucky Swallow Obamacare?" *washingtonpost.com.* The Washington Post. 11 July 2013. Web. ‹http://www.washingtonpost.com/blogs/wonkblog/wp/2013/07/11/will-bourbon-help-kentucky-swallow-obamacare/›.

[163] Department of Health and Human Services. "Health Insurance Marketplace: November Enrollment Report." DHHS Office of the Assistant Secretary for Planning and Evaluation Issue Brief. 13 November 2013 Web. ‹http://aspe.hhs.gov/health/reports/2013/marketplaceenrollment/rpt_enrollment.pdf›. (8).

[164] Northrop Grumman. "Long Endurance Multi-Intelligence Vehicle (LEMV)." NorthorpGrumman.com. 2013. Northrop Grumman. 13 Nov. 2013. Web. ‹http://www.northropgrumman.com/Capabilities/lemv/Pages/default.aspx›.

[165] Hennigan, W.J., "Army lets air out of battlefield spyship project," *Los Angeles Times*, 23 October 2013. Web. ⟨http://www.latimes.com/business/la-fi-blimp-fire-sale-20131023,0,3497521.story#axzz2jlihKJbW⟩.

[166] Army News Service. "First flight test successful for Army's Long Endurance Multi-Intelligence Vehicle air vehicle." *Army.mil*. United States Army. 8 August 2012. Web. ⟨http://www.army.mil/article/85175/⟩.

[167] Army News Service. "First flight test successful for Army's Long Endurance Multi-Intelligence Vehicle air vehicle." *Army.mil*. United States Army. 8 August 2012. Web. ⟨http://www.army.mil/article/85175/⟩.

[168] GAO. *Defense Acquisitions: Future Aerostat and Airship Investment Decisions Drive Oversight and Coordination Needs*. GAO-13-81. Report to the Subcommittee on Emerging Threats and Capabilities, Committee on Armed Services. US Senate. October 2012. Web. ⟨http://www.gao.gov/assets/650/649661.pdf⟩.

[169] GAO. *Defense Acquisitions: Future Aerostat and Airship Investment Decisions Drive Oversight and Coordination Needs*. GAO-13-81. Report to the Subcommittee on Emerging Threats and Capabilities, Committee on Armed Services. US Senate. October 2012. Web. ⟨http://www.gao.gov/assets/650/649661.pdf⟩.

[170] Moore, Kirk, "Army Pulls Plug on Airship Project," *military.com*. Asbury Park Press, April 2. 2013, Web. ⟨http://www.military.com/daily-news/2013/04/02/army-pulls-plug-on-airship-project.html⟩.

[171] Moore, Kirk, "Army Pulls Plug on Airship Project," *military.com*. Asbury Park Press, April 2. 2013, Web. ⟨http://www.military.com/daily-news/2013/04/02/army-pulls-plug-on-airship-project.html⟩.

[172] Matthews, William. "Deflated: America's Airship Revolution is Threatened by Mishaps, Delays, Funding Cuts." *DefenseNews.com*. Gannett Government Media Corporation. 1 May 2012. Web. ⟨http://www.defensenews.com/article/20120501/C4ISR01/305010009/⟩.

[173] Hennigan, W.J., "Army Lets Air Out of Battlefield Spyship Project." *LATimes.com*. Los Angeles Times. 23 October 2013, ⟨http://www.latimes.com/business/la-fi-blimp-fire-sale-20131023,0,3497521.story#axzz2jlihKJbW⟩.

[174] Kirk, Chris. "Who's Been Most Shut Down by the Shutdown? Which federal agencies are untouched, and which are ghost towns?" *slate.com*. The Slate Group. The Washington Post Company. 1 October 2013. Web. ⟨http://www.slate.com/articles/news_and_politics/slate_labs/2013/10/federal_government_shutdown_agencies_with_the_most_furloughs.html⟩.

[175] The Washington Post. "Impact of a Government Shutdown." *Washingtonpost.com*. The Washington Post. Published 25 September 2013; Updated 2 October 2013. Web. ⟨http://www.washingtonpost.com/wp-srv/special/politics/2013-shutdown-federal-department-impact/?hpid=zl⟩.

[176] Moore, Jack. "Sequestration Tracker: Guide to Agency Furloughs." *Federalnewsradio.com*. Federal News Radio. 22 August 2013. Web. ⟨http://www.federalnewsradio.com/1104/3237795/Sequestration-Tracker-Guide-to-agency-furloughs⟩.

[177] Ziegler, Maseena. "NASA Will Pay $18,000 To Watch You Rest In Bed—Really." *Forbes.com*. Forbes.com LLC. 18 September 2013. Web. ⟨ http://www.forbes.com/sites/crossingborders/2013/09/18/nasa-will-pay-18000-to-watch-you-rest-in-bed-for-real/⟩.

[178] NASA. "Countermeasure and Functional Testing (CFT) Study," *bedreststudy.jsc.nasa.gov*. NASA. Updated 7 March 2013. Web. ⟨https://bedreststudy.jsc.nasa.gov/cft.aspx⟩.

[179] Hlavaty, Craig . "NASA Needs Volunteers To Stay In Bed for 15 Weeks Straight." *Chron.com*. Houston Chronicle. 18 September 2013. Web. ⟨http://www.chron.com/news/article/NASA-needs-volunteers-to-stay-in-bed-for-15-weeks-4821188.php?cmpid=hpfc#photo-5202164⟩.

[180] Hlavaty, Craig . "NASA Needs Volunteers To Stay In Bed for 15 Weeks Straight." *Chron.com*. Houston Chronicle. 18 September 2013. Web. ⟨http://www.chron.com/news/article/NASA-needs-volunteers-to-stay-in-bed-for-15-weeks-4821188.php?cmpid=hpfc#photo-5202164⟩.

[181] Moore, Charles. "NASA Seeks Paid Volunteers for Bed Rest Study at University of Texas Medical Branch Galveston."*bionews-tx.com*. BIO News Texas. 20 September 2013. Web. ⟨http://bionews-tx.com/news/2013/09/20/nasa-seeks-paid-volunteers-for-bed-rest-study-at-university-of-texas-medical-branch-galveston/⟩.

[182] Ziegler, Maseena. "NASA Will Pay $18,000 To Watch You Rest In Bed—Really." *Forbes.com*. Forbes.com LLC. 18 September 2013. Web. ⟨ http://www.forbes.com/sites/crossingborders/2013/09/18/nasa-will-pay-18000-to-watch-you-rest-in-bed-for-real/⟩.

[183] Hlavaty, Craig . "NASA Needs Volunteers To Stay In Bed for 15 Weeks Straight." *Chron.com*. Houston Chronicle. 18 September 2013. Web. ⟨http://www.chron.com/news/article/NASA-needs-volunteers-to-stay-in-bed-for-15-weeks-4821188.php?cmpid=hpfc#photo-5202164⟩.

[184] NASA. "Countermeasure and Functional Testing (CFT) Study," *bedreststudy.jsc.nasa.gov*. NASA. Updated 7 March 2013. Web. ⟨https://bedreststudy.jsc.nasa.gov/cft.aspx⟩.

[185] Prigg, Mark. "Thousands of Astronauts Enter Race to Take Part In '1,000-Day Mission To Mars' As NASA Says Red Planet Is 'Top Priority.'" *Dailymail.co.uk*. Associated Newspapers Ltd. 6 May 2013. Web. <http://www.dailymail.co.uk/sciencetech/article-2320344/Charles-Bolden-NASA-chief-says-manned-mission-Mars-priority--happen-2033.html>.

[186] Halvorson, Todd. "Manned Mission to Mars an Unlikely Proposition; Current Limits on Exposure to Radiation Make Chances of Flight in Near Future Pretty Slim." *FloridaToday.com*. Florida Today. 22 September 2013. Web. <http://www.floridatoday.com/article/20130922/SPACE/309220026/Manned-mission-Mars-an-unlikely-proposition>.

[187] Website of the International Trade Administration, "2012 Winners of MDCP Awards," Accessed 25 November 2013, <http://ita.doc.gov/td/mdcp/active.html>.USASpending.gov. "Prime Award Spending Data." Last modified 10 November 2013.
http://usaspending.gov/search?form_fields=%7B%22search_term%22%3A%22American+Association+of+Independent+Music%22%7D .

[188] Karp, Hannah. "Uncle Sam Helps Indie-Rock Bands Drum Up Fans Abroad." *Wsj.com*. Dow Jones & Company. 3 May 2013. Web. <http://online.wsj.com/news/articles/SB10001424127887324582004578457490606789014>.

[189] Karp, Hannah. "Uncle Sam Helps Indie-Rock Bands Drum Up Fans Abroad." *Wsj.com*. Dow Jones & Company. 3 May 2013. Web. <http://online.wsj.com/news/articles/SB10001424127887324582004578457490606789014>.

[190] Ugwu, Reggie, "Q&A: A2IM President Rich Bengloff Talks Export Mission to Brazil." *Billboard*.com. Billboard. 29 April 2013. <http://www.billboard.com/biz/articles/news/global/1560023/qa-a2im-president-rich-bengloff-talks-export-mission-to-brazil>.

[191] Karp, Hannah. "Uncle Sam Helps Indie-Rock Bands Drum Up Fans Abroad." *Wsj.com*. Dow Jones & Company. 3 May 2013. Web. <http://online.wsj.com/news/articles/SB10001424127887324582004578457490606789014>.

[192] Christman, Ed. "Universal Music Still Market Top Dog in 2012," *billboard.com*. Billboard. 3 January 2013 Web. <http://www.billboard.com/biz/articles/news/1510504/universal-music-still-market-top-dog-in-2012>.

[193] Karp, Hannah. "Uncle Sam Helps Indie-Rock Bands Drum Up Fans Abroad." *Wsj.com*. Dow Jones & Company. 3 May 2013. Web. <http://online.wsj.com/news/articles/SB10001424127887324582004578457490606789014>.

[194] A2IM. News. *A2IM Takes Indies to South America*. *A2im.org*. American Association of Independent Music, 15 Apr. 2013. Web. <http://a2im.org/2013/04/15/a2im-takes-indies-to-south-america/>.

[195] A2IM. News. *A2IM Takes Indies to South America*. *A2im.org*. American Association of Independent Music, 15 Apr. 2013. Web. <http://a2im.org/2013/04/15/a2im-takes-indies-to-south-america/>.

[196] Ugwu, Reggie, "Q&A: A2IM President Rich Bengloff Talks Export Mission to Brazil." *Billboard*.com. Billboard. 29 April 2013. <http://www.billboard.com/biz/articles/news/global/1560023/qa-a2im-president-rich-bengloff-talks-export-mission-to-brazil>.

[197] A2IM. News. *A2IM Brazil Trade Mission: The Participants in Their Own Words and Pictures*. *A2im.org*. American Association of Independent Music, 22 Apr. 2013. Web. <http://a2im.org/tag/mdcp-grant/page/2/>.

[198] Karp, Hannah. "Uncle Sam Helps Indie-Rock Bands Drum Up Fans Abroad." *Wsj.com*. Dow Jones & Company. 3 May 2013. Web. <http://online.wsj.com/news/articles/SB10001424127887324582004578457490606789014>.

[199] Karp, Hannah. "Uncle Sam Helps Indie-Rock Bands Drum Up Fans Abroad." *Wsj.com*. Dow Jones & Company. 3 May 2013. Web. <http://online.wsj.com/news/articles/SB10001424127887324582004578457490606789014>.

[200] A2IM. News. *A2IM Brazil Trade Mission: The Participants in Their Own Words and Pictures*. *A2im.org*. American Association of Independent Music, 22 Apr. 2013. Web. <http://a2im.org/tag/mdcp-grant/page/2/>.

[201] Karp, Hannah. "Uncle Sam Helps Indie-Rock Bands Drum Up Fans Abroad." *Wsj.com*. Dow Jones & Company. 3 May 2013. Web. <http://online.wsj.com/news/articles/SB10001424127887324582004578457490606789014>.

[202] Website of the American Association of Independent Music. Invitation from AsIM and Daryl Friedman "A Breakfast Reception in Support of Congressman Jerry Nadler." Web. <http://www.a2im.org/downloads/NadlerBFastPosterALTVERSION.pdf>.

[203] Staff of Senator Coburn note that while Facebook's U.S. pretax profit was $1.1 billion, $568 million was recognized in foreign pretax losses, as noted on the 10-K. These amounts netted to a total of $494M in total pretax profit. Please refer to page 84 of the FY12 10-K.

[204] Facebook, Inc. FY Form 10-K for the period ending December 31, 2012. (filed Feb. 2 2013). Web. <http://www.sec.gov/Archives/edgar/data/1326801/000132680113000003/fb-12312012x10k.htm>. (82).

[205] Facebook, Inc. FY Form 10-K for the period ending December 31, 2012. (filed Feb. 2 2013). Web. <http://www.sec.gov/Archives/edgar/data/1326801/000132680113000003/fb-12312012x10k.htm>. (54).
A difference of $22 million exists between $451 million reported on the 10-K and CTJ's figure of $429 million, which includes only federal and state taxes while the 10-K includes all levels of taxation (ie foreign).

[206] Singer, Anne. "Facebook's Multi-Billion Dollar Tax Break: Executive-Pay Tax Break Slashes Income Taxes on Facebook-- and Other Fortune 500 Companies." *Ctj.org.* Citizens for Tax Justice. 14 February 2013. Web. ‹http://ctj.org/ctjreports/2013/02/facebooks_multi-billion_dollar_tax_break_executive-pay_tax_break_slashes_income_taxes_on_facebook--.php#_ftn2›.

[207] Stock option deduction was independently calculated by adding the $1.03B fiscal year tax savings and the $2.17B tax carryforward for a total expected deduction of $3.2 if Facebook continues to generate appropriate income levels over the deductions phrase-out period.

[208] Using the $2.17 billion in carry-forward deductions, and still have a remaining $1.07 billion to spare for their 2014 tax bill.

[209] "Re: HHS Healthbeat: Calm down." Audio blog comment. *Hhs.gov.* US Department of Health & Human Services, 19 Nov. 2013. Web. ‹http://www.hhs.gov/news/healthbeat/2013/11/calm-down.html›.

[210] Lian Bloch, Claudia M. Haase, and Robert W. Levenson, "Emotion Regulation Predicts Marital Satisfaction," Emotion, American Psychological Association, November 4, 2013.

[211] Lian Bloch, Claudia M. Haase, and Robert W. Levenson, "Emotion Regulation Predicts Marital Satisfaction," Emotion, American Psychological Association, November 4, 2013.

[212] Lian Bloch, Claudia M. Haase, and Robert W. Levenson, "Emotion Regulation Predicts Marital Satisfaction: Appendix," Emotion, American Psychological Association, November 4, 2013.

[213] Lian Bloch, Claudia M. Haase, and Robert W. Levenson, "Emotion Regulation Predicts Marital Satisfaction," Emotion, American Psychological Association, November 4, 2013.

[214] NIH Grant 5T32MH020006.

[215] Senate Office of Education and Training "Course Catalog: Benefits of a Good Night's Sleep." Web. ‹http://lms.senate.gov/index.cfm/showCourseDetails/backTo/showCourses/courseID/364a8c382992f231bda180030d12fcaf/pgTitle/Course%20Catalog/›.

[216] Senate Office of Education and Training "Course Catalog: Pressure Point Therapy Workshop." Web. ‹http://lms.senate.gov/index.cfm/showCourseDetails/backTo/showCourses/courseID/554ed60f4941416c0b15882a246fbe02/pgTitle/Course%20Catalog/›.

[217] Moody, Chris, "Federal government typo of the day," Federal government typo of the day," *news.yahoo.com.* ABC News Network. 16 March 2012 web. ‹http://news.yahoo.com/blogs/ticket/federal-government-typo-day-205417924.html›.

[218] Senate Office of Education and Training "Course Catalog: Assert Yourself: Speak Up with Tact Rather than Suffer in Silence." Web. ‹http://lms.senate.gov/index.cfm/showCourseDetails/backTo/showCourses/courseID/37228fb7cd264c4edc1443b8ff0efadf/pgTitle/Course%20Catalog/›.

[219] Senate Office of Education and Training "Course Catalog: Small Talk: Breaking the Ice in Social Situations." Web. ‹http://lms.senate.gov/index.cfm/showCourseDetails/backTo/showCourses/courseID/3dafd6a343c534c6404f7d263e4a2155/pgTitle/Course%20Catalog/›.

[220] Senate Office of Education and Training "Course Catalog: That's Not What I Meant!" Web. ‹http://lms.senate.gov/index.cfm/showCourseDetails/backTo/showCourses/courseID/b3b02a23982cf7ae3a0b280e3a5dbd4e/pgTitle/Course%20Catalog/›.

[221] Senate Office of Education and Training "Course Catalog: Be Curious, Not Furious." Web. ‹http://lms.senate.gov/index.cfm/showCourseDetails/backTo/showCourses/courseID/e755350c475d371b9ed32b47f3dd4409/pgTitle/Course%20Catalog/›.

[222] Senate Office of Education and Training "Course Catalog: EAP: Forgiveness." Web. ‹http://lms.senate.gov/index.cfm/showCourseDetails/backTo/showCourses/courseID/364a8c382992f231bda180030d38cf0d/pgTitle/Course%20Catalog/›.

[223] Senate Office of Education and Training "Course Catalog: Making Subjects and Verbs Agree. ‹http://lms.senate.gov/index.cfm/showCourseDetails/backTo/showCourses/courseID/ee6523eadbb306b184623149e00b9730/pgTitle/Course%20Catalog/›.

[224] Wexler, Alexandra."U.S. Loses $53.3 Million on Sugar Deal." *Wsj.com.* Dow Jones & Company. 30 September 2013. Web. ‹http://online.wsj.com/article/SB10001424052702303918804579107672636781520.html›.

[225] Coalition for Sugar Reform. Web. ‹http://www.sugarreform.org›.

[226] Wexler, Alexandra."U.S. Loses $53.3 Million on Sugar Deal." *Wsj.com.* Dow Jones & Company. 30 September 2013. Web. ‹http://online.wsj.com/article/SB10001424052702303918804579107672636781520.html›.

[227] Wexler, Alexandra."U.S. Loses $53.3 Million on Sugar Deal." *Wsj.com.* Dow Jones & Company. 30 September 2013. Web. ‹http://online.wsj.com/article/SB10001424052702303918804579107672636781520.html›.

[228] Wexler, Alexandra. "U.S. Loses $53.3 Million on Sugar Deal." *Wsj.com.* Dow Jones & Company. 30 September 2013. Web. ‹http://online.wsj.com/article/SB10001424052702303918804579107672636781520.html›.

[229] Congressional Budget Office. "CBO's May 2013. Baseline for Farm Programs. *Cbo.gov. Congressional Budget Office.* 14 May 2013. Web. ‹http://cbo.gov/sites/default/files/cbofiles/attachments/44202_USDAMandator%20FarmPrograms.pdf›.

[230] Wexler, Alexandra. "U.S. Loses $53.3 Million on Sugar Deal." *Wsj.com.* Dow Jones & Company. 30 September 2013. Web. ‹http://online.wsj.com/article/SB10001424052702303918804579107672636781520.html›.

[231] Wohlgenant, Michael, and Vincent H. Smith, "Bitter Sweet. How Big Sugar Robs You." *American.*com American Enterprise Institute. 14 February 2012. Web. ‹http://www.american.com/archive/2012/february/bitter-sweet-how-big-sugar-robs-you›.

[232] Associated Press. "American Crystal Sugar to Default on USDA Loan." *Finance.yahoo.com.* The Associated Press. 1 October 2013. Web. ‹http://www.miamiherald.com/2013/10/01/v-print/3662881/american-crystal-sugar-to-default.html›.

[233] Associated Press. "American Crystal Sugar to Default on USDA Loan." *Finance.yahoo.com.* The Associated Press. 1 October 2013. Web. ‹http://www.miamiherald.com/2013/10/01/v-print/3662881/american-crystal-sugar-to-default.html›.

[234] Wexler, Alexandra. "U.S. Loses $53.3 Million on Sugar Deal." *Wsj.com.* Dow Jones & Company. 30 September 2013. Web. ‹http://online.wsj.com/article/SB10001424052702303918804579107672636781520.html›.

[235] Wohlgenant, Michael, and Vincent H. Smith, "Bitter Sweet. How Big Sugar Robs You." *American.*com American Enterprise Institute. 14 February 2012. Web. ‹http://www.american.com/archive/2012/february/bitter-sweet-how-big-sugar-robs-you›.

[236] Wohlgenant, Michael, and Vincent H. Smith, "Bitter Sweet. How Big Sugar Robs You." *American.*com American Enterprise Institute. 14 February 2012. Web. ‹http://www.american.com/archive/2012/february/bitter-sweet-how-big-sugar-robs-you›.

[237] Sokolove, Sofia. "Trash Dance Creator's Latest Electrifying Piece has Austin Energy Linemen Pole Dancing." *Austin.culturemap.com.* CultureMap LLC. 6 September 2013. Web. ‹http://austin.culturemap.com/news/arts/09-06-13-austin-energy-dudes-dance-up-poles-for-powerup-allison-orrs-latest-grand-performance/›.

[238] Forklift Danceworks website. "PowerUP - a performance by the employees and machinery of Austin Energy." *Forkliftdanceworks.com.* Forklift Danceworks. September 2013. Web. ‹http://www.forkliftdanceworks.org/powerup-performance-employees-and-machinery-austin-energy›.

[239] Scheiner, Eric. "Feds Help Fund Pole Dancing – For Linemen." *Cnsnews.com.* Cybercast News Service. 8 May 2013. Web. ‹ http://cnsnews.com/news/article/feds-help-fund-pole-dancing-linemen›.

[240] Sullivan, Patricia. "$1 million bus stop opens in Arlington," *washingtionpost.com.* The Washington Post. 21 March 2013. Web. ‹http://articles.washingtonpost.com/2013-03-24/local/37989853_1_high-capacity-bus-construction-streetcar›.

[241] Sullivan, Patricia. "$1 million bus stop opens in Arlington," *washingtionpost.com.* The Washington Post. 21 March 2013. Web. ‹http://articles.washingtonpost.com/2013-03-24/local/37989853_1_high-capacity-bus-construction-streetcar›.

[242] "Transit Capital Program: Columbia Pike Super Stops," Arlington County, http://www.arlingtonva.us/departments/ManagementAndFinance/cip_09_adopted/07/file65997.pdf, accessed November 21, 2013.

[243] Sullivan, Patricia. "$1 million bus stop opens in Arlington," *washingtionpost.com.* The Washington Post. 21 March 2013. Web. ‹http://articles.washingtonpost.com/2013-03-24/local/37989853_1_high-capacity-bus-construction-streetcar›.

[244] Sullivan, Patricia. "$1 million bus stop opens in Arlington," *washingtionpost.com.* The Washington Post. 21 March 2013. Web. ‹http://articles.washingtonpost.com/2013-03-24/local/37989853_1_high-capacity-bus-construction-streetcar›.

[245] Sullivan, Patricia. "$1 million bus stop opens in Arlington," *washingtionpost.com.* The Washington Post. 21 March 2013. Web. ‹http://articles.washingtonpost.com/2013-03-24/local/37989853_1_high-capacity-bus-construction-streetcar›.

[246] Rousselot, Peter. "Peter's Take: New Spending Needed to Increase High School Capacity." *ARLnow.com.* Local News Now LLC. 24 October 2013. Web. ‹ http://www.arlnow.com/2013/10/24/peters-take-new-spending-needed-to-increase-high-school-capacity/›.

[247] Sullivan, Patricia. "$1 million bus stop opens in Arlington," *washingtionpost.com.* The Washington Post. 21 March 2013. Web. ‹http://articles.washingtonpost.com/2013-03-24/local/37989853_1_high-capacity-bus-construction-streetcar›.

[248] Sullivan, Patricia. "$1 million bus stop opens in Arlington," *washingtionpost.com.* The Washington Post. 21 March 2013. Web. ‹http://articles.washingtonpost.com/2013-03-24/local/37989853_1_high-capacity-bus-construction-streetcar›.

[249] Information received from Arlington County, via the Congressional Research Service. 15 November 2013.

[250] Information received from Arlington County, via the Congressional Research Service. 15 November 2013.

[251] Information received from Arlington County, via the Congressional Research Service. 15 November 2013.

[252] Doren, Jenny. "$1M Arlington bus stop eyed by investigators," *wjla.com*. ABC 7 News – WJLA, 26 June 2013. Web. ‹http://www.wjla.com/articles/2013/06/-1m-arlington-bus-stop-eyed-by-investigators-90591.html›.

[253] Wilonsky, Robert. "Is it a book? Is it a TV show? It's a Superhero Boom!" *dallasnews.com*. The Dallas Morning News Inc. 14 October 2013. Web. ‹http://www.dallasnews.com/entertainment/television/headlines/20131014-is-it-a-book-is-it-a-tv-show-its-a-superhero-boom.ece›.

[254] PBSarts. "Superheroes: A Never-Ending Episode Guide."*pbs.org*. Public Broadcasting Service. Web. ‹http://www.pbs.org/arts/programs/superheroes-never-ending-battle/superheroes-episode-guide/›. Accessed 4 December 2013.

[255] ShopPBS. "Superheroes: A Never-Ending Battle DVD." *shoppbs.com*. Public Broadcasting Service. Web. ‹http://www.shoppbs.org/product/index.jsp?productId=23148226&cp=2809871.24995996&utm_source=PBS&utm_campaign=pbs_content_pbsarts_superheroes_buydvdmodule&utm_medium=Link&parentPage=family›. Accessed 4 December 2013.

[256] USAspending.gov website, accessed December 4, 2013.

[257] USAspending.gov website, accessed December 4, 2013.

[258] National Endowment for the Humanities. "Superheroes: A Never-Ending Battle." *neh.gov*. National Endowment for the Humanities. 15 October 2013. Web. ‹http://www.neh.gov/events/superheroes-never-ending-battle›.

[259] Genie Awards Database, Academy of Canadian Cinema and Television. *Academy.ca*. Web. ‹http://www.academy.ca/hist/history.cfm?stitle=comic+book+confidential&awyear=0&winonly=1&awards=1&rtype=2&curstep=4&submit.x=60&submit.y=12›. Accessed 4 December 2013.

[260] The White House. Office of the Press Secretary. "President and Mrs. Bush Attend Presentation of the 2008 National Medals of Arts and National Humanities Medals." Press release. Whitehouse.gov. 17 Nov. 2008. ‹http://georgewbush-whitehouse.archives.gov/news/releases/2008/11/20081117-2.html›.

[261] Comichron. "Comic Book Sales by Year," *comichron.com*. The Comics Chronicles. Web. ‹http://www.comichron.com/yearlycomicssales.html›. Accessed 4 December 2013.

[262] Box Office Mojo. "Superhero 1978-Present." *Boxofficemojo.com*. Box Office Mojo. Web. ‹http://boxofficemojo.com/genres/chart/?id=superhero.htm›. Accessed 4 December 2013.

[263] Harrington, Wallace. "Superman and the War Years; The Battle of Europe Within the Pages Of Superman Comics." *supermanhomepage.com*. Superman Homepage. Web. ‹http://www.supermanhomepage.com/comics/comics.php?topic=articles/supes-war›.

[264] Farenthold, David A., "Federal Employee Mike Marsh's Mission: Get Himself Fired, and His Agency Closed." *Washingtonpost.com*. The Washington Post. 26 September 2013. Web. ‹http://articles.washingtonpost.com/2013-09-26/politics/42423034_1_economic-development-agency-washington-post-alaska-afl-cio›.

[265] Letter from Denali Commission Office of Inspector General to Ranking Member Tom Coburn. September 25, 2013.

[266] Farenthold, David A., "Federal Employee Mike Marsh's Mission: Get Himself Fired, and His Agency Closed." *Washingtonpost.com*. The Washington Post. 26 September 2013. Web. ‹http://articles.washingtonpost.com/2013-09-26/politics/42423034_1_economic-development-agency-washington-post-alaska-afl-cio›.

[267] Letter from Denali Commission Office of Inspector General to Ranking Member Tom Coburn. September 25, 2013.

[268] Farenthold, David A., "Federal Employee Mike Marsh's Mission: Get Himself Fired, and His Agency Closed." *Washingtonpost.com*. The Washington Post. 26 September 2013. Web. ‹http://articles.washingtonpost.com/2013-09-26/politics/42423034_1_economic-development-agency-washington-post-alaska-afl-cio›.

[269] Denali Commission of Alaska. "About Us." *Denali.gov*. The Denali Commission. Web. ‹http://www.denali.gov/about-us›.

[270] Denali Commission of Alaska. "About Us." *Denali.gov*. The Denali Commission. Web. ‹http://www.denali.gov/about-us›.

[271] Denali Commission of Alaska. "About Us." *Denali.gov*. The Denali Commission. Web. ‹http://www.denali.gov/about-us›.

[272] U.S. House. Committee on Appropriations. *Energy and Water Development Appropriations Bill, 2014, (to Accompany H.R.2609) Together with Additional Views*. (113 H. Rpt. 135). Text from: Thomas.loc.gov. ‹http://thomas.loc.gov/cgi-bin/cpquery/?&sid=cp113InZRb&r_n=hr135.113&dbname=cp113&&sel=TOC_381588&›.

[273] Letter from Denali Commission Office of Inspector General to Ranking Member Tom Coburn. 25 September 2013.

[274] Letter from Denali Commission Office of Inspector General to Ranking Member Tom Coburn. 25 September 2013. (1).

[275] Letter from Denali Commission Office of Inspector General to Ranking Member Tom Coburn. 25 September 2013. (1).

[276] Letter from Denali Commission Office of Inspector General to Ranking Member Tom Coburn. 25 September 2013

[277] Letter from Denali Commission Office of Inspector General to Ranking Member Tom Coburn. 25 September 2013.

[278] Vilsack, Thomas J. "Sequestration of USDA's Operations." Letter to Senator Barbara Mikulski. 5 Feb. 2013. MS. Senate Committee on Appropriations, Washington, D.C..

[279] USDA Agricultural Marketing Service "Fiscal Year 2013 Description of Funded Projects." USDA Agricultural Marketing Service, Fruit and Vegetable Programs, Specialty Crop Block Grant Program. 26 September 2013. Web. <http://www.ams.usda.gov/AMSv1.0/getfile?dDocName=STELPRDC5105139>.

[280] USDA Agricultural Marketing Service "Fiscal Year 2013 Description of Funded Projects." USDA Agricultural Marketing Service, Fruit and Vegetable Programs, Specialty Crop Block Grant Program. 26 September 2013. Web. <http://www.ams.usda.gov/AMSv1.0/getfile?dDocName=STELPRDC5105139>.

[281] USDA Agricultural Marketing Service "Fiscal Year 2013 Description of Funded Projects." USDA Agricultural Marketing Service, Fruit and Vegetable Programs, Specialty Crop Block Grant Program. 26 September 2013. Web. <http://www.ams.usda.gov/AMSv1.0/getfile?dDocName=STELPRDC5105139>.

[282] USDA Agricultural Marketing Service "Fiscal Year 2013 Description of Funded Projects." USDA Agricultural Marketing Service, Fruit and Vegetable Programs, Specialty Crop Block Grant Program. 26 September 2013. Web. <http://www.ams.usda.gov/AMSv1.0/getfile?dDocName=STELPRDC5105139>.

[283] USDA Agricultural Marketing Service "Fiscal Year 2013 Description of Funded Projects." USDA Agricultural Marketing Service, Fruit and Vegetable Programs, Specialty Crop Block Grant Program. 26 September 2013. Web. <http://www.ams.usda.gov/AMSv1.0/getfile?dDocName=STELPRDC5105139>.

[284] USDA Agricultural Marketing Service "Fiscal Year 2013 Description of Funded Projects." USDA Agricultural Marketing Service, Fruit and Vegetable Programs, Specialty Crop Block Grant Program. 26 September 2013. Web. <http://www.ams.usda.gov/AMSv1.0/getfile?dDocName=STELPRDC5105139>.

[285] Ye Hee Lee, Michelle, "Tempe Housing Complex for Deaf Under Fire." *Azcentral.com*. Arizona Republic. 28 September 2013. <http://www.azcentral.com/community/tempe/articles/20130925tempe-housing-deaf-under-fire.html>.

[286] La Jeunesse, William, and Jennifer Girdon. "Feds Try in Eliminate Housing for the Deaf – At Complex for the Hearing Impaired." *Foxnews.com*. Fox News 21 October 2013. Web. <http://www.foxnews.com/politics/2013/10/21/feds-try-to-eliminate-housing-for-deaf-at-complex-built-for-hearing-impaired>.

[287] Against Persons with Disabilities, Barriers at Every Step, Office of Policy Development and Research, United States Department of Housing and Urban Development, June 2005.

[288] La Jeunesse, William and Jennifer Girdon. "Feds Try in Eliminate Housing for the Deaf – At Complex for the Hearing Impaired." *Foxnews.com*. Fox News 21 October 2013. Web. <http://www.foxnews.com/politics/2013/10/21/feds-try-to-eliminate-housing-for-deaf-at-complex-built-for-hearing-impaired>.

[289] Ye Hee Lee, Michelle. "Tempe Housing Complex for Deaf Under Fire." *Azcentral.com*. Arizona Republic. 28 September 2013. <http://www.azcentral.com/community/tempe/articles/20130925tempe-housing-deaf-under-fire.html>.

[290] Website of Apache ASL Trails, "Welcome to Apache ASL Trails." Web. <http://apacheasltrails.com/main.html>. accessed 7 November 2013.

[291] KSAZ Fox10. "Tempe Apartments for the Deaf Accused of Discrimination," *myfoxphoenix.com*. Fox Television Stations, Inc. and World now. KSAZ Fox 10 (Phoenix, Arizona), 26 October 2013. Web. <http://www.myfoxphoenix.com/story/23751124/2013/10/21/tempe-apartments-for-the-deaf-accused-of-discrimination>.

[292] La Jeunesse, William, and Jennifer Girdon. "Feds Try in Eliminate Housing for the Deaf – At Complex for the Hearing Impaired." *Foxnews.com*. Fox News 21 October 2013. Web. <http://www.foxnews.com/politics/2013/10/21/feds-try-to-eliminate-housing-for-deaf-at-complex-built-for-hearing-impaired>.

[293] Website of the National Association of the Deaf, Letter from NAD to the Department of Housing and Urban Development Secretary, Shawn Donovan, 25 April 2013. *Nad.org*. National Association for the Death. Web. <http://www.nad.org/nad-writes-letter-housing-and-urban-development>.

[294] KSAZ Fox10. "Tempe Apartments for the Deaf Accused of Discrimination," *myfoxphoenix.com*. Fox Television Stations, Inc. and World now. KSAZ Fox 10 (Phoenix, Arizona), 26 October 2013. Web.

[295] Cruz, Crystal, "Deaf Group Living In Tempe Fears Federal Government Could Break Them Up." *Azfamily.com*.KTVK Inc. 9 July 2012. Web. <http://www.azfamily.com/news/Deaf-group-living-together-in-Tempe-fears-federeal-government-will-break-them-up-161524345.html>.

[296] Dellorto, Danielle. "Wounded Fort Hood Soldier Describes 'Swift, Tactical' Gunman." *CNN.com*. CNN. 11 November 2011. Web. <http://www.cnn.com/2009/US/11/11/fort.hood.wounded.soldier/>.

[297] Friedman, Scott. "Accused Fort Hood Shooter Paid $278,000 While Awaiting Trial." *NBCDFW.com*. NBC 5, Dallas-Fort Worth. Web. <http://www.nbcdfw.com/investigations/Accused-Fort-Hood-Shooter-Paid-278000-While-Awaiting-Trial-208230691.html>.

[298] Senate Committee on Homeland Security & Governmental Affairs. "A Ticking Time Bomb: Counterterrorism Lessons from the U.S. Government's Failure to Prevent the Fort Hood Attack." A Special Report by Joseph I. Lieberman, Chairman, and Susan M. Collins, Ranking Member. Washington, D.C. 3 February 2011. Print.

[299] Friedman, Scott. "Accused Fort Hood Shooter Paid $278,000 While Awaiting Trial." *NBCDFW.com*. NBC 5, Dallas-Fort Worth. Web. <http://www.nbcdfw.com/investigations/Accused-Fort-Hood-Shooter-Paid-278000-While-Awaiting-Trial-208230691.html>.

[300] Friedman, Scott. "Accused Fort Hood Shooter Paid $278,000 While Awaiting Trial." *NBCDFW.com*. NBC 5, Dallas-Fort Worth. Web. <http://www.nbcdfw.com/investigations/Accused-Fort-Hood-Shooter-Paid-278000-While-Awaiting-Trial-208230691.html>.

[301] Friedman, Scott. "Accused Fort Hood Shooter Paid $278,000 While Awaiting Trial." *NBCDFW.com*. NBC 5, Dallas-Fort Worth. Web. <http://www.nbcdfw.com/investigations/Accused-Fort-Hood-Shooter-Paid-278000-While-Awaiting-Trial-208230691.html>.

[302] Friedman, Scott. "Accused Fort Hood Shooter Paid $278,000 While Awaiting Trial." *NBCDFW.com*. NBC 5, Dallas-Fort Worth. Web. <http://www.nbcdfw.com/investigations/Accused-Fort-Hood-Shooter-Paid-278000-While-Awaiting-Trial-208230691.html>.

[303] NBC 5 Dallas-Fort Worth. "Cost of Jailing Hassan: About $548,000 So Far." *NBCDFW.com*. NBC 5, Dallas-Fort Worth. Web. <http://www.nbcdfw.com/investigations/Cost-of-Jailing-Hasan-About-548000-So-Far-211316621.html>.

[304] Office of Management and Budget. *USAspending.gov*. Accessed 12 November 2013. Web. <http://www.usaspending.gov/explore?tab=By+Prime+Awardee&typeofview=complete&pageno=4&fiscal_year=all&piid=NNH13CH20B>.

[305] NASA Employee and Organizational Excellence Branch. "Congressional Operations Seminar for NASA (held annually)." *EOEB.HQ.NASA.gov*. NASA. 2013. Web. <http://eoeb.hq.nasa.gov/training/congressional.html>.

[306] NASA Employee and Organizational Excellence Branch. "Congressional Operations Seminar for NASA (held annually)." *EOEB.HQ.NASA.gov*. NASA. 2013. Web. <http://eoeb.hq.nasa.gov/training/congressional.html>.

[307] Office of Management and Budget. *USAspending.gov*. Accessed 12 November 2013. Web. <http://www.usaspending.gov/explore?tab=By+Prime+Awardee&typeofview=complete&pageno=4&fiscal_year=all&piid=NNH13CH20B>.

[308] Office of Management and Budget. *USAspending.gov*. Accessed 12 November 2013. Web. <http://www.usaspending.gov/explore?tab=By+Prime+Awardee&typeofview=complete&pageno=4&fiscal_year=all&piid=NNH13CH20B>.

[309] Library of Congress. "Legislation of the U.S. Congress – 113th" Congress.gov. Accessed 20 November 2013

[310] Cilliza, Chris. "The Fix: Surprise! This is the Least Productive Congress Ever," *WashingtonPost.com*. The Washington Post. 3 August 2013. Web. <http://www.washingtonpost.com/blogs/the-fix/wp/2013/08/03/surprise-this-is-the-least-productive-congress-ever-video/?tid=rssfeed>.

[311] Newport, Frank. "Congress' Job Approval Falls to 11% Amid Gov't Shutdown; Americans' Approval of Their Own Representative Averages 44%," *Gallup.com*. GallupPolitics. 7 October 2013. Web. <http://www.gallup.com/poll/165281/congress-job-approval-falls-amid-gov-shutdown.aspx>.

[312] *The Exonomist/YouGov Poll*, Weekly Tracking. November 30 – December 2, 2013. http://d25d2506sfb94s.cloudfront.net/cumulus_uploads/document/59s5m3yaxz/trackingreport_alladults.pdf

[313] Newport, Frank. "Congress' Job Approval Falls to 11% Amid Gov't Shutdown; Americans' Approval of Their Own Representative Averages 44%," *Gallup.com*. GallupPolitics. 7 October 2013. Web. <http://www.gallup.com/poll/165281/congress-job-approval-falls-amid-gov-shutdown.aspx>.

[314] "Drop the money here: Officials say growth in Silver Spring is 'smart,'" *Gazette.net*. The Gazette. 2 May 1997. Web. <http://webcache.googleusercontent.com/search?q=cache:http://ww2.gazette.net/gazette_archive/1997/199718/montgomerycty/county/a56585-1.html>.

[315] "Drop the money here: Officials say growth in Silver Spring is 'smart,'" *Gazette.net*. The Gazette. 2 May 1997. Web. <http://webcache.googleusercontent.com/search?q=cache:http://ww2.gazette.net/gazette_archive/1997/199718/montgomerycty/county/a56585-1.html>.

[316] "Drop the money here: Officials say growth in Silver Spring is 'smart,'" *Gazette.net*. The Gazette. 2 May 1997. Web. <http://webcache.googleusercontent.com/search?q=cache:http://ww2.gazette.net/gazette_archive/1997/199718/montgomerycty/county/a56585-1.html>.

[317] Turque, Bill, "Silver Spring Transit Center's inspectors ran poor concrete tests, report says," *washingtonpost.com*. The Washington Post. 26 March 2013. Web. <http://www.washingtonpost.com/local/silver-spring-transit-centers-inspectors-ran-poor-concrete-tests-report-says/2013/03/26/846fa820-931c-11e2-a3le-14700e2724e4_story.html>.

[318] Orlin, Glenn, "Memorandum: Action," Montgomery County Council. 29 March 2013. Web. <http://montgomerycountymd.granicus.com/MetaViewer.php?meta_id=48018&view=&showpdf=1>.

[319] Orlin, Glenn, "Memorandum: Action," Montgomery County Council. 29 March 2013. Web. <http://montgomerycountymd.granicus.com/MetaViewer.php?meta_id=48018&view=&showpdf=1>.

[320] PBS. "Wonders of the World database: Empire State Building," *pbs.org.* PBS/WGBH. <http://www.pbs.org/wgbh/buildingbig/wonder/structure/empire_state.html>. Accessed 11 December 2013.

[321] "Montgomery Council Committee to Discuss Silver Spring Transit Center on Mon, Jan. 30," *montgomerycountymd.gov.* Montgomery County Government. 27 January 2012. Web. <http://www6.montgomerycountymd.gov/Apps/Council/PressRelease/PR_details.asp?PrID=8210>.

[322] "Silver Spring Transit Center Structural Evaluation of Superstructure," *montgomerycountymd.gov.* Montgomery County Government. 15 March 2013. Web. <http://www6.montgomerycountymd.gov/content/dgs/resources/SSTC-Report-March-15-2013.pdf,>.

[323] Di Caro, Martin, "Foulger Responds to Reported Defects in Silver Spring Transit Center," *WAMU.org.* WAMU 88.5 American University Radio. 28 March 2013. Web. <http://wamu.org/news/13/03/28/ foulger_responds_to_ reported_ defects_ in_ silver_spring_transit_center>.

[324] Rose, Kara. "Fougler-Pratt 'outraged' about treatment from Montgomery over transit center," *Gazette.net.* The Gazette. 28 March 2013. Web. <http://www.gazette.net/article /20130328/NEWS /130328823/foulger-pratt-x2018-outraged-x2019-about-treatment-from&template=gazette>.

[325] Rose, Kara. "Montgomery County awaits word from Silver Spring Transit Center inspector," *Gazette.net.* The Gazette. 9 April 2013. Web. <http://www.gazette.net/article/20130409/NEWS /130409260/1124 /montgomery-county-awaits-word-from-silver-spring-transit-center&template =gazette>.

[326] Rose, Kara. "Montgomery County awaits word from Silver Spring Transit Center inspector," *Gazette.net.* The Gazette. 9 April 2013. Web. <http://www.gazette.net/article/20130409/NEWS /130409260/1124 /montgomery-county-awaits-word-from-silver-spring-transit-center&template =gazette>.

[327] Wine Communications Group. "Family Winemakers and Stonebridge Research Awarded China Market Research Grant by USDA; Project to generate sales and marketing approach for California fine wines." *Winebusiness.com.* Wine Communications Group. 3 May 2013. Web. <http://www.winebusiness.com/news/?go=getArticle&dataid=116036>.

[328] "SPECIALTY CROP BLOCK GRANT AWARDS 2013," Washington State Department of Agriculture, 26 September 2013. Web. <http://agr.wa.gov/Grants/docs/2013WSDASCBGAwards.pdf>.

[329] "SPECIALTY CROP BLOCK GRANT AWARDS 2013," Washington State Department of Agriculture, 26 September 2013. Web. <http://agr.wa.gov/Grants/docs/2013WSDASCBGAwards.pdf>.

[330] "SPECIALTY CROP BLOCK GRANT AWARDS 2013," Washington State Department of Agriculture, 26 September 2013. Web. <http://agr.wa.gov/Grants/docs/2013WSDASCBGAwards.pdf>.

[331] "SPECIALTY CROP BLOCK GRANT AWARDS 2013," Washington State Department of Agriculture, 26 September 2013. Web. <http://agr.wa.gov/Grants/docs/2013WSDASCBGAwards.pdf>.

[332] Wei, Yu. "Is China Really Ready for Napa's Higher-End Wines?" *us.chinadaily.com.cn.* China Daily Information Co. 22 August 2013. <http://usa.chinadaily.com.cn/2013-08/22/content_16913514.htm>.

[333] SPECIALTY CROP BLOCK GRANT AWARDS 2013," Washington State Department of Agriculture, 26 September 2013. Web. <http://agr.wa.gov/Grants/docs/2013WSDASCBGAwards.pdf>.

[334] SPECIALTY CROP BLOCK GRANT AWARDS 2013," Washington State Department of Agriculture, 26 September 2013. Web. <http://agr.wa.gov/Grants/docs/2013WSDASCBGAwards.pdf>.

[335] SPECIALTY CROP BLOCK GRANT AWARDS 2013," Washington State Department of Agriculture, 26 September 2013. Web. <http://agr.wa.gov/Grants/docs/2013WSDASCBGAwards.pdf>.

[336] Burkitt, Laurie and Chow, Jason. "China as a Vast Wine Market; Australian Vintner Plans to Open Outlets in Country to Create a Taste for Luxury Brands." *Wsj.com.* Dow Jones & Company, Inc. 24 March 2013. <http://online.wsj.com/news/articles/SB10001424127887324373204578375902196479138>.

[337] Wei, Yu. "Is China Really Ready for Napa's Higher-End Wines?" *us.chinadaily.com.cn.* China Daily Information Co. 22 August 2013. <http://usa.chinadaily.com.cn/2013-08/22/content_16913514.htm>.

[338] Department of the Treasury. "MAJOR FOREIGN HOLDERS OF TREASURY SECURITIES," Department of the Treasury/Federal Reserve Board Web. <http://www.treasury.gov/resource-center/data-chart-center/tic/Documents/mfh.txt>. Accessed 23 September 2013.

[339] National Oceanic and Atmospheric Administration. *Hurricane/Post-Tropical Cyclone Sandy, 22-29 October 2012.* Service Assessment. Department of Commerce. May 2013. National Weather Service, Department of Commerce. May 2013. Web. <http://www.nws.noaa.gov/os/assessments/pdfs/Sandy13.pdf; The total program use amounts to $47.6 billion (appropriated net of sequester and set aside), Task Force PMO. Monthly Financial Update. Financial Report #21. September 16, 2013. United States Department of Housing and Urban Development.

[340] Kusisto, Laura. "Distribution of Sandy Aid Irks the City." *Wsj.com*. The Wall Street Journal. 22 October 2013. Web. <http://online.wsj.com/news/articles/SB10001424052702303448104579149502255313262>.

[341] U.S. Department of Housing and Urban Development letter to Ranking Member Tom A. Coburn. June 28, 2013.

[342] Hakim, Danny. "Ad Effort Selling State as a Business Haven is Criticized."*Nytimes.com*. The New York Times Company. Web. 2 May 2013. Web. <http://wap.nytimes.com/2013/05/04/nyregion/new-york-states-ads-to-attract-business-also-drawcomplaints.html>.

[343] Hakim, Danny. "Ad Effort Selling State as a Business Haven is Criticized."*Nytimes.com*. The New York Times Company. Web. 2 May 2013. Web. <http://wap.nytimes.com/2013/05/04/nyregion/new-york-states-ads-to-attract-business-also-drawcomplaints.html>.

[344] Associated Press. "Gov. Christie, 'Jersey Shore' Cast Reopen State's Beaches Post-Sandy." *Foxnews.com*. Associated Press. 24 May 2013. Web. <http://www.foxnews.com/us/2013/05/24/gov-christie-jersey-shore-cast-reopen-state-beaches-post-sandy/>.

[345] Diamond, Michael. "Jersey Shore Tourism Struggled to Come Back From Sandy." *Usatoday.com*. Gannett. 2 September 2013. Web. <http://www.usatoday.com/story/news/nation/2013/09/02/sandy-jersey-shore-tourism/2755785/>.

[346] Parnass, Sarah. "Hillary Clinton Endures Brusque Questioning at Hearings," *abcnews.com*. World News. 23 January 2013. <http://abcnews.go.com/Politics/OTUS/hillary-clinton-endures-brusque-questioning-hearings/story?id=18292329>.

[347] Solicitation No. S-BE200-12-R-0046, p. 10.

[348] Solicitation No. S-BE200-12-R-0046. January 9, 2013. pp.15-16.

[349] Harrington, Elizabeth. "Safe from Sequester: $704,198 for Gardening at NATO Ambassador's Home," *CNSNews.com*. Cybercast News Service. 9 April 9, 2013. <http://cnsnews.com/news/article/safe-sequester-704198-gardening-nato-ambassador-s-home>.

[350] Harrington, Elizabeth. "Safe from Sequester: $704,198 for Gardening at NATO Ambassador's Home," *CNSNews.com*. Cybercast News Service. 9 April 9, 2013. <http://cnsnews.com/news/article/safe-sequester-704198-gardening-nato-ambassador-s-home>.

[351] Harrington, Elizabeth. "Safe from Sequester: $704,198 for Gardening at NATO Ambassador's Home," *CNSNews.com*. Cybercast News Service. 9 April 9, 2013. <http://cnsnews.com/news/article/safe-sequester-704198-gardening-nato-ambassador-s-home>.

[352] Borenstein, Seth. "Spending Cuts May Deep-Six Crucial Flood Gauges." *bigstory.AP.org*. The Associated Press. 25 April 2013. Web. <http://bigstory.ap.org/article/spending-cuts-may-deep-six-crucial-flood-gauges>.

[353] Borenstein, Seth. "Spending Cuts May Deep-Six Crucial Flood Gauges." *bigstory.AP.org*. The Associated Press. 25 April 2013. Web. <http://bigstory.ap.org/article/spending-cuts-may-deep-six-crucial-flood-gauges>.

[354] US Geological Survey. "USGS UAS Missions: Planned." *Rmgsc.cr.usgs.gov*. U.S. Department of the Interior, US Geological Survey. Modified 21 November 2013. Web. <http://rmgsc.cr.usgs.gov/UAS/missions.shtml?current=3>.

[355] Brean, Henry. "Drones to Spy on Southern Nevada Wildlife, Not People." *Reviewjournal.com*. Las Vegas Review-Journal. Stephens Media LLC. 4 June 2013. Web. <http://www.reviewjournal.com/news/water-environment/drones-spy-southern-nevada-wildlife-not-people>.

[356] Hood, Grace. "Over Grand County Drones Are Bird Watching, Not People Watching." *Kunc.org*. KUNC 91.5 Community Radio for Northern Colorado. 25 April 2013. Web. <http://kunc.org/post/over-grand-county-drones-are-bird-watching-not-people-watching>.

[357] Hood, Grace. "Over Grand County Drones Are Bird Watching, Not People Watching." *Kunc.org*. KUNC 91.5 Community Radio for Northern Colorado. 25 April 2013. Web.<http://kunc.org/post/over-grand-county-drones-are-bird-watching-not-people-watching>.

[358] Farrell, Sean Patrick. "A Drone's-Eye View of Nature," *nytimes.com*. The New York Times Company. 6 May 2013. Web. <http://www.nytimes.com/2013/05/07/science/drones-offer-a-safer-clearer-look-at-the-natural-world.html?_r=0>.

[359] Brean, Henry. "Drones to Spy on Southern Nevada Wildlife, Not People." *Reviewjournal.com*. Las Vegas Review-Journal. Stephens Media LLC. 4 June 2013. Web. <http://www.reviewjournal.com/news/water-environment/drones-spy-southern-nevada-wildlife-not-people>.

[360] Farrell, Sean Patrick. "A Drone's-Eye View of Nature," *nytimes.com*. The New York Times Company. 6 May 2013. Web. <http://www.nytimes.com/2013/05/07/science/drones-offer-a-safer-clearer-look-at-the-natural-world.html?_r=0>.

[361] Brean, Henry. "Drones to Spy on Southern Nevada Wildlife, Not People." *Reviewjournal.com*. Las Vegas Review-Journal. Stephens Media LLC. 4 June 2013. Web. <http://www.reviewjournal.com/news/water-environment/drones-spy-southern-nevada-wildlife-not-people>.

[362] Doughton, Sandi. "Northwest Scientists Using Drones to Spy on Nature." *Seattletimes.com*. The Seattle Times. 16 July 2013. Web. <http://seattletimes.com/html/localnews/2021405556_dronessciencexml.html>.

[363] US Geological Survey National Unmanned Aircraft Systems Project Office. "Overview." *Rmgsc.cr.usgs.gov*. DOI, USGS, National UAS Project Office. Web. Modified 18 October 2013. Web. ‹http://rmgsc.cr.usgs.gov/UAS/›.

[364] Farrell, Sean Patrick. "A Drone's-Eye View of Nature," *nytimes.com*. The New York Times Company. 6 May 2013. Web. ‹http://www.nytimes.com/2013/05/07/science/drones-offer-a-safer-clearer-look-at-the-natural-world.html?_r=0›.

[365] Malewitz, Jim. "For Flood Forecasting, Sequestration Less Painful than Predicted." *Pewstates.org*. Stateline. 7 August 2013. Web. ‹http://www.pewstates.org/projects/stateline/headlines/for-flood-forecasting-sequestration-less-painful-than-predicted-85899495896›.

[366] Malewitz, Jim. "For Flood Forecasting, Sequestration Less Painful than Predicted." *Pewstates.org*. Stateline. 7 August 2013. Web. ‹http://www.pewstates.org/projects/stateline/headlines/for-flood-forecasting-sequestration-less-painful-than-predicted-85899495896›.

[367] Brean, Henry. "Drones to Spy on Southern Nevada Wildlife, Not People." *Reviewjournal.com*. Las Vegas Review-Journal. Stephens Media LLC. 4 June 2013. Web. ‹http://www.reviewjournal.com/news/water-environment/drones-spy-southern-nevada-wildlife-not-people›.

[368] Brean, Henry. "Drones to Spy on Southern Nevada Wildlife, Not People." *Reviewjournal.com*. Las Vegas Review-Journal. Stephens Media LLC. 4 June 2013. Web. ‹http://www.reviewjournal.com/news/water-environment/drones-spy-southern-nevada-wildlife-not-people›.

[369] Nogueras, David. "OSU Plans Drone Flights for Potato Study Near Hermiston." *Opb.org*. Oregon Public Broadcasting. 11 April 2013. Web. ‹http://www.opb.org/news/article/osu-plans-drone-flights-for-potato-study-near-hermiston/›.

[370] Fish, Sandra. "Already Stinging from Sequestration, Coloradans Fear More Cuts." *America.aljazeera.com*. Al Jazeera America. 26 September 2013. Web. ‹http://america.aljazeera.com/articles/2013/9/26/already-feeling-sequestrationstingcoloradansfearmorefederalcuts.html›.

[371] Hayward, Mark. "Manchester airport remains in dark over solar-panel glare solution | New Hampshire Energy." *Unionleader.com*. New Hampshire Union Leader. Aug. 2013. Web. ‹http://www.unionleader.com/article/20130807/NEWS05/130809503›.

[372] Hayward, Mark. "Manchester airport remains in dark over solar-panel glare solution | New Hampshire Energy." *Unionleader.com*. New Hampshire Union Leader. Aug. 2013. Web. ‹http://www.unionleader.com/article/20130807/NEWS05/130809503›.

[373] Hayward, Mark. "Manchester airport remains in dark over solar-panel glare solution | New Hampshire Energy." *Unionleader.com*. New Hampshire Union Leader. Aug. 2013. Web. ‹http://www.unionleader.com/article/20130807/NEWS05/130809503›.

[374] Hayward, Mark. "Manchester airport remains in dark over solar-panel glare solution | New Hampshire Energy." *Unionleader.com*. New Hampshire Union Leader. Aug. 2013. Web. ‹http://www.unionleader.com/article/20130807/NEWS05/130809503›.

[375] Manchester Boston Regional Airport. "Solar Project." Holiday 2012 Newsletter. *Flymanchester.com*. MBRA. Web. ‹http://www.flymanchester.com/newsletters/holiday-2012/solar-project›.

[376] Manchester Boston Regional Airport. "Solar Project." Holiday 2012 Newsletter. *Flymanchester.com*. MBRA. Web. ‹http://www.flymanchester.com/newsletters/holiday-2012/solar-project›.

[377] Federal Aviation Administration. *Technical Guidance for Evaluating Selected Solar Technologies on Airports*. FAA Office of Airports, Office of Airport Planning and Programming. *FAA.gov*. Washington, D.C.. November 2010. NOTE: As of 23 Oct. 2013, FAA is reviewing multiple sections of the report. Web.

[378] Federal Aviation Administration. *Technical Guidance for Evaluating Selected Solar Technologies on Airports*. FAA Office of Airports, Office of Airport Planning and Programming. *FAA.gov*. Washington, D.C.. November 2010. NOTE: As of 23 Oct. 2013, FAA is reviewing multiple sections of the report. Web. ‹http://www.faa.gov/airports/environmental/policy_guidance/media/airport_solar_guide_print.pdf›

[379] HMMH. "Project Experience: FAA Solar Guidance for Airports." *Hmmh.com*. Harris Miller Miller & Hanson Inc..‹http://www.hmmh.com/solar_power_faa_solar_guidance.html›.

[380] WMUR ABC9. "Solar panel glare causes problems for flight controllers." *wmur.com*. WMUR-TV ABC9 30 Aug. 2012. Web. ‹http://www.wmur.com/news/nh-news/Solar-panel-glare-causes-problems-for-flight-controllers/-/9857858/16430964/-/tdfn90z/-/index.html›.

[381] US Department of State Office of Inspector General. *Inspection of the Bureau of International Information Programs*. ISP-I-13-28. Office of Inspections, DHS OIG. May 2013. Web. ‹http://oig.state.gov/documents/organization/211193.pdf›.

[382] U.S. Department of State "Bureau of International Information Programs." Web. ‹http://www.state.gov/r/iip/›.

[383] US Department of State Office of Inspector General. *Inspection of the Bureau of International Information Programs.* ISP-I-13-28. Office of Inspections, DHS OIG. May 2013. Web.

[384] US Department of State Office of Inspector General. *Inspection of the Bureau of International Information Programs.* ISP-I-13-28. Office of Inspections, DHS OIG. May 2013. Web.

[385] Cooper, Steve. "Dealing With Facebook's Unfriendly New Algorithm." *Forbes.com.* Forbes. 30 November 2012. Web. ‹http://www.forbes.com/sites/stevecooper/2012/11/30/dealing-with-facebooks-unfriendly-new-algorithm/›.

[386] US Department of State Office of Inspector General. *Inspection of the Bureau of International Information Programs.* ISP-I-13-28. Office of Inspections, DHS OIG. May 2013. Web. ‹http://oig.state.gov/documents/organization/211193.pdf›.

[387] US Department of State Office of Inspector General. *Inspection of the Bureau of International Information Programs.* ISP-I-13-28. Office of Inspections, DHS OIG. May 2013. Web. ‹http://oig.state.gov/documents/organization/211193.pdf›.

[388] Green Ninja Website. "About the Green Ninja."*greenninja.org.* Green Ninja. 2013. Web. ‹http://www.greenninja.org/about.html›.

[389] Slager, Boris. "SJSU's Green Ninja Fights Climate Change." *Spartandaily.com.* The Spartan Daily. 18 April 2012. ‹http://spartandaily.com/72699/sjsus-green-ninja-fights-climate-change›.

[390] Green Ninja Website. "About the Green Ninja."*greenninja.org.* Green Ninja. 2013. Web. ‹http://www.greenninja.org/about.html›.

[391] Holst, Amanda. "Green Ninja Gains Momentum." *Blogs.sjsu.edu.* San Jose State University Today. 19 February 2012. Web. ‹http://blogs.sjsu.edu/today/2012/green-ninja-gains-momentum/›.

[392] Holst, Amanda. "Green Ninja Gains Momentum." *Blogs.sjsu.edu.* San Jose State University Today. 19 February 2012. Web. ‹http://blogs.sjsu.edu/today/2012/green-ninja-gains-momentum/›.

[393] Green Ninja YouTube channel, http://www.youtube.com/greenninjatv/ .

[394] Ninja, Green. "A Kickstart for the New Year." Weblog post.*OurGreenNinja.com.* 7 Jan. 2013. Web. ‹http://ourgreenninja.wordpress.com/2013/01/07/a-kickstart-for-the-new-year/›.

[395] Slager, Boris. "SJSU's Green Ninja Fights Climate Change." *Spartandaily.com.* The Spartan Daily. 18 April 2012. ‹http://spartandaily.com/72699/sjsus-green-ninja-fights-climate-change›.

[396] The U.S. Office of Special Counsel is an independent federal investigative and prosecutorial agency. OSC authorities come from four federal statutes: the Civil Service Report Act, the Whistleblower Protection Act, the Hatch Act, and the Uniformed Services Employment and Reemployment Rights Act.

[397] U.S. Office of Special Counsel report to the President. October 31, 2013. OSC File No. DI-13-0002. Web. ‹http://www.osc.gov/documents/press/2013/pr13_10.pdf›.

[398] U.S. Office of Special Counsel report to the President. October 31, 2013. OSC File No. DI-13-0002. Web. ‹http://www.osc.gov/documents/press/2013/pr13_10.pdf›.

[399] U.S. Office of Special Counsel report to the President. October 31, 2013. OSC File No. DI-13-0002. Web. ‹http://www.osc.gov/documents/press/2013/pr13_10.pdf›.

[400] The Situation Room is utilized to supply the Commissioner and headquarters executive staff members with crucial information, including news on significant events that occur at any CBP office.

[401] Wax-Thibodeaux, Emily. "Homeland Security Workers Routinely Boost Pay With Unearned Overtime, Report Says." *Washingtonpost.com.* The Washington Post. 31 October 2013. Web. ‹http://www.washingtonpost.com/politics/homeland-security-workers-routinely-boost-pay-with-unearned-overtime-report-says/2013/10/31/3d33f6e4-3fdf-11e3-9c8b-e8deeb3c755b_story.html›.

[402] Wax-Thibodeaux, Emily. "Homeland Security Workers Routinely Boost Pay With Unearned Overtime, Report Says." *Washingtonpost.com.* The Washington Post. 31 October 2013. Web. ‹http://www.washingtonpost.com/politics/homeland-security-workers-routinely-boost-pay-with-unearned-overtime-report-says/2013/10/31/3d33f6e4-3fdf-11e3-9c8b-e8deeb3c755b_story.html›.

[403] According to information provided by the Air Force.

[404] Aleniana Aermacchi. "C-27J Spartan Tactical Transport Aircraft."*aleniana.com.* Alenia Aermacchi North America. 13 Nov. 2013. Web. ‹http://www.aleniana.com/c-27j-spartan-tactical-transport-aircraft›.

[405] Cost-Benefit Analysis for Buying More C-27J Aircraft

[406] Cost-Benefit Analysis for Buying More C-27J Aircraft

[407] Dayton Daily News. "New Air Force Planes Go Directly to 'Boneyard.' *Military.com.* Military Advantage. 7 October 2013. Web. ‹http://www.military.com/daily-news/2013/10/07/new-air-force-planes-go-directly-to-boneyard.html›.

[408] Virtanen, Michael. "Spoils of War: U.S. Police Getting Leftover Armor-protected 18-ton Trucks from War in Iraq." *Washingtonpost.com.* The Washington Post. 24 November 2013. Web. ‹http://www.washingtonpost.com/politics/more-

defense-surplus-equipment-heading-to-local-police-departments-aclu-concerned/2013/11/24/44051418-555a-11e3-ba82-16ed03681809_story.html>.

[409] Guenther, Ryan. "Ohio State University Police Bring in Military Vehicle." *thelantern.com.* The Lantern, 26 September 2013. Web. <http://thelantern.com/2013/09/ohio-state-university-police-bring-in-military-vehicle/>.

[410] Nevada Daily Mail. "Bates County Sheriff's Office New Rescue Vehicle," *nevadadailymail.com.* Nevada Daily Mail. 23 November 2013. Web. <http://www.nevadadailymail.com/story/2026938.html>.

[411] Virtanen, Michael. "Spoils of War: U.S. Police Getting Leftover Armor-protected 18-ton Trucks from War in Iraq." *Washingtonpost.com.* The Washington Post. 24 November 2013. Web. <http://www.washingtonpost.com/politics/more-defense-surplus-equipment-heading-to-local-police-departments-aclu-concerned/2013/11/24/44051418-555a-11e3-ba82-16ed03681809_story.html>.

[412] Virtanen, Michael. "Spoils of War: U.S. Police Getting Leftover Armor-protected 18-ton Trucks from War in Iraq." *Washingtonpost.com.* The Washington Post. 24 November 2013. Web. <http://www.washingtonpost.com/politics/more-defense-surplus-equipment-heading-to-local-police-departments-aclu-concerned/2013/11/24/44051418-555a-11e3-ba82-16ed03681809_story.html>.

[413] Virtanen, Michael. "Spoils of War: U.S. Police Getting Leftover Armor-protected 18-ton Trucks from War in Iraq." *Washingtonpost.com.* The Washington Post. 24 November 2013. Web. <http://www.washingtonpost.com/politics/more-defense-surplus-equipment-heading-to-local-police-departments-aclu-concerned/2013/11/24/44051418-555a-11e3-ba82-16ed03681809_story.html>.

[414] Mack, Justin. "West Lafayette Police Acquire Military Vehicle," *jconline.com.* Journal and Courier Online. 31 October 2013. Web. <http://www.jconline.com/article/20131031/NEWS/310310038/?nclick_check=1>.

[415] Mack, Justin. "West Lafayette Police Acquire Military Vehicle," *jconline.com.* Journal and Courier Online. 31 October 2013. Web. <http://www.jconline.com/article/20131031/NEWS/310310038/?nclick_check=1>.

[416] Nevada Daily Mail. "Bates County Sheriff's Office New Rescue Vehicle," *nevadadailymail.com.* Nevada Daily Mail. 23 November 2013. Web. <http://www.nevadadailymail.com/story/2026938.html>.

[417] U.S. Census Bureau . "State & County Quickfacts: Bates County, Missouri." *Census.gov* Web. <http://quickfacts.census.gov/qfd/states/29/29013.html>. Accessed 26 November 2013.

[418] Virtanen, Michael. "Spoils of War: U.S. Police Getting Leftover Armor-protected 18-ton Trucks from War in Iraq." *Washingtonpost.com.* The Washington Post. 24 November 2013. Web. <http://www.washingtonpost.com/politics/more-defense-surplus-equipment-heading-to-local-police-departments-aclu-concerned/2013/11/24/44051418-555a-11e3-ba82-16ed03681809_story.html>.

[419] Virtanen, Michael. "Spoils of War: U.S. Police Getting Leftover Armor-protected 18-ton Trucks from War in Iraq." *Washingtonpost.com.* The Washington Post. 24 November 2013. Web. <http://www.washingtonpost.com/politics/more-defense-surplus-equipment-heading-to-local-police-departments-aclu-concerned/2013/11/24/44051418-555a-11e3-ba82-16ed03681809_story.html>.

[420] Guenther, Ryan. "Ohio State University Police Bring in Military Vehicle." *thelantern.com.* The Lantern, 26 September 2013. Web. <http://thelantern.com/2013/09/ohio-state-university-police-bring-in-military-vehicle/>.

[421] Preston, Benjamin. "Police Are Getting the Military's Leftover Armored Trucks." Web log post. *Wheels.blog.nytimes.com.* The New York Times Wheels Blog, 11 Oct. 2013. Web. <http://wheels.blogs.nytimes.com/2013/10/11/police-are-getting-the-militarys-leftover-armored-trucks/?_r=1>.

[422] U.S. Air Force, "US Air Force Expeditionary Combat Support System (ECSS)." *Acc.dau.mil.* Acquisition Community Connection. 14 February 2012. Web. <https://acc.dau.mil/CommunityBrowser.aspx?id=111768>.

[423] Perera, David. "Air Force Cancels ECSS." *Fiercegovermentit.com.* FierceMarkets. 29 November 2012. <http://www.fiercegovernmentit.com/pages/air-force-statement-ecss-cancelation>.

[424] GAO. *Information Technology: Key Federal Agencies Need to Address Potentially Duplicative Investments.* Report No. GAO-13-718, September 2013. Web. <http://www.gao.gov/products/GAO-13-718>.

[425] GAO. *Information Technology: Key Federal Agencies Need to Address Potentially Duplicative Investments.* Report No. GAO-13-718, September 2013. Web. <http://www.gao.gov/products/GAO-13-718>.

[426] GAO. *Information Technology: Key Federal Agencies Need to Address Potentially Duplicative Investments.* Report No. GAO-13-718, September 2013. Web. <http://www.gao.gov/products/GAO-13-718>.

[427] GAO. *Information Technology: Key Federal Agencies Need to Address Potentially Duplicative Investments.* Report No. GAO-13-718, September 2013. Web. <http://www.gao.gov/products/GAO-13-718>.

[428] GAO. *Information Technology: Key Federal Agencies Need to Address Potentially Duplicative Investments.* Report No. GAO-13-718, September 2013. Web. <http://www.gao.gov/products/GAO-13-718>.

[429] O'Connell, Michael, "More oversight needed to achieve billions of dollars in IT savings," *federalnewsradio.com*. Federal News Radio. 12 November 2013. Web. ‹http://www.federalnewsradio.com/245/3503291/GAO-reports-on-IT-reveal-duplicate-spending-lack-of-transparency›.

[430] O'Connell, Michael, "More oversight needed to achieve billions of dollars in IT savings," *federalnewsradio.com*. Federal News Radio. 12 November 2013. Web. ‹http://www.federalnewsradio.com/245/3503291/GAO-reports-on-IT-reveal-duplicate-spending-lack-of-transparency›.

[431] Website of the Office of the Secretary of Defense, "Pentagon Tours," accessed December 12, 2013, Web. ‹http://pentagontours.osd.mil›.

[432] Wise, David J. *FEDERAL REAL PROPERTY: National Strategy and Better Data Needed to Improve Management of Excess and Underutilized Property*. Rep. no. GAO-12-645. Governmental Accountability Office, 20 June 2012. Web. ‹http://www.gao.gov/products/GAO-12-645›. There is 450 million square feet in underutilized federal buildings.

[433] Wise, David J. *FEDERAL REAL PROPERTY: National Strategy and Better Data Needed to Improve Management of Excess and Underutilized Property*. Rep. no. GAO-12-645. Governmental Accountability Office, 20 June 2012. Web. ‹http://www.gao.gov/products/GAO-12-645›.

[434] Wise, David J. *FEDERAL REAL PROPERTY: National Strategy and Better Data Needed to Improve Management of Excess and Underutilized Property*. Rep. no. GAO-12-645. Governmental Accountability Office, 20 June 2012. Web. ‹http://www.gao.gov/products/GAO-12-645›.

[435] Wise, David J. FEDERAL REAL PROPERTY: National Strategy and Better Data Needed to Improve Management of Excess and Underutilized Property. Rep. no. GAO-12-645. Governmental Accountability Office, 20 June 2012. Web. ‹http://www.gao.gov/products/GAO-12-645›.

[436] AP. "Army to Cut Brigades at 10 U.S. Bases." *CBSnews.com*. Associated Press. 25 June 2013. Web. ‹http://www.cbsnews.com/8301-201_162-57590979/army-to-cut-brigades-at-10-u.s-bases/›.

[437] Elliot, Stuart. "Army Tries Reality Style for Recruitment." *Nytimes.com*. New York Times. 21 May 2013. Web. ‹http://www.nytimes.com/2013/05/22/business/media/army-tries-a-reality-style-for-recruitment.html›.

[438] Elliot, Stuart. "Army Tries Reality Style for Recruitment." *Nytimes.com*. New York Times. 21 May 2013. Web. ‹http://www.nytimes.com/2013/05/22/business/media/army-tries-a-reality-style-for-recruitment.html›.

[439] Kurtz, Annalyn. "Army plans to launch a reality TV show," *Money.CNN.com* CNNMoney. 21 May 2013. Web. ‹http://money.cnn.com/2013/05/21/news/economy/army-reality-tv/index.html›.

[440] https://www.facebook.com/StartingStrong

Elliot, Stuart. "Army Tries Reality Style for Recruitment." *Nytimes.com*. New York Times. 21 May 2013. Web. ‹http://www.nytimes.com/2013/05/22/business/media/army-tries-a-reality-style-for-recruitment.html›.

[442] Elliot, Stuart. "Army Tries Reality Style for Recruitment." *Nytimes.com*. New York Times. 21 May 2013. Web. ‹http://www.nytimes.com/2013/05/22/business/media/army-tries-a-reality-style-for-recruitment.html›.

[443] Under the Radar. "Will 'Starting Strong' Recruit the Next Generation?,"*Military.com*. Military Advantage. 19 July, 2013. Web. ‹http://undertheradar.military.com/?s=Starting+Strong›.

[444] US Army. "Starting Strong Episode 1: Avionic Mechanic (15N)." Online Video Clip. *YouTube.com*. YouTube. 2 June 2013. Web. ‹http://www.youtube.com/watch?v=h19kEnB8Rs4›.

[445] US Army. "Starting Strong Episode 1: Avionic Mechanic (15N)." Online Video Clip. *YouTube.com*. YouTube. 2 June 2013. Web. ‹http://www.youtube.com/watch?v=h19kEnB8Rs4›.

[446] Under the Radar. "Will 'Starting Strong' Recruit the Next Generation?,"*Military.com*. Military Advantage. 19 July, 2013. Web. ‹http://undertheradar.military.com/?s=Starting+Strong›.

[447] Sopko, John M. "Management Alert: Command and Control Facility at Camp Leatherneck." Letter to Defense Secretary Chuck Hagel. 8 July 2013. MS. SIGAR, Arlington, VA. Web. ‹http://www.sigar.mil/pdf/alerts/SIGAR%20SP-13-7.pdf›.

[448] Sopko, John M. "Management Alert: Command and Control Facility at Camp Leatherneck." Letter to Defense Secretary Chuck Hagel. 8 July 2013. MS. SIGAR, Arlington, VA. Web. ‹http://www.sigar.mil/pdf/alerts/SIGAR%20SP-13-7.pdf›.

[449] Curtis, Kris. *Department Of Transportation and Public Facilities Knik Arm Bridge and Toll Authority Knik Arm Crossing Project*. Audit. no. 25-30068-13. Juneau, AK: Alaska State Legislature, Legislative Budget and Audit Committee, Division of Legislative Audit, 2013. Web. ‹http://www.legaudit.state.ak.us/pages/audits/2013/pdf/30068rpt.pdf›.

[450] Demer, Lisa, "KABATA plows on with bridge in legislative limbo," *and.com*. Anchorage Daily News, 2 November 2013. Web. ‹http://www.adn.com/2013/11/02/3155504/kabata-plowing-on-and-over-businesses.html›.

[451] Grosvold, Lacie. "Anchorage Business Slated for Demolition Get Reprieve," *ktuu.com*. KTUU-TV NBC2. 14 November 2013. Web. ‹http://www.ktuu.com/news/news/anchorage-businesses-slated-for-demolition-get-reprieve/-/21043658/22973898/-/pkgt9e/-/index.html›.

[452] Demer, Lisa, "KABATA plows on with bridge in legislative limbo," *and.com*. Anchorage Daily News, 2 November 2013. Web. ‹http://www.adn.com/2013/11/02/3155504/kabata-plowing-on-and-over-businesses.html›.

[453] Curtis, Kris. *Department Of Transportation and Public Facilities Knik Arm Bridge and Toll Authority Knik Arm Crossing Project*. Audit. no. 25-30068-13. Juneau, AK: Alaska State Legislature, Legislative Budget and Audit Committee, Division of Legislative Audit, 2013. Web. ‹http://www.legaudit.state.ak.us/pages/audits/2013/pdf/30068rpt.pdf›.

[454] Demer, Lisa, "KABATA plows on with bridge in legislative limbo," *and.com*. Anchorage Daily News, 2 November 2013. Web. ‹http://www.adn.com/2013/11/02/3155504/kabata-plowing-on-and-over-businesses.html›.

[455] Information provided by the Federal Highway Administration (FHWA), November 18, 2013.

[456] Hope, Heather. "Oklahoma Families Left With Uncertainty After Food Stamp Cuts." *Newson6.com*. WeoldNow and KOTV. 1 November 2013. Web. ‹http://www.newson6.com/story/23856093/oklahoma-families-left-with-uncertainty-after-food-stamp-cuts›.

[457] LeFlore, Jeanne. "Local Winery Benefits from USDA Grant." *Mcalesternews.com*. McAlester News-Capital. 25 June 2013. Web. ‹http://www.mcalesternews.com/x182748545/Local-winery-benefits-from-USDA-grant›.

[458] LeFlore, Jeanne. "Local Winery Benefits from USDA Grant." *Mcalesternews.com*. McAlester News-Capital. 25 June 2013. Web. ‹http://www.mcalesternews.com/x182748545/Local-winery-benefits-from-USDA-grant›.

[459] LeFlore, Jeanne. "Local Winery Benefits from USDA Grant." *Mcalesternews.com*. McAlester News-Capital. 25 June 2013. Web. ‹http://www.mcalesternews.com/x182748545/Local-winery-benefits-from-USDA-grant›.

[460] "Public Law 111-11, Omnibus Public Land Management Act of 2009." (111 Stat. 11; Date 3/30/2009; enacted H.R. 146). Text from: Government Printing Office Website. ‹http://www.gpo.gov/fdsys/pkg/PLAW-111publ11/pdf/PLAW-111publ11.pdf›.

[461] Mroz, Jacqueline. "The Great Falls: Power for Another Revolution?" *nytimes.com*. The New York Times Company. 27 March 2009. Web. ‹http://www.nytimes.com/2009/03/29/nyregion/new-jersey/29fallsnj.html?pagewanted=all›.

[462] US Department of the Interior, NPS, Northeast Region. "Chapter Three: Designation Analysis." *Great Falls Historic District: Paterson, New Jesrsey*. Philadelphia: National Park Service Division of Planning & Special Studies,2006. Web. ‹http://parkplanning.nps.gov/document.cfm?parkId=261&projectId=16673&documentID=17397›.

[463] US Department of the Interior, NPS, Northeast Region. "Chapter Three: Designation Analysis." *Great Falls Historic District: Paterson, New Jesrsey*. Philadelphia: National Park Service Division of Planning & Special Studies,2006. Web. ‹http://parkplanning.nps.gov/document.cfm?parkId=261&projectId=16673&documentID=17397›.

[464] Malinconico, Joe. "Great Falls National Park Remains Open During Federal Shutdown." *Northjersey.com*. North Jersey Media Group. Press, 1 October 2013. Web. ‹http://www.northjersey.com/news/Great_Falls_National_Park_remains_open_during_federal_shutdown.html›.

[465] August 8, 2013 trip to Paterson Great Falls National Historic Park by staff of Senator Tom Coburn.

[466] Kelly, Mike. "Trash Piling Up at Great Falls; Site Was Approved in '09 for Historic Park." *Northjersey.com*. North Jersey Media Group. 28 March 2011. Web. ‹http://www.northjersey.com/columnists/Trash_piling_up_at_site_approved_in_09_for_historic_park.html›.

[467] Health and Human Services. "Contingency Staffing Plan for Operations in the Absence of Enacted Annual Appropriations." *Hhs.gov*. Department of Health and Human Services. Web. ‹http://www.hhs.gov/budget/fy2014/fy2014contingency_staffing_plan-rev2.pdf›.

[468] Substance Abuse and Mental Health Services Administration. SAMHSA Press Office. *SAMHSA Honors Community and Entertainment Leaders at 2013 Voice Awards for Giving a Voice to Behavioral Health Recovery.Www.samhsa.gov*. SAMHSA, 26 Sept. 2013. Web. ‹http://www.samhsa.gov/newsroom/advisories/1309262617.aspx›.

[469] Substance Abuse and Mental Health Services Administration. SAMHSA Press Office. *SAMHSA Honors Community and Entertainment Leaders at 2013 Voice Awards for Giving a Voice to Behavioral Health Recovery.Samhsa.gov*. SAMHSA, 26 Sept. 2013. Web. ‹http://www.samhsa.gov/newsroom/advisories/1309262617.aspx›.

[470] Substance Abuse and Mental Health Services Administration. "Voice Awards Live Webcast." 25 September 2013. Web. ‹http://www.samhsa.gov/voiceawards/#sthash.LebYNDVt.dpuf›.

[471] Subcommittee on Oversight and Investigations. "Examining SAMHSA's Role in Delivering Services to the Severely Mentally Ill." *Democrats.energycommerce.house.gov*. House Committee on Energy and Commerce. 22 May 2013. Web ‹http://democrats.energycommerce.house.gov/sites/default/files/documents/Transcript-OI-SAMHSA-Mentally-Ill-Services-2013-5-22.pdf›. Preliminary Transcript (57-59).

[472] Subcommittee on Oversight and Investigations. "Examining SAMHSA's Role in Delivering Services to the Severely Mentally Ill." *Democrats.energycommerce.house.gov*. House Committee on Energy and Commerce. 22 May 2013. Web

‹http://democrats.energycommerce.house.gov/sites/default/files/documents/Transcript-OI-SAMHSA-Mentally-Ill-Services-2013-5-22.pdf›. Preliminary Transcript (57-59).

[473] Subcommittee on Oversight and Investigations. "Examining SAMHSA's Role in Delivering Services to the Severely Mentally Ill." *Democrats.energycommerce.house.gov*. House Committee on Energy and Commerce. 22 May 2013. Web. ‹http://democrats.energycommerce.house.gov/sites/default/files/documents/Transcript-OI-SAMHSA-Mentally-Ill-Services-2013-5-22.pdf›. Preliminary Transcript (46).

[474] Subcommittee on Oversight and Investigations. "Examining SAMHSA's Role in Delivering Services to the Severely Mentally Ill." *Democrats.energycommerce.house.gov*. House Committee on Energy and Commerce. 22 May 2013. Web ‹http://democrats.energycommerce.house.gov/sites/default/files/documents/Transcript-OI-SAMHSA-Mentally-Ill-Services-2013-5-22.pdf›. Preliminary Transcript (67).

[475] Subcommittee on Oversight and Investigations. "Examining SAMHSA's Role in Delivering Services to the Severely Mentally Ill." *Democrats.energycommerce.house.gov*. House Committee on Energy and Commerce. 22 May 2013. Web ‹http://democrats.energycommerce.house.gov/sites/default/files/documents/Transcript-OI-SAMHSA-Mentally-Ill-Services-2013-5-22.pdf›. Preliminary Transcript (71).

[476] Subcommittee on Oversight and Investigations. "Examining SAMHSA's Role in Delivering Services to the Severely Mentally Ill." *Democrats.energycommerce.house.gov*. House Committee on Energy and Commerce. 22 May 2013. Web ‹http://democrats.energycommerce.house.gov/sites/default/files/documents/Transcript-OI-SAMHSA-Mentally-Ill-Services-2013-5-22.pdf›. Preliminary Transcript (102).

[477] DOJ IG. *Review Of Department Of Justice Airfares And Booking Fees October 2012 Through June 2013*. Rep. no. 13-39. Washington, D.C.: DOJ OIG, September 2013. Web. ‹ http://www.justice.gov/oig/reports/2013/a1339.pdf›.

[478] DOJ IG. *Review Of Department Of Justice Airfares And Booking Fees October 2012 Through June 2013*. Rep. no. 13-39. Washington, D.C.: DOJ OIG, September 2013. Web. ‹ http://www.justice.gov/oig/reports/2013/a1339.pdf›.

[479] DOJ IG. *Review Of Department Of Justice Airfares And Booking Fees October 2012 Through June 2013*. Rep. no. 13-39. Washington, D.C.: DOJ OIG, September 2013. Web. ‹ http://www.justice.gov/oig/reports/2013/a1339.pdf›.

[480] DOJ IG. *Review Of Department Of Justice Airfares And Booking Fees October 2012 Through June 2013*. Rep. no. 13-39. Washington, D.C.: DOJ OIG, September 2013. Web. ‹ http://www.justice.gov/oig/reports/2013/a1339.pdf›.

[481] Government Accountability Office. *Department of Justice: Executives' Use of Aircraft for Nonmission Purposes* Rep no. GAO-13-235 26 February 2013. Web. ‹http://www.gao.gov/products/GAO-13-235›.

[482] NASA, https://prod.nais.nasa.gov/cgibin/npdv/contract.cgi, accessed November 22, 2013.

[483] Peckham, Matt. "NASA-Funded 3D Food Printer: Could It End World Hunger," *Time.com*. Time. Inc. 24 May 2013.Web. ‹http://newsfeed.time.com/2013/05/24/nasa-funded-3d-food-printer-could-it-end-world-hunger/›.

[484] NASA, https://prod.nais.nasa.gov/cgibin/npdv/contract.cgi, accessed November 22, 2013.

[485] The Engineer. "In Future You May Print Your Own Food Using This Food Printer,"." Weblog post. *Wonderfulengineering.com/*. Wonderful Engineering, 30 June 2013. Web. ‹http://wonderfulengineering.com/in-future-you-may-print-your-own-food-using-this-food-printer/›..

[486] NASA, https://prod.nais.nasa.gov/cgibin/npdv/contract.cgi, accessed November 22, 2013.

[487] The Engineer. "In Future You May Print Your Own Food Using This Food Printer,"." Weblog post. *Wonderfulengineering.com/*. Wonderful Engineering, 30 June 2013. Web. ‹http://wonderfulengineering.com/in-future-you-may-print-your-own-food-using-this-food-printer/›.

[488] Plusnick-Masti, Ramit. "NASA Builds Menu For Planned Mars Mission in 2030s," *ap.com* . The Associated Press. 17 July 2012. Web. ‹http://bigstory.ap.org/article/nasa-builds-menu-planned-mars-mission-2030s›.

[489] Schwartz, Ariel. "Why NASA Just Spent $125,000 To Fund A 3-D Pizza Printer Prototype." *FastCoexist.com*. Fast Company & Inc. 3 June 2013. Web. ‹http://www.fastcoexist.com/1682194/why-nasa-just-spent-125000-to-fund-a-3-d-pizza-printer-prototype›.

[490] Waugh, Rob. "Tofu Bacon, Peanut Butter Cookies and French Fries: Nasa Menu Suggests Mars Astronauts May Be Too Fat To Get Out Of Capsule On Arrival." *DailyMail.co.uk*. Associated Newspapers Ltd. 25 July 2012. Web. ‹http://www.dailymail.co.uk/sciencetech/article-2178697/Nasa-menu-suggests-Mars-astronauts-fat-capsule-arrival.html›.

[491] Office of Congresswoman Betsy McCollum. U.S. House of Representatives. *McCollum: National Guard's $26 Million Sponsoring NASCAR's Dale Earnhardt Jr. Results in ZERO Recruits*. *Mccollum.house.gov*. N.p., 18 May 2012. Web. ‹http://mccollum.house.gov/press-release/mccollum-national-guard%E2%80%99s-26-million-sponsoring-nascar%E2%80%99s-dale-earnhardt-jr-results›.

[492] Office of Congresswoman Betsy McCollum. U.S. House of Representatives. *McCollum: National Guard's $26 Million Sponsoring NASCAR's Dale Earnhardt Jr. Results in ZERO Recruits*. *Mccollum.house.gov*. N.p., 18 May 2012. Web.

‹http://mccollum.house.gov/press-release/mccollum-national-guard%E2%80%99s-26-million-sponsoring-nascar%E2%80%99s-dale-earnhardt-jr-results›.

[493] The Associated Press. "Military Sports Sponsorships Debate Could Impact Dale Earnhardt Jr. and National Guard." *Washington.cbslocal.com*. The Associated Press. 18 July 2012. Web. ‹http://washington.cbslocal.com/2012/07/18/military-sports-sponsorships-debate-could-impact-dale-earnhardt-jr-and-national-guard/›.

[494] Statement of Work, August 2, 2013, http://apps.federaltimes.com/projects/files/future-of-stamps.pdf, page 1.

[495] "The Popcorn Report: Faith Popcorn on the Future of Your Company, Your World, Your Life," *Amazon.com*. Amazon.com. Web, ‹http://www.amazon.com/The-Popcorn-Report-Future-Company/dp/B000C4SGNM/ref=sr_1_2?ie=UTF8&qid=1386968471&sr=8-2&keywords=faith+popcorn›.

[496] Faith Popcorn's 2006 Predictions, Creating Control, January 1, 2006, http://www.faithpopcorn.com/faith-popcorns-2006-prediction-creating-control/

[497] Faith Popcorn's 2006 Predictions, Creating Control, January 1, 2006, http://www.faithpopcorn.com/faith-popcorns-2006-prediction-creating-control/

[498] Faith Popcorn's 2006 Predictions, Creating Control, January 1, 2006, http://www.faithpopcorn.com/faith-popcorns-2006-prediction-creating-control/

[499] Statement of Work, August 2, 2013, http://apps.federaltimes.com/projects/files/future-of-stamps.pdf, page 9.

[500] Statement of Work, August 2, 2013, http://apps.federaltimes.com/projects/files/future-of-stamps.pdf, page 9.

[501] Statement of Work, August 2, 2013, http://apps.federaltimes.com/projects/files/future-of-stamps.pdf, page 1.

[502] Statement of Work, August 2, 2013, http://apps.federaltimes.com/projects/files/future-of-stamps.pdf, page 1.

[503] Statement of Work, August 2, 2013, http://apps.federaltimes.com/projects/files/future-of-stamps.pdf, page 1.

[504] Badenhausen, Kurt. "Tiger Woods Is Back On Top Of The World's Highest-Paid Athletes." *Forbes.com*. Forbes.com LLC. Web. ‹http://www.forbes.com/sites/kurtbadenhausen/2013/06/05/tiger-woods-is-back-on-top-of-the-worlds-highest-paid-athletes/›.

[505] Senator Tom Coburn, M.D. *Wastebook 2012*. Office of Senator Tom Coburn. *Coburn.senate.gov*. Web. ‹http://www.coburn.senate.gov/public/index.cfm?a=Files.Serve&File_id=b7b23f66-2d60-4d5a-8bc5-8522c7e1a40e›.

[506] United States Department of Treasury. Internal Revenue Service. "2010 Return of Organization Exempt from Income Tax (Form990): PGA Tour, Inc." Form 990 filed by PGA Tour, Inc.

[507] 26 USC § 7701, Public Law 99-514

[508] Nesbit, Jeff. 1986. PGA tour receives hefty boost from the Senate. *The Philadelphia Inquirer*, July 3, 1986.

[509] TiqIQBlog. "The Masters Tickets Out Pricing Other Majors." Web log post. *TiqIQ.com*. N.p., Feb. 2013. Web. ‹http://blog.tiqiq.com/2013/02/the-masters-tickets-out-pricing-other-majors/›.

[510] Title VIII, Subtitle D, Section 409A of Public Law 108-357

[511] Simpson, Glenn R. "PGA Tour Golfers Hit It on the Green In Regulation(s)." *wsj.com*. The Wall Street Journal. 14 October 2004. Web. ‹ http://online.wsj.com/news/articles/SB109771287850844910 ›.

[512] Werfel, Daniel I. "Agency Use of Official Time." Letter to The Honorable Charles Boustany Jr., M.D., Chairman, Subcommittee on Oversight. 29 July 2013. *Waysandmeans.house.gov*. House Ways and Means Committee. Web. ‹http://waysandmeans.house.gov/uploadedfiles/boustany_7_29.pdf›.

[513] "Official Time" (5 USC §713, 7 January 2011). Text from : GPO. Web. ‹http://www.gpo.gov/fdsys/pkg/USCODE-2010-title5/html/USCODE-2010-title5-partIII-subpartF-chap71-subchapIV-sec7131.htm›.

[514] Werfel, Daniel I. "Agency Use of Official Time." Letter to The Honorable Charles Boustany Jr., M.D., Chairman, Subcommittee on Oversight. 29 July 2013. *Waysandmeans.house.gov*. House Ways and Means Committee. Web. ‹http://waysandmeans.house.gov/uploadedfiles/boustany_7_29.pdf›.

[515] Bedard, Paul. "Furloughs? IRS Sends Staff to Vegas for Union Training." *Washingtonexaminer.com*. Washington Examiner. 18 April 2013. Web. ‹http://washingtonexaminer.com/furloughs-irs-sends-staff-to-vegas-for-union-training/article/2527565›.

[516] Bedard, Paul. "Furloughs? IRS Sends Staff to Vegas for Union Training." *Washingtonexaminer.com*. Washington Examiner. 18 April 2013. Web. ‹http://washingtonexaminer.com/furloughs-irs-sends-staff-to-vegas-for-union-training/article/2527565›.

[517] Americans for Limited Government Freedom of Information Files Website: "Treasury Department Full Time Official Time Personnel." *Internal Revenue Service Responsive Records*. 6 June 2013. *Algfoiafiles.com*. Accessed Via Web. ‹http://algfoiafiles.com/images/a/ad/IRS_Responsive_Records_w_06.06.13.PDF›.

[518] Coburn, Tom A., M.D., and Gingrey, Phil. "IRS Protection of Official Time Over National Priorities." Letter to the Honorable Daniel I. Werfel. 27 Jan. 2013. *Coburn.senate.gov*. Office of Senator Tom Coburn, M.D. Web. ‹http://www.coburn.senate.gov/public/index.cfm?a=Files.Serve&File_id=1abcf8f7-4ecf-45b7-854f-4bf152842cea›.

[519] The Strong. Press Room. *The Strong® Receives Museums for America Grant from Institute of Museum and Library Services. Thestrong.org.* The Strong, 13 Sept. 2013. Web. <http://www.thestrong.org/press/releases/1969/12/4638-strong-receives-imls-grant>.

[520] The Strong. Press Room. *The Strong® Receives Museums for America Grant from Institute of Museum and Library Services. Thestrong.org.* The Strong, 13 Sept. 2013. Web. <http://www.thestrong.org/press/releases/1969/12/4638-strong-receives-imls-grant>.

[521] The Strong. Press Room. *The Strong® Receives Museums for America Grant from Institute of Museum and Library Services. Thestrong.org.* The Strong, 13 Sept. 2013. Web. <http://www.thestrong.org/press/releases/1969/12/4638-strong-receives-imls-grant>.

[522] The Strong. Press Room. *The Strong® Receives Museums for America Grant from Institute of Museum and Library Services. Thestrong.org.* The Strong, 13 Sept. 2013. Web. <http://www.thestrong.org/press/releases/1969/12/4638-strong-receives-imls-grant>.

[523] The Strong. Press Room. *The Strong® Receives Museums for America Grant from Institute of Museum and Library Services. Thestrong.org.* The Strong, 13 Sept. 2013. Web. <http://www.thestrong.org/press/releases/1969/12/4638-strong-receives-imls-grant>.

[524] The Strong. Press Room. *The Strong® Receives Museums for America Grant from Institute of Museum and Library Services. Thestrong.org.* The Strong, 26 July 2013. Web. <http://www.thestrong.org/press/releases/2012/07/4364-strong-receives-museums-america-grant-imls>.

[525] The Strong. Press Room. *The Strong® Receives Museums for America Grant from Institute of Museum and Library Services. Thestrong.org.* The Strong, 13 Sept. 2013. Web. <http://www.thestrong.org/press/releases/1969/12/4638-strong-receives-imls-grant>.

[526] National Museum of Play. "Exhibits: eGameRevolution." *Museumofplay.org.* The Strong. Web. <http://www.museumofplay.org/see-do/exhibits/egamerevolution?utm_source=homepage&utm_medium=panel&utm_campaign=home-panels-general>.

[527] National Museum of Play. "International Center for the History of Electronic Games Virtual Tour." Web. <http://www.museumofplay.org/360/egamerevolution-2/index.html>.

[528] MuseumofPlay. "Space Chase: In Another Galaxy Weekend at The Strong." Online Video Clip. *YouTube.*com. YouTube, 15 October 2013. Web. <http://www.youtube.com/watch?v=ax9Mg5p7aEE&feature=share&list=UU8DF0j2qeO98>.

[529] FedBizOpps. "Department of State 2013 Production and Supply Contract for Lead-Free Crystal and Glass Tabletop Ware." Solicitation No. SAQMMA13R0126 . 8 February 2013. Web. <https://www.fbo.gov/?s=opportunity&mode=form&id=92d284b329ff2b588d876b3e9f4c063a&tab=core&_cview>

[530] FedBizOpps. "Department of State 2013 Production and Supply Contract for Lead-Free Crystal and Glass Tabletop Ware." Solicitation No. SAQMMA13R0126 . 8 February 2013. Web. <https://www.fbo.gov/?s=opportunity&mode=form&id=92d284b329ff2b588d876b3e9f4c063a&tab=core&_cview>

[531] The Commons Online. "Rich Earth Institute gets USDA Grant for Urine Reclamation Project." *Commonsnews.org.* The Commons. Issue no. 194. 13 March 2013. Web. <http://www.commonsnews.org/site/site05/story.php?articleno=7129&page=1#.UjjMVcakqtY>.

[532] The Urine Brigade. "Donate Urine." *Richearthinstitute.org.* The Rich Earth Institute. Web.< http://richearthinstitute.org/?page_id=655>.

[533] Rich Earth Institute. "Urine Nutrient Reclamation Project–Technical Details," *richearthinstitutue.org.* The Rich Earth Institute. Web. <http://richearthinstitute.org/?page_id=27>.

[534] Rich Earth Institute. "Urine Nutrient Reclamation Project–Technical Details," *richearthinstitutue.org.* The Rich Earth Institute. Web. <http://richearthinstitute.org/?page_id=27>.

[535] Baker, Issac Nichols. "Closing the Cycle; Rich Earth Institute Breaks Ground with First-ever U.S. Field Trial Using Human Urine as a Fertilizer." *Commonsnews.org.* The Commons. Issue no. 165 15 August 2012. Web. <http://www.commonsnews.org/site/site05/story.php?articleno=5906&page=1#.Ukn0cIakqtY>.

[536] Baker, Issac Nichols. "Closing the Cycle; Rich Earth Institute Breaks Ground with First-ever U.S. Field Trial Using Human Urine as a Fertilizer." *Commonsnews.org.* The Commons. Issue no. 165 15 August 2012. Web. <http://www.commonsnews.org/site/site05/story.php?articleno=5906&page=1#.Ukn0cIakqtY>.

[537] Karush, Becky. "Looking for a New Source of Fertilizer? Urine Luck." *Reformer.com.* The Brattleboro Reformer. 20 April 2013. Web. <http://www.reformer.com/latestnews/ci_23067779/looking-new-source-fertilizer-urine-luck>.

[538] The Commons Online. "Rich Earth Institute gets USDA Grant for Urine Reclamation Project." *Commonsnews.org.* The Commons. Issue no. 194. 13 March 2013. Web. <http://www.commonsnews.org/site/site05/story.php?articleno=7129&page=1#.UjjMVcakqtY>.

[539] Rich Earth Institute. "Urine Nutrient Reclamation Project." *Richearthinstitute.org.* The Rich Earth Institute. <http://richearthinstitute.org/?page_id=399>.

[540] American Chemical Society. "Human Urine As a Safe, Inexpensive Fertilizer for Food Crops." *ScienceDaily.com* Science Daily, LLC. 8 October 2007. Web. <http://www.sciencedaily.com/releases/2007/10/071008093608.htm>.

[541] Mallapaty, Smriti. "Liquid Gold: Farmers in Nepal Find Resourceful Way to Fertilize Crops." *Environmentalhealthenws.org.* Environmental Health Sciences. 17 December 2012. Web. <http://www.environmentalhealthnews.org/ehs/news/2012/urine-as-fertilizer>.

[542] Carolyn Colwell, "Human Urine Safe, Productive Fertilizer," HealthDay News, October 8, 2007.

[543] Pradhan, Surendra K., Anne-Marja Nerg, Annalena Sjöblom, Jarmo K. Holopainen, and Helvi Heinonen-Tanski. *Journal of Agricultural and Food Chemistry* 55.21 (21 November 2007): 8567-663. *American Chemical Society.* Web. <http://pubs.acs.org/doi/full/10.1021/jf0717891>.

[544] American Chemical Society. "Human Urine As a Safe, Inexpensive Fertilizer for Food Crops." *ScienceDaily.com* Science Daily, LLC. 8 October 2007. Web. <http://www.sciencedaily.com/releases/2007/10/071008093608.htm>.

[545] Keese, Susan. "Brattleboro Group Researches Innovative Fertilizer Application." *Vpr.net.* Vermont Public Radio. 8 March 2013. Web. <http://www.vpr.net/news_detail/97732/brattleboro-group-researches-innovative-fertilizer/>.

[546] Flock, Elizabeth. "Monument To Jim Clyburn, Southern University Turns Into Boondoggle." Web log post. USnews.com. 8 Mar. 2013. <http://www.usnews.com/news/blogs/washington-whispers/2013/03/08/monument-to-jim-clyburn-southern-university-turns-into-boondoggle>.

[547] FoxNews.com. "South Carolina University Project Chugs Along After 15 Years, $24M Cost to Taxpayers." *Foxnews.com.* FOX News Network, LLC. 24 March 2013. Web. <http://www.foxnews.com/politics/2013/03/24/clyburn-transportation-center-turns-into-15-year-government-boondoggle/>.

[548] South Carolina General Assembly Legislative Audit Council, *Review of Construction of the James E. Clyburn University Transportation Center and Transportation Center Program Expenditures.* Rep. no. LAC/10-4. Columbia, SC: South Carolina General Assembly, 2011. *Lac.sc.gov.* June 2011. SC State University. <http://lac.sc.gov/LAC_Reports/2011/Documents/SCSU.pdf>. (5).

[549] South Carolina General Assembly Legislative Audit Council, *Review of Construction of the James E. Clyburn University Transportation Center and Transportation Center Program Expenditures.* Rep. no. LAC/10-4. Columbia, SC: South Carolina General Assembly, 2011. *Lac.sc.gov.* June 2011. SC State University. <http://lac.sc.gov/LAC_Reports/2011/Documents/SCSU.pdf>. (5-6).

[550] South Carolina General Assembly Legislative Audit Council, *Review of Construction of the James E. Clyburn University Transportation Center and Transportation Center Program Expenditures.* Rep. no. LAC/10-4. Columbia, SC: South Carolina General Assembly, 2011. *Lac.sc.gov.* June 2011. SC State University. <http://lac.sc.gov/LAC_Reports/2011/Documents/SCSU.pdf>. (5, 8).

[551] South Carolina General Assembly Legislative Audit Council, *Review of Construction of the James E. Clyburn University Transportation Center and Transportation Center Program Expenditures.* Rep. no. LAC/10-4. Columbia, SC: South Carolina General Assembly, 2011. *Lac.sc.gov.* June 2011. SC State University. <http://lac.sc.gov/LAC_Reports/2011/Documents/SCSU.pdf>. (8).

[552] Linder-Altman, Dale "12 years Later...Transportation Center May Get off the Ground." *Thetandd.com.* The Times and Democrat. 18 July 2010. Web. <http://thetandd.com/news/local/article_4573afd6-9135-11df-8736-001cc4c03286.html>.

[553] South Carolina General Assembly Legislative Audit Council, *Review of Construction of the James E. Clyburn University Transportation Center and Transportation Center Program Expenditures.* Rep. no. LAC/10-4. Columbia, SC: South Carolina General Assembly, 2011. *Lac.sc.gov.* June 2011. SC State University. <http://lac.sc.gov/LAC_Reports/2011/Documents/SCSU.pdf>. (12-13).

[554] South Carolina General Assembly Legislative Audit Council, *Review of Construction of the James E. Clyburn University Transportation Center and Transportation Center Program Expenditures.* Rep. no. LAC/10-4. Columbia, SC: South Carolina General Assembly, 2011. *Lac.sc.gov.* June 2011. SC State University. <http://lac.sc.gov/LAC_Reports/2011/Documents/SCSU.pdf>. (13).

[555] South Carolina General Assembly Legislative Audit Council, *Review of Construction of the James E. Clyburn University Transportation Center and Transportation Center Program Expenditures.* Rep. no. LAC/10-4. Columbia, SC: South Carolina General Assembly, 2011. *Lac.sc.gov.* June 2011. SC State University. <http://lac.sc.gov/LAC_Reports/2011/Documents/SCSU.pdf>. (26).

[556] South Carolina General Assembly Legislative Audit Council, *Review of Construction of the James E. Clyburn University Transportation Center and Transportation Center Program Expenditures.* Rep. no. LAC/10-4. Columbia, SC: South Carolina General

Assembly, 2011. *Lac.sc.gov.* June 2011. SC State University. <http://lac.sc.gov/LAC_Reports/2011/Documents/SCSU.pdf>. (49-40).

[557] South Carolina General Assembly Legislative Audit Council, *Review of Construction of the James E. Clyburn University Transportation Center and Transportation Center Program Expenditures.* Rep. no. LAC/10-4. Columbia, SC: South Carolina General Assembly, 2011. *Lac.sc.gov.* June 2011. SC State University. <http://lac.sc.gov/LAC_Reports/2011/Documents/SCSU.pdf>. (48-49).

[558] South Carolina General Assembly Legislative Audit Council, *Review of Construction of the James E. Clyburn University Transportation Center and Transportation Center Program Expenditures.* Rep. no. LAC/10-4. Columbia, SC: South Carolina General Assembly, 2011. *Lac.sc.gov.* June 2011. SC State University. <http://lac.sc.gov/LAC_Reports/2011/Documents/SCSU.pdf>. (48-49).

[559] Knich, Diane. "Transportation Center Stalled." *Postandcourier.com.* The Post and Courier. 23 March 2012. Web. <http://www.postandcourier.com/article/20100614/PC1602/30614997>.

[560] "Alumni Foundation to Induct Clyburn into Hall of Fame." *Theitem.com.* The Item. 4 October 2005. Web. <http://www.theitem.com/news01/alumni-foundation-to-induct-clyburn-into-hall-of-fame/article_681956e0-e17f-523f-a7c0-8f748806d36e.html>.

[561] South Carolina General Assembly Legislative Audit Council, *Review of Construction of the James E. Clyburn University Transportation Center and Transportation Center Program Expenditures.* Rep. no. LAC/10-4. Columbia, SC: South Carolina General Assembly, 2011. *Lac.sc.gov.* June 2011. SC State University. <http://lac.sc.gov/LAC_Reports/2011/Documents/SCSU.pdf>.

[562] South Carolina General Assembly Legislative Audit Council, *Review of Construction of the James E. Clyburn University Transportation Center and Transportation Center Program Expenditures.* Rep. no. LAC/10-4. Columbia, SC: South Carolina General Assembly, 2011. *Lac.sc.gov.* June 2011. SC State University. <http://lac.sc.gov/LAC_Reports/2011/Documents/SCSU.pdf>. (36-37).

[563] Knich, Diane. "Transportation Center Stalled." *Postandcourier.com.* The Post and Courier. 23 March 2012. Web. <http://www.postandcourier.com/article/20100614/PC1602/30614997>.

[564] Knich, Diane. "Transportation Center Stalled." *Postandcourier.com.* The Post and Courier. 23 March 2012. Web. <http://www.postandcourier.com/article/20100614/PC1602/30614997>.

[565] O'Keefe, Ed. "Senator to Probe Postal Regulatory Commission Travel Schedule," *washingtonpost.com.* The Washington Post. 2 February 2013. Web. <http://www.washingtonpost.com/blogs/federal-eye/post/senator-to-probe-postal-regulatory-commission-travel-schedule/2012/02/08/gIQALQNbzQ_blog.html>.

[566] O'Keefe, Ed. "Senator to Probe Postal Regulatory Commission Travel Schedule," *washingtonpost.com.* The Washington Post. 2 February 2013. Web. <http://www.washingtonpost.com/blogs/federal-eye/post/senator-to-probe-postal-regulatory-commission-travel-schedule/2012/02/08/gIQALQNbzQ_blog.html>.

[567] O'Keefe, Ed. "Senator to Probe Postal Regulatory Commission Travel Schedule," *washingtonpost.com.* The Washington Post. 2 February 2013. Web. <http://www.washingtonpost.com/blogs/federal-eye/post/senator-to-probe-postal-regulatory-commission-travel-schedule/2012/02/08/gIQALQNbzQ_blog.html>.

[568] 39 U.S.C. $407. Gpo.gov.

[569] Documentation provided to the Committee from the Postal Regulatory Commission, May 7, 2013.

[570] "IMLS Grants to Museums in 2013," The Institute of Museum and Library Services website, accessed October 28, 2013; http://www.imls.gov/news/imls_grants_to_museums_2013.aspx .

[571] Lee, Betti. "A Museum for the Child in All of Us." *Examiner.com.* Denver Museum Examiner. 21 May 2009. Web. <http://www.examiner.com/article/a-museum-for-the-child-all-of-us>.

[572] Denver Museum of Miniatures, Dolls, and Toys. "Exhibits." *Dmmdt.org.* Web. <http://www.dmmdt.org/Exhibits.htm>.

[573] Ziegler, Kristin. "Denver Doll and Toys Museum Rekindles Childhood Magic." *Outfrontonline.com.* Out Front. 23 September 2013. Web. <http://outfrontonline.com/social/high-society/dolls-toy-museum-rekindles-childhood-magic/>.

[574] Denver Museum of Miniatures, Dolls, and Toys. "History." *Dmmdt.org.* Web. <http://www.dmmdt.org/History.htm>.

[575] Institute of Museum and Library Services. News. *IMLS Grants to Museums in 2013. Imlus.gov.* The Institute of Museum and Library Services, 2013. Web. <http://www.imls.gov/news/imls_grants_to_museums_2013.aspx>.

[576] "Inventory Manager at the Denver Museum of Miniatures, Dolls, and Toys," The Colorado-Wyoming Association of Museums website. 10 October 2013. Web. <http://www.cwam-us.org/inventory-manager-at-the-denver-museum-of-miniatures-dolls-and-toys/>.

[577] The Denver Museum of Miniatures, Dolls and Toys Facebook page, accessed October 28, 2013; <https://www.facebook.com/pages/Denver-Museum-of-Miniatures-Dolls-and-Toys/177398786500>.

[578] "Links to Other Museums' Websites," The Denver Museum of Miniatures, Dolls and Toy. Web. ‹http://www.dmmdt.org/museums.htm›.

[579] Hess, Hannah. "Smithsonian Feeling the Budget-Cutting Pain." *Rollcall.com*. CQ Roll Call. 28 October 2013. Web. ‹http://www.rollcall.com/news/smithsonian_feeling_the_budget_cutting_pain-228677-1.html›.

[580] Shaw, Allison and Kathryn Kelly. "Link El Nino, local rainfall, and migration timing in a tropical migratory species," *Global Change Biology*, 19:3283-3290.

[581] NASA Contract Number NNX13AH19G, FY obligations for FY2013. Information accessible from ‹https://prod.nais.nasa.gov›.

[582] Shaw, Allison and Kathryn Kelly. "Link El Nino, local rainfall, and migration timing in a tropical migratory species," Global Change Biology, 19:3283-3290.

[583] National Geographic. "Red Crab." *Animals.nationalgeographic.com*. National Geographic Society. Web. ‹http://animals.nationalgeographic.com/animals/invertebrates/red-crab/›.

[584] Shaw, Allison and Kathryn Kelly. "Link El Nino, local rainfall, and migration timing in a tropical migratory species," *Global Change Biology*, 19:3283-3290.

[585] Unless otherwise noted, all data cited is derived from FERDI 2011 data provided to the Office of Senator Tom Coburn, February 2013. Assuming a more modest two percent annual increase in funds owed in the following years, in 2013 federal employees will fail to pay an estimated $3.66 billion in federal taxes—while simultaneously collecting a federal paycheck.

[586] These figures do not include federal employees with ongoing installment agreements to repay their taxes owed.

[587] Tanzi, Alex. "U.S. Banknotes Monthly Production Figures for Sept.," *Bloomberg.com*, Bloomberg L.P. 22 October 2013. Web. ‹http://www.bloomberg.com/news/2013-10-02/u-s-banknotes-monthly-production-figures-for-sept-table-.html›.

[588] Wolman, David. "A Blunder at the Money Factory." *NewYorker.com*. Condé Nast. 13 August 2013. Web. ‹http://www.newyorker.com/online/blogs/newsdesk/2013/08/blunder-at-the-money-factory.html›.

[589] Wolman, David. "A Blunder at the Money Factory." *NewYorker.com*. Condé Nast. 13 August 2013. Web. ‹http://www.newyorker.com/online/blogs/newsdesk/2013/08/blunder-at-the-money-factory.html›.

[590] U.S.Currency Exchange. Press Release. *Federal Reserve Board Issues Redesigned $100 Note. Newmoney.gov*. Department of the Treasury, 8 Oct. 2013. Web. ‹http://www.newmoney.gov/stakeholder/media/release_10082013.htm›.

[591] Wolman, David. "A Blunder at the Money Factory." *NewYorker.com*. Condé Nast. 13 August 2013. Web. ‹http://www.newyorker.com/online/blogs/newsdesk/2013/08/blunder-at-the-money-factory.html›.

[592] Sportelli, Natalie. "Bureau Gives New Meaning to Blowing Hundred Dollar Bills," *CNBC.com*. CNBC. 13 August 2013. Web. ‹http://www.cnbc.com/id/100960164›.

[593] Wolman, David. "A Blunder at the Money Factory." *NewYorker.com*. Condé Nast. 13 August 2013. Web. ‹http://www.newyorker.com/online/blogs/newsdesk/2013/08/blunder-at-the-money-factory.html›.

[594] Borge, Vanessa. "Mishap At The Money Factory Delays $100 Bill Release," *Miami.cbslocal.com*. CBSMiami/CNN 6 September 2013. ‹http://miami.cbslocal.com/2013/09/06/mishap-at-the-money-factory-delays-100-bill-release/›.

[595] Borge, Vanessa. "Mishap At The Money Factory Delays $100 Bill Release," *Miami.cbslocal.com*. CBSMiami/CNN 6 September 2013. ‹http://miami.cbslocal.com/2013/09/06/mishap-at-the-money-factory-delays-100-bill-release/›. This total, however, does not include the costs to inspect, correct, produce, transport, and secure all the additional money that will replace the botched notes.

[596] Wolman, David. "A Blunder at the Money Factory." *NewYorker.com*. Condé Nast. 13 August 2013. Web. ‹http://www.newyorker.com/online/blogs/newsdesk/2013/08/blunder-at-the-money-factory.html›.

[597] Dillon, Jay. "New $100 Bill Has Ink Well, More Color, 3-D," *okcofx.com*. FOX25 OKOH-TV Oklahoma City. 26 September 2013. Updated 3 October 2013. Web. ‹http://www.okcfox.com/story/23540164/new-100-bill-has-ink-well-more-color-3-d›.

[598] Borge, Vanessa. "Mishap At The Money Factory Delays $100 Bill Release," *Miami.cbslocal.com*. CBSMiami/CNN 6 September 2013. ‹http://miami.cbslocal.com/2013/09/06/mishap-at-the-money-factory-delays-100-bill-release/›.

[599] Dillon, Jay. "New $100 Bill Has Ink Well, More Color, 3-D," *okcofx.com*. FOX25 OKOH-TV Oklahoma City. 26 September 2013. Updated 3 October 2013. Web. ‹http://www.okcfox.com/story/23540164/new-100-bill-has-ink-well-more-color-3-d›.

[600] Yerich, Larry. "Alaskan Brewery Caps Bottles and Costs with USDA Energy Grant." Blogs.usda.gov. 24 Jan. 2013. USDA. 13 Nov. 2013 ‹http://blogs.usda.gov/2013/01/24/alaskan-brewery-caps-bottles-and-costs-with-usda-energy-grant/›.

[601] Ibid.

[602] David Jesse, "Pell Grant Scammers Ripping off Michigan Colleges for Millions," *detroitfreepress.com*. Gannett. 17 February 2013. ‹http://www.freep.com/article/20130217/NEWS06/302170251/Pilfering-Pell-Grants-Scammers-ripping-off-colleges-for-millions?odyssey=tab|topnews|text|FRONTPAGE›.

[603] Kelly Field, "Education Department Chases 'Pell Runners' Who Threaten Aid Program," THE CHRONICLE OF HIGHER EDUCATION, Aug. 28, 2011, http://chronicle.com/article/Education-Department-Chases/128821/.

[604] David Jesse, "Pell Grant Scammers Ripping off Michigan Colleges for Millions," *detroitfreepress.com.* Gannett. 17 February 2013. <http://www.freep.com/article/20130217/NEWS06/302170251/Pilfering-Pell-Grants-Scammers-ripping-off-colleges-for-millions?odyssey=tab|topnews|text|FRONTPAGE>.

[605] *U.S.* Department of Education, *Federal Pell Grant Program,* <http://www2.ed.gov/programs/fpg/index.html>.

[606] Jesse, David. "Pell Grant Scammers Ripping off Michigan Colleges for Millions," *detroitfreepress.com.* Gannett. 17 February 2013. <http://www.freep.com/article/20130217/NEWS06/302170251/Pilfering-Pell-Grants-Scammers-ripping-off-colleges-for-millions?odyssey=tab|topnews|text|FRONTPAGE>.

[607] Jesse, David. "Pell Grant Scammers Ripping off Michigan Colleges for Millions," *detroitfreepress.com.* Gannett. 17 February 2013. <http://www.freep.com/article/20130217/NEWS06/302170251/Pilfering-Pell-Grants-Scammers-ripping-off-colleges-for-millions?odyssey=tab|topnews|text|FRONTPAGE>.

[608] Field, Kelly. "Education Department Chases 'Pell Runners' Who Threaten Aid Program." *chronicle.com.* The Chronicle of Higher Education. 28 August 2011. Web. <http://chronicle.com/article/Education-Department-Chases/128821/>. For example, a semester of tuition at Oakland Community College is $891, so a student would have more than $1,850 left after the school takes tuition out of the Pell Grant. *Id.* It's not surprising, then, that Pell Runners looks for the cheapest community colleges to exploit.

[609] Will, Madeline. "Government and Colleges Crack Down on Pell Grant Fraud." *Dailytarheel.com.* DTH Publishing Corp. University of North Carolina. 8 September 2011. Web. <http://www.dailytarheel.com/index.php/article/2011/09/pell_runners_0906>.

[610] Jesse, David. "Pell Grant Scammers Ripping off Michigan Colleges for Millions," *detroitfreepress.com.* Gannett. 17 February 2013. <http://www.freep.com/article/20130217/NEWS06/302170251/Pilfering-Pell-Grants-Scammers-ripping-off-colleges-for-millions?odyssey=tab|topnews|text|FRONTPAGE>.

[611] Jesse, David. "Pell Grant Scammers Ripping off Michigan Colleges for Millions," *detroitfreepress.com.* Gannett. 17 February 2013. <http://www.freep.com/article/20130217/NEWS06/302170251/Pilfering-Pell-Grants-Scammers-ripping-off-colleges-for-millions?odyssey=tab|topnews|text|FRONTPAGE>.

[612] *See, e.g.,* Jesse, David. "Pell Grant Scammers Ripping off Michigan Colleges for Millions," *detroitfreepress.com.* Gannett. 17 February 2013. <http://www.freep.com/article/20130217/NEWS06/302170251/Pilfering-Pell-Grants-Scammers-ripping-off-colleges-for-millions?odyssey=tab|topnews|text|FRONTPAGE>; Will, Madeline. "Government and Colleges Crack Down on Pell Grant Fraud." *Dailytarheel.com.* DTH Publishing Corp. University of North Carolina. 8 September 2011. Web. <http://www.dailytarheel.com/index.php/article/2011/09/pell_runners_0906>; Ullman, Ellen, and Matthew Dembicki. "Fighting Pell Grant Fraud." *Ccdaily.com.* American Association of Community Colleges. 7 December 2011. Web. <http://www.ccdaily.com/pages/campus-issues/fighting-pell-grant-fraud.aspx>.

[613] Johnson, Brent, "Poverty in N.J. reaches 52-year High, New Report Shows." *Nj.com.* Newark Star-Ledger. New Jersey On-Line LLC. 8 September 2013. Web. <http://www.nj.com/politics/index.ssf/2013/09/poverty_in_nj_reaches_52-year_high_new_report_shows.html>.

[614] Malinconico, Joe, "Paterson Mayor to State: Without Transition Aid, City Will Sink." *Northjersey.com.* Paterson <Press. North Jersey Media Group. 6 November 2013. Web. http://www.northjersey.com/news/Paterson_mayor_to_state_Without_transition_aid_city_will_sink.html?c=y&page=1>.

[615] Malinconico, Joe, "Paterson Mayor to State: Without Transition Aid, City Will Sink." *Northjersey.com.* Paterson <Press. North Jersey Media Group. 6 November 2013. Web. http://www.northjersey.com/news/Paterson_mayor_to_state_Without_transition_aid_city_will_sink.html?c=y&page=1>.

[616] Malinconico, Joe, "Paterson Mayor to State: Without Transition Aid, City Will Sink." *Northjersey.com.* Paterson Press. North Jersey Media Group. 6 November 2013. Web. <http://www.northjersey.com/news/Paterson_mayor_to_state_Without_transition_aid_city_will_sink.html?c=y&page=1>.

[617] Zillow. "82 N 3rd St., Paterson, NJ 07522," *Zillow.com.* Zillow. Web. <http://www.zillow.com/homedetails/82-N-3rd-St-Paterson-NJ-07522/39753115_zpid/>.

[618] Malinconico, Joe, "Paterson Mayor to State: Without Transition Aid, City Will Sink." *Northjersey.com.* Paterson <Press. North Jersey Media Group. 6 November 2013. Web. http://www.northjersey.com/news/Paterson_mayor_to_state_Without_transition_aid_city_will_sink.html?c=y&page=1>.

[619] Steward, Tom. "MN airport a No-Fly Zone for Daily Commercial Service Despite Federal Grant." *Watchdog.org.* Franklin Center for Government & Public Integrity. 31 May 2013. Web. <http://watchdog.org/87811/mn-airport-a-no-fly-zone-for-daily-commercial-service-despite-federal-grant/>.

[620] Steward, Tom. "MN airport a No-Fly Zone for Daily Commercial Service Despite Federal Grant." *Watchdog.org*. Franklin Center for Government & Public Integrity. 31 May 2013. Web. ‹http://watchdog.org/87811/mn-airport-a-no-fly-zone-for-daily-commercial-service-despite-federal-grant/›.

[621] Steward, Tom. "MN airport a No-Fly Zone for Daily Commercial Service Despite Federal Grant." *Watchdog.org*. Franklin Center for Government & Public Integrity. 31 May 2013. Web. ‹http://watchdog.org/87811/mn-airport-a-no-fly-zone-for-daily-commercial-service-despite-federal-grant/›.

[622] Greater St. Cloud Air Service. Greater St. Cloud Development Corporation. Web. ‹http://www.letsgostc.com/›.

[623] Greater St. Cloud Air Service. Greater St. Cloud Development Corporation. Web ‹http://www.letsgostc.com/partners/›.

[624] Steward, Tom. "MN airport a No-Fly Zone for Daily Commercial Service Despite Federal Grant." *Watchdog.org*. Franklin Center for Government & Public Integrity. 31 May 2013. Web. ‹http://watchdog.org/87811/mn-airport-a-no-fly-zone-for-daily-commercial-service-despite-federal-grant/›.

[625] National Science Foundation. "BIR Phase I: Contemporary Studies of the Zombie Apocalypse: An Online Game to Teach Mathematical Thinking to Middle School Students." SF Grant #1315412. National Science Foundation. 29 May 2013. Web. ‹ http://www.nsf.gov/awardsearch/showAward?AWD_ID=1315412&HistoricalAwards=false›.

[626] National Science Foundation. "BIR Phase I: Contemporary Studies of the Zombie Apocalypse: An Online Game to Teach Mathematical Thinking to Middle School Students." SF Grant #1315412. National Science Foundation. 29 May 2013. Web. ‹ http://www.nsf.gov/awardsearch/showAward?AWD_ID=1315412&HistoricalAwards=false›.

[627] National Science Foundation. "BIR Phase I: Contemporary Studies of the Zombie Apocalypse: An Online Game to Teach Mathematical Thinking to Middle School Students." SF Grant #1315412. National Science Foundation. 29 May 2013. Web. ‹ http://www.nsf.gov/awardsearch/showAward?AWD_ID=1315412&HistoricalAwards=false›.

[628] National Science Foundation. "BIR Phase I: Contemporary Studies of the Zombie Apocalypse: An Online Game to Teach Mathematical Thinking to Middle School Students." SF Grant #1315412. National Science Foundation. 29 May 2013. Web. ‹ http://www.nsf.gov/awardsearch/showAward?AWD_ID=1315412&HistoricalAwards=false›.

[629] North Carolina Public Schools. "FY 2013-2014 North Carolina Public Salary Schedules."*ncpublicschools.org*. Web. ‹http://www.ncpublicschools.org/docs/fbs/finance/salary/schedules/2013-14schedules.pdf›. Accessed 6 Dec. 2013.

[630] USASpending.gov. "Prime Award Spending Data: Triad Digital Media." Web. ‹http://usaspending.gov/search?form_fields=%7B%22search_term%22%3A%22triad+digital+media%22%7D›.

[631] Triad Interactive Media. "Math Monster Mystery: A Web-based Suite of Math Games for 3rd to 5th Graders." Web. ‹http://www.triadinteractivemedia.com/m3/›.

[632] Triad Interactive Media, "PlatinuMath: An Online Formative Assessment Math Game for Preservice Elementary Teachers." Web. ‹http://www.triadinteractivemedia.com/platinumath/›.

[633] John Sbardellati, "J. Edgar Hoover Goes to the Movies: The FBI and the Origins of Hollywood's Cold War," Cornell University Press, May 1, 2012.

[634] Goodman, Alana. "FBI Goes Hollywood." *Freebeacon.com*. The Washington Free Beacon. 12 April 2013. Web. ‹http://freebeacon.com/fbi-goes-hollywood›.

[635] FBI Office of Investigative Publicity and Public Affairs. *Working with the FBI: A Guide for Writers, Authors, and Producers*. Federal Bureau of Investigation. October 2008 Web. ‹http://www.fbi.gov/news/stories/2008/october/a-guide-for-writers-authors-and-producers›.

[636] FBI Office of Investigative Publicity and Public Affairs. *Working with the FBI: A Guide for Writers, Authors, and Producers*. Federal Bureau of Investigation. October 2008 Web. ‹http://www.fbi.gov/news/stories/2008/october/a-guide-for-writers-authors-and-producers›.

[637] Bond, Paul. "FBI Seminar a Hit with Hollywood." *Washingtonpost.com*. Reuters. 11 January 2007. Web. ‹http://www.washingtonpost.com/wp-dyn/content/article/2007/01/11/AR2007011100092_pf.html›.

[638] Goodman, Alana. "FBI Goes Hollywood." *Freebeacon.com*. The Washington Free Beacon. 12 April 2013. Web. ‹http://freebeacon.com/fbi-goes-hollywood›.

[639] Box Office Mojo. "Shooter." Web. ‹http://www.boxofficemojo.com/movies/?id=shooter.htm›.

[640] Box Office Mojo. "The Kingdom." Web. ‹http://www.boxofficemojo.com/movies/?id=kingdom.htm›.

[641] Box Office Mojo. "Breach." Web. ‹http://www.boxofficemojo.com/movies/?id=breach.htm›.

[642] Hicks, Josh. "FBI Hinting at 10-day Shutdown if Sequester Continues." *Washingtonpost.com*. The Washington Post. 18 September 2013. Web. ‹http://www.washingtonpost.com/blogs/federal-eye/wp/2013/09/18/fbi-hinting-at-10-day-shutdown-if-sequester-continues/›.

[643] Correspondence from U.S. Attorney General Eric H. Holder, Jr., to Senate Appropriations Committee Chair Senator Barbara Mikulski, page 2, February 1, 2013.

[644] Adams, Scott "Movie Star Who Needs to Shoot a Door Off Its Hinges? Then Scott Nelson is Your Man...," *independent.co.uk.* The Independent. 20 June 2012. Web. ‹http://www.independent.co.uk/news/world/americas/movie-star-who-needs-to-shoot-a-door-off-its-hinges-then-scott-nelson-is-your-man-7866618.html›.

[645] FBI Office of Investigative Publicity and Public Affairs. *Working with the FBI: A Guide for Writers, Authors, and Producers.* Federal Bureau of Investigation. October 2008 Web. ‹http://www.fbi.gov/news/stories/2008/october/a-guide-for-writers-authors-and-producers›.

[646] Wenzl, Roy. "K-State Researcher: Slow-Growing Grasses Affect Cattle." *Kansas.com.* The Wichita Eagle. 24 June 2013. Web. ‹http://www.kansas.com/2013/06/24/2861072/k-state-researcher-slow-growing.html.

[647] Kansas State University. "University Team Receives USDA Grant To Help Develop Solutions For Beef Cattle Grazing Systems." News Release. *K-state.edu.* Kansas State University News and Editorial Services. 13 May 2013. Web. ‹http://www.k-state.edu/media/newsreleases/may13/grazing51313.html›.

[648] Kansas State University. "University Team Receives USDA Grant To Help Develop Solutions For Beef Cattle Grazing Systems." News Release. *K-state.edu.* Kansas State University News and Editorial Services. 13 May 2013. Web. ‹http://www.k-state.edu/media/newsreleases/may13/grazing51313.html›.

[649] Kansas State University. "University Team Receives USDA Grant To Help Develop Solutions For Beef Cattle Grazing Systems." News Release. *K-state.edu.* Kansas State University News and Editorial Services. 13 May 2013. Web. ‹http://www.k-state.edu/media/newsreleases/may13/grazing51313.html›.

[650] Kansas State University. "University Team Receives USDA Grant To Help Develop Solutions For Beef Cattle Grazing Systems." News Release. *K-state.edu.* Kansas State University News and Editorial Services. 13 May 2013. Web. ‹http://www.k-state.edu/media/newsreleases/may13/grazing51313.html›.

[651] U.S. Environmental Protection Agency Office of Inspector General. *Early Warning Report: Main EPA Headquarters Warehouse in Landover, Maryland, Requires Immediate EPA Attention.* Report No. 13-P-0272. EPA OIG. Washington, D.C. 31 May 2013. Print.

[652] U.S. Environmental Protection Agency Office of Inspector General. *Early Warning Report: Main EPA Headquarters Warehouse in Landover, Maryland, Requires Immediate EPA Attention.* Report No. 13-P-0272. EPA OIG. Washington, D.C. 31 May 2013. Print.

[653] U.S. Environmental Protection Agency Office of Inspector General "Observations at EPA Warehouse, Landover, MD," *EPA OIG.* Presentation. 16 May 2013. Web. ‹http://www.epa.gov/oig/reports/2013/20130531-13-P-0272_briefing.pdf›.

[654] Walsh, Michael, "Major EPA warehouse a huge 'man cave' at taxpayers' expense: report," *nydailynews.com.* New York Daily News. 7 June 2013. Web. ‹http://www.nydailynews.com/news/national/major-epa-warehouse-huge-man-cave-taxpayers-expense-report-article-1.1366042#ixzz2ghUbfLiZ›.

[655] Bernstein, Lenny, "Workers Turned EPA Warehouse In Landover Into Personal Rec Rooms, Audit Finds." *WashingtonPost.com.* The Washington Post. 5 June 2013. Web. ‹http://articles.washingtonpost.com/2013-06-05/national/39760554_1_warehouse-passports-report›.

[656] U.S. Environmental Protection Agency Office of Inspector General. *Early Warning Report: Main EPA Headquarters Warehouse in Landover, Maryland, Requires Immediate EPA Attention.* Report No. 13-P-0272. EPA OIG. Washington, D.C. 31 May 2013. Print.

[657] U.S. Environmental Protection Agency Office of Inspector General. *Early Warning Report: Main EPA Headquarters Warehouse in Landover, Maryland, Requires Immediate EPA Attention.* Report No. 13-P-0272. EPA OIG. Washington, D.C. 31 May 2013. Print.

[658] Katz, Eric. "Secret Man Caves Found in EPA Warehouse." *Govexec.com.* Government Executive. 4 June 2013. Web. ‹http://www.govexec.com/contracting/2013/06/secret-man-caves-found-epa-warehouse/64202/?oref=govexec_today_nl›.

[659] DoD Readiness and Environmental Protection Integration Program. "2013 REPI Challenge Fact Sheet." *Repi.mil.* Department of Defense. June 2013. Web. ‹http://www.repi.mil/Portals/44/Documents/REPI_Challenge/REPIChallenge2013.pdf›.

[660] DoD Readiness and Environmental Protection Integration Program. "2013 REPI Challenge Fact Sheet." *Repi.mil.* Department of Defense. June 2013. Web. ‹http://www.repi.mil/Portals/44/Documents/REPI_Challenge/REPIChallenge2013.pdf›.

[661] Springer, Dan, "Military Spending Millions To Protect Gophers, While Workers Go On Furlough." *FoxNews.com.* Fox News Network, LLC. 14 July 2013. Web. ‹http://www.foxnews.com/politics/2013/07/14/military-spending-millions-to-protect-gophers-while-workers-go-on-furlough/›.

[662] State of Florida. Media Center. *Governor, Florida Cabinet, Approve 21,000 Acre Purchase to Buffer Eglin Air Force Base. Flgov.com.* State of Florida, 20 Aug. 2013. Web. ‹http://www.flgov.com/2013/08/20/governor-florida-cabinet-approve-21000-acre-purchase-to-buffer-eglin-air-force-base/›.

[663] State of Florida. Media Center. *Governor, Florida Cabinet, Approve 21,000 Acre Purchase to Buffer Eglin Air Force Base. Flgov.com.* State of Florida, 20 Aug. 2013. Web. ‹http://www.flgov.com/2013/08/20/governor-florida-cabinet-approve-21000-acre-purchase-to-buffer-eglin-air-force-base/›.

[664] Grant Search: Centralia Cultural Society," Art Works: The National Endowment for the Arts," http://apps.nea.gov/GrantSearch/SearchResults.aspx, accessed November 13, 2013.

[665] Mainstage. "About the Story: Mooseltoe." *Artistsofmainstage.com*. Web. ‹http://www.artistsofmainstage.com/shows/Mooseltoe/mooseltoewebsite/Abouttheproduction.html›.

[666] Mainstage. "About the Story: Mooseltoe." *Artistsofmainstage.com*. Web. ‹http://www.artistsofmainstage.com/shows/Mooseltoe/mooseltoewebsite/Abouttheproduction.html›.

[667] Alan, Marc. Butler University Newsroom. *Butler Receives $2.9 Million Grant to Create a New Kind of Science Museum. News.butler.edu.* Butler University, 23 Sept. 2013. Web. ‹https://news.butler.edu/blog/2013/09/butler-receives-2-9-million-grant-to-create-a-new-kind-of-science-museum/›.

[668] Alan, Marc. Butler University Newsroom. *Butler Receives $2.9 Million Grant to Create a New Kind of Science Museum. News.butler.edu.* Butler University, 23 Sept. 2013. Web. ‹https://news.butler.edu/blog/2013/09/butler-receives-2-9-million-grant-to-create-a-new-kind-of-science-museum/›.

[669] Alan, Marc. Butler University Newsroom. *Butler Receives $2.9 Million Grant to Create a New Kind of Science Museum. News.butler.edu.* Butler University, 23 Sept. 2013. Web. ‹https://news.butler.edu/blog/2013/09/butler-receives-2-9-million-grant-to-create-a-new-kind-of-science-museum/›..

[670] IU Bloomington. Newsroom. *Center for Urban Health to lead Research on Grant to Create Science Museum Tied to Waterways. News.indiana.edu.* Indiana University Bloomington, 27 September 2013. 2013. ‹http://news.indiana.edu/releases/center-for-urban-health.shtml›.

[671] IU Bloomington. Newsroom. *Center for Urban Health to lead Research on Grant to Create Science Museum Tied to Waterways. News.indiana.edu.* Indiana University Bloomington, 27 September 2013. 2013. ‹http://news.indiana.edu/releases/center-for-urban-health.shtml›.

[672] Webster, Richard A., "Program to Move Homes from LSU-VA Hospital Site, Rehab Them, Remains in Disarray." NOLA.com. NOLA Media Group. 24 November 2012. Web. ‹http://www.nola.com/politics/index.ssf/2012/11/program_to_move_homes_from_lsu.html›.

[673] Webster, Richard A., "Program to Move Homes from LSU-VA Hospital Site, Rehab Them, Remains in Disarray." NOLA.com. NOLA Media Group. 24 November 2012. Web. ‹http://www.nola.com/politics/index.ssf/2012/11/program_to_move_homes_from_lsu.html›.

[674] Webster, Richard A., "Program to Move Homes from LSU-VA Hospital Site, Rehab Them, Remains in Disarray." NOLA.com. NOLA Media Group. 24 November 2012. Web. ‹http://www.nola.com/politics/index.ssf/2012/11/program_to_move_homes_from_lsu.html›.

[675] Webster, Richard A., "Program to Move Homes from LSU-VA Hospital Site, Rehab Them, Remains in Disarray." NOLA.com. NOLA Media Group. 24 November 2012. Web. ‹http://www.nola.com/politics/index.ssf/2012/11/program_to_move_homes_from_lsu.html›.

[676] Gadbois, Karen, "Slow-mo House-Moving Saga: a Status Report on a What Seemed a Dandy Idea," *thelensnola.org*. The Lens. 4 April 2013. Web. ‹http://thelensnola.org/2013/04/04/slow-mo-house-moving-saga-a-status-report-on-a-what-seemed-a-dandy-idea/›.

[677] Webster, Richard A., "Program to Move Homes from LSU-VA Hospital Site, Rehab Them, Remains in Disarray." NOLA.com. NOLA Media Group. 24 November 2012. Web. ‹http://www.nola.com/politics/index.ssf/2012/11/program_to_move_homes_from_lsu.html›.

[678] Webster, Richard A., "Program to Move Homes from LSU-VA Hospital Site, Rehab Them, Remains in Disarray." NOLA.com. NOLA Media Group. 24 November 2012. Web. ‹http://www.nola.com/politics/index.ssf/2012/11/program_to_move_homes_from_lsu.html›.

[679] Gadbois, Karen, "Slow-mo House-Moving Saga: a Status Report on a What Seemed a Dandy Idea," *thelensnola.org*. The Lens. 4 April 2013. Web. ‹http://thelensnola.org/2013/04/04/slow-mo-house-moving-saga-a-status-report-on-a-what-seemed-a-dandy-idea/›.

[680] Gadbois, Karen, "Slow-mo House-Moving Saga: a Status Report on a What Seemed a Dandy Idea," *thelensnola.org*. The Lens. 4 April 2013. Web. ‹http://thelensnola.org/2013/04/04/slow-mo-house-moving-saga-a-status-report-on-a-what-seemed-a-dandy-idea/›.

[681] Gadbois, Karen, "Slow-mo House-Moving Saga: a Status Report on a What Seemed a Dandy Idea," *thelensnola.org*. The Lens. 4 April 2013. Web. ‹http://thelensnola.org/2013/04/04/slow-mo-house-moving-saga-a-status-report-on-a-what-seemed-a-dandy-idea/›.

[682] Gadbois, Karen, "Slow-mo House-Moving Saga: a Status Report on a What Seemed a Dandy Idea," *thelensnola.org*. The Lens. 4 April 2013. Web. ‹http://thelensnola.org/2013/04/04/slow-mo-house-moving-saga-a-status-report-on-a-what-seemed-a-dandy-idea/›.

[683] Webster, Richard A., "Program to Move Homes from LSU-VA Hospital Site, Rehab Them, Remains in Disarray." *NOLA.com*. NOLA Media Group. 24 November 2012. Web. ‹http://www.nola.com/politics/index.ssf/2012/11/program_to_move_homes_from_lsu.html›.

[684] Webster, Richard A., "Program to Move Homes from LSU-VA Hospital Site, Rehab Them, Remains in Disarray." *NOLA.com*. NOLA Media Group. 24 November 2012. Web. ‹http://www.nola.com/politics/index.ssf/2012/11/program_to_move_homes_from_lsu.html›.

[685] Gadbois, Karen, "Slow-mo House-Moving Saga: a Status Report on a What Seemed a Dandy Idea," *thelensnola.org*. The Lens. 4 April 2013. Web. ‹http://thelensnola.org/2013/04/04/slow-mo-house-moving-saga-a-status-report-on-a-what-seemed-a-dandy-idea/›.

[686] Gadbois, Karen, "Slow-mo House-Moving Saga: a Status Report on a What Seemed a Dandy Idea," *thelensnola.org*. The Lens. 4 April 2013. Web. ‹http://thelensnola.org/2013/04/04/slow-mo-house-moving-saga-a-status-report-on-a-what-seemed-a-dandy-idea/›.

[687] Webster, Richard A., "Program to Move Homes from LSU-VA Hospital Site, Rehab Them, Remains in Disarray." NOLA.com. NOLA Media Group. 24 November 2012. Web. ‹http://www.nola.com/politics/index.ssf/2012/11/program_to_move_homes_from_lsu.html›.

[688] Brown, Shelley, " FOX8 Investigates: New Developments in Historic House-moving Project." *Fox8Live.com*. WorldNow and WVUE. 28 June 2012. Web. ‹http://www.fox8live.com/story/18908861/fox-8-investigates-new-developments-in-historic-house-moving-project?clienttype=printable›.

[689] Webster, Richard A., "Program to Move Homes from LSU-VA Hospital Site, Rehab Them, Remains in Disarray." NOLA.com. NOLA Media Group. 24 November 2012. Web. ‹http://www.nola.com/politics/index.ssf/2012/11/program_to_move_homes_from_lsu.html›.

[690] USDA Rural Development. Office of Legislative and Public Affairs. *Value-Added Producer Grants Support Local Producers, Biobased Initiatives. Rurdev.usda.gov.* USDA, 1 May 2013. Web. ‹http://www.rurdev.usda.gov/STELPRD4020424_print.html›..

[691] USDA Rural Development. Office of Legislative and Public Affairs. *Value-Added Producer Grants Support Local Producers, Biobased Initiatives. Rurdev.usda.gov.* USDA, 1 May 2013. Web. ‹http://www.rurdev.usda.gov/STELPRD4020424_print.html›.

[692] Associated Press. "Changing Demographics Influencing Taste Buds; Salsa Beats Ketchup!" *myfoxdc.com*. WTTG Fox 5. 18 October 2013. Web. ‹http://www.myfoxdc.com/story/23718477/changing-demographics-influencing-taste-buds#axzz2i0786QWR›.

[693] USDA Rural Development. Office of Legislative and Public Affairs. *Value-Added Producer Grants Support Local Producers, Biobased Initiatives. Rurdev.usda.gov.* USDA, 1 May 2013. Web. ‹http://www.rurdev.usda.gov/STELPRD4020424_print.html›.

[694] USDA Rural Development. Office of Legislative and Public Affairs. *Value-Added Producer Grants Support Local Producers, Biobased Initiatives. Rurdev.usda.gov.* USDA, 1 May 2013. Web. ‹http://www.rurdev.usda.gov/STELPRD4020424_print.html›.

[695] National Register of Historic Places Inventory. "Nomination Form for Federal Properties: Perry Point Mansion and House and Mill." *Msa.maryland.gov*. DOI NPS. Web. ‹http://msa.maryland.gov/megafile/msa/stagsere/se1/se5/006000/006400/006485/pdf/msa_se5_6485.pdf›.

[696] Fritze, John. "Aged Grist Mill Awaits Scarce Federal Funds." *Baltimoresun.com*. The Baltimore Sun. 8 February 2013. Web. ‹http://articles.baltimoresun.com/2013-02-08/news/bs-md-fed-historic-buildings-20130208_1_grist-mill-federal-agencies-office-buildings›.

[697] BES Design/Build. "Grist Mill & Mansion." *Bes-design-build.com*. BES Design/Build. Web. ‹http://bes-design-build.com/?page_id=80›.

[698] FedBizOpps. "Perry Point MD project # 512A5-10-335, Mansion and Grist Mill Construction and Rehabilitation." Solicitation No. VA24513B0113. Awarded 20 June 2013. Web. ‹https://www.fbo.gov/index?s=opportunity&mode=form&tab=core&id=0f3bf4d167b3e4b3ad0540771e2af61a&_cview=0›.

[699] FedBizOpps. "Perry Point MD project # 512A5-10-335, Mansion and Grist Mill Construction and Rehabilitation." Solicitation No. VA24513B0113. Awarded 20 June 2013. Web. ‹https://www.fbo.gov/index?s=opportunity&mode=form&tab=core&id=0f3bf4d167b3e4b3ad0540771e2af61a&_cview=0›.

[700] Sullivan, Michael J. *Federal Real Property, Improved Data Needed to Strategically Manage Historic Buildings, Address Multiple Challenges*. Rep. no. GAO-13-35. GAO, 11 Dec. 2012. Web. ‹http://www.gao.gov/products/GAO-13-35›.

[701] Fritze, John. "Aged Grist Mill Awaits Scarce Federal Funds." *Baltimoresun.com*. The Baltimore Sun. 8 February 2013. Web. ‹http://articles.baltimoresun.com/2013-02-08/news/bs-md-fed-historic-buildings-20130208_1_grist-mill-federal-agencies-office-buildings›.

[702] National Science Foundation. "Update to Important Notice No. 133." IN-133A. Arlington, VA, 17 July 2013. Web. ‹http://www.nsf.gov/pubs/2013/in133a/in133a.jsp?org=NSF›.

[703] National Science Foundation. "Update to Important Notice No. 133." IN-133A. Arlington, VA, 17 July 2013. Web. ‹http://www.nsf.gov/pubs/2013/in133a/in133a.jsp?org=NSF›.

[704] Kikim Media, LLC. "Full-Scale Development: In Defense of Food." Award Abstract #1224172. National Science Foundation. 7 September 2012. Web. ‹http://www.nsf.gov/awardsearch/showAward?AWD_ID=1224172&HistoricalAwards=false›.

[705] Pollan, Michael. "About Michael Pollan." *Michaelpollan.com*, Web. ‹http://michaelpollan.com/press-kit/›. Accessed 25 October 2013.

[706] "Kikim Media, LLC "Kikim Media Begins Production of In Defense of Food." Kikim Media Projects – News Release, 23 July 2013. ‹http://www.kikim.com/xml/projects.php?projectId=88›.

[707] Grummer, Ric. "'InDefense of Food' is short on science." *Host.madison.com*. Wisconsin State Journal, 23 September 2009. Web. ‹http://host.madison.com/news/opinion/mailbag/in-defense-of-food-is-short-on-science/article_87f51ea8-a892-11de-936b-001cc4c002e0.html›.

[708] Kikim Media, LLC. "Full-Scale Development: In Defense of Food." Award Abstract #1224172. National Science Foundation. 7 September 2012. Web.

[709] Kikim Media, LLC. "Full-Scale Development: In Defense of Food." Award Abstract #1224172. National Science Foundation. 7 September 2012. Web.

[710] See website: http://www.fldoe.org/

[711] Fineout, Gary. "Florida Using Federal Grant Money to Settle Lawsuit." *Tbo.com*. Tampa Media Group, LLC. 24 May 2013. Web. ‹http://tbo.com/ap/technology/fla-using-federal-grant-money-to-settle-lawsuit-ap_technology33df7ec12cbe45729a908da846ade35c›.

[712] Fineout, Gary. "Florida Using Federal Grant Money to Settle Lawsuit." *Tbo.com*. Tampa Media Group, LLC. 24 May 2013. Web. ‹http://tbo.com/ap/technology/fla-using-federal-grant-money-to-settle-lawsuit-ap_technology33df7ec12cbe45729a908da846ade35c›.

[713] Tomassini, Jason, and Nikhita Venugopal. "Common-Core Deal in Florida Sparks Legal Feud." *Edweek.org*. Editorial Projects in Education. 13 November 2012. Web. ‹http://www.edweek.org/ew/articles/2012/11/14/12infinity.h32.html?tkn=XZNFE9KgXmiSwpfZ7JtDs3m0sQyZeL%2BN2mql›.

[714] Fineout, Gary. "Florida Using Federal Grant Money to Settle Lawsuit." *Tbo.com*. Tampa Media Group, LLC. 24 May 2013. Web. ‹http://tbo.com/ap/technology/fla-using-federal-grant-money-to-settle-lawsuit-ap_technology33df7ec12cbe45729a908da846ade35c›..

[715] Tomassini, Jason, and Nikhita Venugopal. "Common-Core Deal in Florida Sparks Legal Feud." *Edweek.org*. Editorial Projects in Education. 13 November 2012. Web. ‹http://www.edweek.org/ew/articles/2012/11/14/12infinity.h32.html?tkn=XZNFE9KgXmiSwpfZ7JtDs3m0sQyZeL%2BN2mql›.

[716] Tomassini, Jason, and Nikhita Venugopal. "Common-Core Deal in Florida Sparks Legal Feud." *Edweek.org*. Editorial Projects in Education. 13 November 2012. Web. ‹http://www.edweek.org/ew/articles/2012/11/14/12infinity.h32.html?tkn=XZNFE9KgXmiSwpfZ7JtDs3m0sQyZeL%2BN2mql›.

[717] "Fineout, Gary. "Florida Using Federal Grant Money to Settle Lawsuit." *Tbo.com*. Tampa Media Group, LLC. 24 May 2013. Web. ‹http://tbo.com/ap/technology/fla-using-federal-grant-money-to-settle-lawsuit-ap_technology33df7ec12cbe45729a908da846ade35c›.

[718] Fineout, Gary. "Florida Using Federal Grant Money to Settle Lawsuit." *Tbo.com*. Tampa Media Group, LLC. 24 May 2013. Web. ‹http://tbo.com/ap/technology/fla-using-federal-grant-money-to-settle-lawsuit-ap_technology33df7ec12cbe45729a908da846ade35c›.

[719] Kahn Academy Website. "about." *Khanacaedmy.org*. Kahn Academy. 2013. Web. ‹https://www.khanacademy.org/about›.

[720] Data on portraits obtained from USASpending.gov.

[721] Data on portraits obtained from USASpending.gov.

[722] Office of Management and Budget. USA Spending.gov Contract # DEMA0006433, "Painting for the Department of Energy." *Usaspending.gov*. 23 Sept. 2013. Web. ‹http://usaspending.gov/explore?fiscal_year=all&comingfrom=searchresults&piid=DEMA0006433&typeofview=complete›.

[723] Office of Management and Budget. USA Spending.gov. Contract # NNH13PY08P, "Painting of Deputy Administrator Portrait." *Usaspending.gov*. 25 Oct. 2013. Web. ‹http://usaspending.gov/explore?fiscal_year=all&comingfrom=searchresults&piid=NNH13PY08P&typeofview=complete›.

[724] Department of Homeland Security. DHS Press Office. *DHS Unveils Official Portrait of Former Secretary Tom Ridge. Dhs.gov.* DHS, 23 May 2013. Web. <http://www.dhs.gov/news/2013/05/23/dhs-unveils-official-portrait-former-secretary-tom-ridge>.

[725] Staff interview with contracted firm, Oct. 18, 2013.

[726] Office of Management and Budget. USASpending.gov. Contract # DU100A12P0011, "The Objective Is To Obtain A High Quality Portrait Of The 14th Secretary Of The U.S. Department of Housing and Urban Development (HUD)." *Usaspending.gov.* 3 June 2013. Web. <http://usaspending.gov/explore?fiscal_year=all&comingfrom=searchresults&piid=DU100A12P0011&typeofview=complete>.

[727] Data on portraits obtained from USASpending.gov.

[728] Office of Management and Budget. USASpending.gov. Contract #HUDCCOPC23165, "Contract Shall Provide 5 3/4 Length Standing Oil Portraits About 30 X 40 on CANVAS. They Would Need to Be Framed in Gold Approximately 4 1/2 to 5' Wide Frame Similar to the Frames Used by the Past Portraits and Ready for HANGING." 30 September 2007. Web. <http://usaspending.gov/explore?fiscal_year=all&comingfrom=searchresults&piid=HUDCCOPC23165&modification=0&typeofview=complete>.

[729] FedBizOpps. "Portrait of Department Secretary." Solicitation No. SA1301-8-RQ-0036, awarded 30 September 2008. Web. <https://www.fbo.gov/index?s=opportunity&mode=form&tab=core&id=b62abd5fef6c04ed5cd42c8fa07f83dc>.

[730] Data on portraits obtained from USASpending.gov.

[731] Data on portraits obtained from USASpending.gov.

[732] McElhatton, Jim. "Picture this: Cabinet portraits for big bucks," *washingtontimes.com.* The Washington Times, LLC. 11 November 2012. Web.<http://www.washingtontimes.com/news/2012/nov/11/picture-this-cabinet-portraits-for-big-bucks/?page=all>.

733 McElhatton, Jim. "Picture this: Cabinet portraits for big bucks," *washingtontimes.com.* The Washington Times, LLC. 11 November 2012. Web.<http://www.washingtontimes.com/news/2012/nov/11/picture-this-cabinet-portraits-for-big-bucks/?page=all>.

[734] NCA. "The History of Coffee." Www.ncausa.org. National Coffee Association. 13 Nov. 2013 Web.<http://www.ncausa.org/i4a/pages/index.cfm?pageid=68>.

[735] Bishop, Hunter. "Kona Coffee Farm Gets Study Grant." *Bigislandnow.com.* Big Island Now. 16 Aug. 2013. Web. <http://bigislandnow.com/2013/08/16/kona-coffee-farm-gets-study-grant/>.

[736] Bishop, Hunter. "Kona Coffee Farm Gets Study Grant." *Bigislandnow.com.* Big Island Now. 16 Aug. 2013. Web. <http://bigislandnow.com/2013/08/16/kona-coffee-farm-gets-study-grant/>.

[737] Laing, Keith. "LaHood: America is One Big Pothole." *TheHill.com.* Capitol Hill Publishing Corp. 6 February 2013. Web. <http://thehill.com/blogs/transportation-report/infrastructure/281461-lahood-america-is-one-big-pothole-right-now>.

[738] Laing, Keith. "LaHood: America is One Big Pothole." *TheHill.com.* Capitol Hill Publishing Corp. 6 February 2013. Web. <http://thehill.com/blogs/transportation-report/infrastructure/281461-lahood-america-is-one-big-pothole-right-now>.

[739] Laing, Keith. "LaHood: America is One Big Pothole." *TheHill.com.* Capitol Hill Publishing Corp. 6 February 2013. Web. <http://thehill.com/blogs/transportation-report/infrastructure/281461-lahood-america-is-one-big-pothole-right-now>.

[740] Hrenchir, Tim. "Federal Grant to Aid Downtown Rossville Makeover." *Cjonline.com.* The Topeka Capital-Journal. 16 June 2013. Web. <http://cjonline.com/news/2013-06-16/federal-grant-aid-downtown-rossville-makeover>.

[741] "Rossville, Kansas." Map. *Google Maps.* 2013.

[742] Hrenchir, Tim. "Federal Grant to Aid Downtown Rossville Makeover." *Cjonline.com.* The Topeka Capital-Journal. 16 June 2013. Web. <http://cjonline.com/news/2013-06-16/federal-grant-aid-downtown-rossville-makeover>.

[743] Hrenchir, Tim. "Federal Grant to Aid Downtown Rossville Makeover." *Cjonline.com.* The Topeka Capital-Journal. 16 June 2013. Web. <http://cjonline.com/news/2013-06-16/federal-grant-aid-downtown-rossville-makeover>.

[744] City of Rossville. "Business Directory." *Rossvillekansas.us.* The City of Rossville, Kansas. Web. <http://www.rossvillekansas.us/business/business-directory>.

[745] Goldberg, Emma. "Media attacks duck genitalia research." *Yaledailynews.com.* Yale Daily News. 2 April 2013. Web. <http://yaledailynews.com/blog/2013/04/02/media-attacks-duck-genitalia-research/>.

[746] H.R. 1, 111th Cong. (enacted).

[747] National Science Foundation. "Conflict, Social Behavior, and Evolution." Award Abstract #0920344. National Science Foundation. 1 December 2010. Web. <http://nsf.gov/awardsearch/showAward?AWD_ID=0920344>.

[748] National Science Foundation. "Conflict, Social Behavior, and Evolution." Award Abstract #0920344. National Science Foundation. 1 December 2010. Web. <http://nsf.gov/awardsearch/showAward?AWD_ID=0920344>.

[749] PolitiFact. "Is the Federal Government Funding a Study on Duck Penises?" *politifact.com.* Tampa Bay Times. 24 March 2013. Web. <http://www.politifact.com/truth-o-meter/statements/2013/mar/22/tweets/federal-government-funding-study-duck-penises/>.

[750] Scheiner, Eric. "$384,949 Federal Study Looks at 'Plasticity in Duck Penis Length.'" *Cnsnews.com*. Cybercast News Service. 19 March 2013. Web ‹http://cnsnews.com/news/article/384949-federal-study-looks-plasticity-duck-penis-length›.

[751] Associated Press. "Thomson Prison Poised to Open, Officials Say." *Journalstandard.com*. Gatehouse Media. 6 September 2013. Web. ‹http://www.journalstandard.com/x914319774/Thomson-prison-poised-to-open-officials-say›.

[752] House Appropriations Committee. Newsroom. *Appropriations Chairman Blasts Obama Administration's Decision to Open Thomson Prison without Approval from Congress. Appropriations.house.gov*. Congressman Hal Rogers, 2 Oct. 2012. Web. ‹http://appropriations.house.gov/news/documentsingle.aspx?DocumentID=310365›.

[753] Office of Congressman Frank Wolf. Press Office. *Wolf: Obama Administration Violates Long-Standing Precedent in Circumventing Congress to Fund Thomson Prison. Wolf.house.gov*. Congressman Frank Wolf, 2 October 2012,

[754] Tareen, Sophia. *"Thomson Prison in Illinois to be Purchased by Federal Government for $165 Million."* huffingtonpost.com. The Huffington Post. 2 October 2012. Web. ‹http://www.huffingtonpost.com/2012/10/02/thomson-prison-illinois_n_1933471.html›.

[755] Tareen, Sophia. *"Thomson Prison in Illinois to be Purchased by Federal Government for $165 Million."* huffingtonpost.com. The Huffington Post. 2 October 2012. Web. ‹http://www.huffingtonpost.com/2012/10/02/thomson-prison-illinois_n_1933471.html›.

[756] Maurer, David C., *Justice Assets Forfeiture Fund: Transparency of Balances and Controls Over Equitable Sharing Should Be Improved*. Rep. no. GAO-12-736. Governmental Accountability Office, 12 July 2012. Web. ‹http://www.gao.gov/products/GAO-12-736›.

[757] Website of the City of Thomson, Illinois. "Thomson Prison." *Thomsonillinois.com*. Web. ‹http://www.thomsonillinois.com/thomson-prison/›.

[758] Associated Press. "Thomson Prison Poised to Open, Officials Say." *Journalstandard.com*. Gatehouse Media. 6 September 2013. Web. ‹http://www.journalstandard.com/x914319774/Thomson-prison-poised-to-open-officials-say›.

[759] Associated Press. "Thomson Prison Would Be Activated by Proposed Budget." *Abclocal.go.com*. ABC Inc., WLS-TV/DT Chicago, IL. 10 April 2013. Web. ‹http://abclocal.go.com/wls/story?id=9060204›.

[760] Department of Justice. "Federal Prison System Federal Bureau of Prisons: FY 2014 Budget Request." *Justice.gov*. Web. ‹http://www.justice.gov/jmd/2014summary/pdf/bop.pdf›. (5).

[761] Department of Justice. "Federal Prison System Federal Bureau of Prisons: FY 2014 Budget Request." *Justice.gov*. Web. ‹http://www.justice.gov/jmd/2014summary/pdf/bop.pdf›. (3).

[762] Office of Senator Dick Durbin. Press Office. *Durbin, Bustos: Senate Committee Calls for Activation of Thomson Prison. Durbin.house.gov*. Senator Dick Durbin. 18 July 2013. Web. ‹http://www.durbin.senate.gov/public/index.cfm/pressreleases?ID=f72c3693-2783-409e-92a5-8e11ed0a54ca›.

[763] The White House. *Digital Government Strategy: Building a 21st Century Platform to Better Serve the American People*. Washington, D.C.: 23 May 2012. Web. ‹http://www.whitehouse.gov/sites/default/files/omb/egov/digital-government/digital-government-strategy.pdf›.

[764] CIO Council. "Creating a Foundation for Mobile Security." Web log post. *Cio.gov*. Chief Information Officers Council, 23 Mar. 2013. Web. ‹https://cio.gov/creating-a-foundation-for-mobile-security/›.

[765] Corbin, Kenneth. "Mobile Connectivity Could Net Feds Productivity Gains." *CIO.com*. CXO Media Inc. 20 August 2013Web. ‹http://www.cio.com/article/738500/Mobile_Connectivity_Could_Net_Feds_Productivity_Gains›.

[766] Corbin, Kenneth. "Mobile Connectivity Could Net Feds Productivity Gains." *CIO.com*. CXO Media Inc. 20 August 2013Web. ‹http://www.cio.com/article/738500/Mobile_Connectivity_Could_Net_Feds_Productivity_Gains›.

[767] Corbin, Kenneth. "Mobile Connectivity Could Net Feds Productivity Gains." *CIO.com*. CXO Media Inc. 20 August 2013Web. ‹http://www.cio.com/article/738500/Mobile_Connectivity_Could_Net_Feds_Productivity_Gains›.

[768] Corbin, Kenneth. "Mobile Connectivity Could Net Feds Productivity Gains." *CIO.com*. CXO Media Inc. 20 August 2013Web. ‹http://www.cio.com/article/738500/Mobile_Connectivity_Could_Net_Feds_Productivity_Gains›.

[769] Corbin, Kenneth. "Mobile Connectivity Could Net Feds Productivity Gains." *CIO.com*. CXO Media Inc. 20 August 2013Web. ‹http://www.cio.com/article/738500/Mobile_Connectivity_Could_Net_Feds_Productivity_Gains›.

[770] Sternstein, Aliya. "The Untested Mobile Security System Defense Just Bought Isn't Functioning at USDA." *Nextgov.com*. National Journal Group. 1 August 2013. ‹http://www.nextgov.com/mobile/2013/08/untested-mobile-security-system-defense-just-bought-isnt-functioning-usda/67868/?oref=ng-channelriver›.

[771] Potential Sources of Mobile Management Solutions," U.S. General Services Administration, May 23, 2013,http://www.gsa.gov/portal/content/171143, accessed November 1, 2013.

[772] Sternstein, Aliya. "The Untested Mobile Security System Defense Just Bought Isn't Functioning at USDA." *Nextgov.com.* National Journal Group. 1 August 2013. ‹http://www.nextgov.com/mobile/2013/08/untested-mobile-security-system-defense-just-bought-isnt-functioning-usda/67868/?oref=ng-channelriver›.

[773] Sternstein, Aliya. "The Untested Mobile Security System Defense Just Bought Isn't Functioning at USDA." *Nextgov.com.* National Journal Group. 1 August 2013. ‹http://www.nextgov.com/mobile/2013/08/untested-mobile-security-system-defense-just-bought-isnt-functioning-usda/67868/?oref=ng-channelriver›.

[774] Sternstein, Aliya. "The Untested Mobile Security System Defense Just Bought Isn't Functioning at USDA." *Nextgov.com.* National Journal Group. 1 August 2013. ‹http://www.nextgov.com/mobile/2013/08/untested-mobile-security-system-defense-just-bought-isnt-functioning-usda/67868/?oref=ng-channelriver›.

[775] Sternstein, Aliya. "The Untested Mobile Security System Defense Just Bought Isn't Functioning at USDA." *Nextgov.com.* National Journal Group. 1 August 2013. ‹http://www.nextgov.com/mobile/2013/08/untested-mobile-security-system-defense-just-bought-isnt-functioning-usda/67868/?oref=ng-channelriver›.

[776] USDA. "Request for Proposal & Performance Work Statement." International Technology Services Next Generation Mobility." *Udga.gov.* USDA." September 2012. ‹http://www.usda.gov/wps/portal/usda/usdahome?navid=DIGITALSTRATEGY›.

[777] Sternstein, Aliya. "The Untested Mobile Security System Defense Just Bought Isn't Functioning at USDA." *Nextgov.com.* National Journal Group. 1 August 2013. ‹http://www.nextgov.com/mobile/2013/08/untested-mobile-security-system-defense-just-bought-isnt-functioning-usda/67868/?oref=ng-channelriver›.

[778] Usaspending.gov. "Prime Award Spending Data: Digital Management Inc." Web. ‹http://www.usaspending.gov/explore?frompage=contracts&tab=By%20Prime%20Awardee&contractorid=113512359&contractorname=DIGITAL%20MANAGEMENT%2C%20INC.&frompage=contracts&comingfrom=searchresults&fiscal_year=all›.

[779] Koetsier, John. "How a tiny Canadian Company Won Security Contracts with Covert 3-letter Agencies Like the NSA, CIA, and FBI," *Venturebeat.com.* VentureBeat. 1 May 2013. Web. ‹http://venturebeat.com/2013/05/01/how-a-tiny-canadian-company-won-security-contracts-with-covert-3-letter-agencies-like-the-nsa-cia-and-fbi/#fq7fPrq8vX7DZmlf.99›.

[780] SIGAR. *Quarterly Report to the United States Congress.* Special Inspector General for Afghanistan Reconstruction. Arlington, VA: 30 October 2013. Web. ‹http://www.sigar.mil/pdf/quarterlyreports/2013-10-30qr.pdf›. Unlike a contract where the principal purpose of the instrument is to acquire property or services for the direct benefit or use of USAID or another U.S. government entity, a cooperative agreement may be used when the principal purpose of the relationship is to transfer money, property, services, or anything of value to the recipient in order to carry out a public purpose of support authorized by federal statute.

[781] Sayed Bilal Sadath Construction Company was established in 2000 and registered with the Ministry of Economics of the Islamic Republic of Afghanistan in 2003. The firm was established to participate in the rehabilitation and development of Afghanistan through the provision of construction, design, and survey services.

[782] SIGAR. *Gardez Hospital: After almost 2 Years, Construction Not Yet Completed because of Poor Contractor Performance, and Overpayments to the Contractor Need to Be Addressed by USAID.* Report No. SIGAR 14-6-IR. Arlington, VA: October, 2013. Web. ‹ http://www.sigar.mil/pdf/inspections/SIGAR%2014-6-IR.pdf›.In September 2008, IOM awarded a contract to Sadat Mohammad Construction Company for Gardez hospital's first phase of construction. The company worked from September 2008 to June 2010, building a boundary wall and deep water well for the hospital.

[783] SIGAR. *Gardez Hospital: After almost 2 Years, Construction Not Yet Completed because of Poor Contractor Performance, and Overpayments to the Contractor Need to Be Addressed by USAID.* Report No. SIGAR 14-6-IR. Arlington, VA: October, 2013. Web. ‹ http://www.sigar.mil/pdf/inspections/SIGAR%2014-6-IR.pdf›.

[784] Before It's News. "US-funded Afghan Hospital Project Bought Gas for $500-a-gallon, Not Market-rate $5." *Beforeitsnews.com.* Before It's News Inc. 24 October 2013. Web. ‹http://beforeitsnews.com/alternative/2013/10/us-funded-afghan-hospital-project-bought-gas-for-500-a-gallon-not-market-rate-5-2803554.html›.

[785] Bier, Jeryl. "Inspector General: Gov't Partner Paid $500 Per Gallon of Gas in Afghanistan." Web log post.*Weeklystandard.com.* The Weekly Standard LLC, 23 Oct. 2013. Web. ‹http://www.weeklystandard.com/blogs/inspector-general-govt-partner-paid-500-gallon-gas-afghanistan_764594.html›.

[786]SIGAR. *Gardez Hospital: After almost 2 Years, Construction Not Yet Completed because of Poor Contractor Performance, and Overpayments to the Contractor Need to Be Addressed by USAID.* Report No. SIGAR 14-6-IR. Arlington, VA: October, 2013. Web. ‹ http://www.sigar.mil/pdf/inspections/SIGAR%2014-6-IR.pdf›.

[787] Anderson, Katie. "Lisbon Dairy Farm Receives $403,000 Grant for Bio-gas Digester." *Watertowndailytimes.com.* The Watertown Daily Times. 14 November 2013. Web. ‹http://www.watertowndailytimes.com/article/20131114/NEWS05/711149803›.

[788] Anderson, Katie. "Lisbon Dairy Farm Receives $403,000 Grant for Bio-gas Digester." *Watertowndailytimes.com*. The Watertown Daily Times. 14 November 2013. Web. <http://www.watertowndailytimes.com/article/20131114/NEWS05/711149803>.

[789] Roy, Suzanne. "BLM Roundup to 'Save' Wild Horses Kills Three Wild Horses." *huffingtonpost.com*. TheHuffingtonpost.com LLC. 7 August 2013. Web. <http://www.huffingtonpost.com/suzanne-roy/blm-roundup-to-save-wild-horses_b_3716764.html>.

[790] Winerip, Michael. "The Wild Horses' Troubled Rescue." *nytimes.com*. The New York Times Company. 17 June 2013. Web.<http://www.nytimes.com/2013/06/17/booming/the-wild-horses-troubled-rescue.html?_r=0>.

[791] Phillips, David. "All the Missing Horses: What Happened to the Wild Horses Tom David Bought From the Gov't?" *propublica.org*. Pro Publica Inc. 28 September 2012. Web.<http://www.propublica.org/article/missing-what-happened-to-wild-horses-tom-davis-bought-from-the-govt>.

[792] Winerip, Michael. "The Wild Horses' Troubled Rescue." *nytimes.com*. The New York Times Company. 17 June 2013. Web.<http://www.nytimes.com/2013/06/17/booming/the-wild-horses-troubled-rescue.html?_r=0>.

[793] Phillips, David. "All the Missing Horses: What Happened to the Wild Horses Tom David Bought From the Gov't?" *propublica.org*. Pro Publica Inc. 28 September 2012. Web.<http://www.propublica.org/article/missing-what-happened-to-wild-horses-tom-davis-bought-from-the-govt>.

[794] Phillips, David. "All the Missing Horses: What Happened to the Wild Horses Tom David Bought From the Gov't?" *propublica.org*. Pro Publica Inc. 28 September 2012. Web.<http://www.propublica.org/article/missing-what-happened-to-wild-horses-tom-davis-bought-from-the-govt>.

[795] Phillips, David. "All the Missing Horses: What Happened to the Wild Horses Tom David Bought From the Gov't?" *propublica.org*. Pro Publica Inc. 28 September 2012. Web.<http://www.propublica.org/article/missing-what-happened-to-wild-horses-tom-davis-bought-from-the-govt>.

[796] Phillips, David. "All the Missing Horses: What Happened to the Wild Horses Tom David Bought From the Gov't?" *propublica.org*. Pro Publica Inc. 28 September 2012. Web.<http://www.propublica.org/article/missing-what-happened-to-wild-horses-tom-davis-bought-from-the-govt>.

[797] Frosch, Dan. "Report Criticizes U.S. Stewardship of Wild Horses." *nytimes.com*. The New York Times Company. 6 June 2013. Web. <http://www.nytimes.com/2013/06/07/us/report-criticizes-us-stewardship-of-wild-horses.html?_r=0>.

[798] Winerip, Michael. "The Wild Horses' Troubled Rescue." *nytimes.com*. The New York Times Company. 17 June 2013. Web.<http://www.nytimes.com/2013/06/17/booming/the-wild-horses-troubled-rescue.html?_r=0>.

[799] Phillips, David. "All the Missing Horses: What Happened to the Wild Horses Tom David Bought From the Gov't?" *propublica.org*. Pro Publica Inc. 28 September 2012. Web.<http://www.propublica.org/article/missing-what-happened-to-wild-horses-tom-davis-bought-from-the-govt>.

[800] Phillips, David. "All the Missing Horses: What Happened to the Wild Horses Tom David Bought From the Gov't?" *propublica.org*. Pro Publica Inc. 28 September 2012. Web.<http://www.propublica.org/article/missing-what-happened-to-wild-horses-tom-davis-bought-from-the-govt>.

[801] Painter, William L., and Jared T. Brown. *FY2013 Supplemental Funding for Disaster Relief*. Rep. no. R42869. Washington, D.C.: Congressional Research Service, 19 February 2013. Web. <http://crs.gov/pages/Reports.aspx?PRODCODE=R42869&Source=search>.

[802] Associated Press "Congress approves $60.4B Sandy aid bill," *silive.com.*. The Staten Island Advance. 28 December 2012. Web. <http://www.silive.com/news/index.ssf/2012/12/senate_approves_604b_hurricane.html>.

[803] HHS. News Office. *HHS Awards Grants for Hurricane Sandy Recovery Research.* US Department of Health and Human Services. 22 October 2013. Web. <http://www.hhs.gov/news/press/2013pres/10/20131022a.html>.

[804] HHS. News Office. *HHS Awards Grants for Hurricane Sandy Recovery Research.* US Department of Health and Human Services. 22 October 2013. Web. <http://www.hhs.gov/news/press/2013pres/10/20131022a.html>.

[805] HHS. News Office. *HHS Awards Grants for Hurricane Sandy Recovery Research.* US Department of Health and Human Services. 22 October 2013. Web. <http://www.hhs.gov/news/press/2013pres/10/20131022a.html>.

[806] McGeehan, Patrick and Griff Palmer, "Displaced by Hurricane Sandy, and Living in Limbo," *nytimes.com*. The New York Times Company. 6 December 2013. Web. <http://www.nytimes.com/2013/12/07/nyregion/displaced-by-hurricane-sandy-and-living-in-limbo-instead-of-at-home.html?_r=0>.

[807] McGeehan, Patrick and Griff Palmer, "Displaced by Hurricane Sandy, and Living in Limbo," *nytimes.com*. The New York Times Company. 6 December 2013. Web. <http://www.nytimes.com/2013/12/07/nyregion/displaced-by-hurricane-sandy-and-living-in-limbo-instead-of-at-home.html?_r=0>.

[808] McGeehan, Patrick and Griff Palmer, "Displaced by Hurricane Sandy, and Living in Limbo," *nytimes.com*. The New York Times Company. 6 December 2013. Web. <http://www.nytimes.com/2013/12/07/nyregion/displaced-by-hurricane-sandy-and-living-in-limbo-instead-of-at-home.html?_r=0>.

[809] U.S. Department of Interior Office of Inspector General. "*Management Of The Coastal Impact Assistance Program, State Of Mississippi*. Report No. ER-IN-MOA-0013-2011. DOI OIG. *Doi.gov/oig*. 27 June 2013. Web. <http://www.doi.gov/oig/news/management-of-the-coastal-impact-assistance-program-state-of-mississippi.cfm>.

[810] U.S. Department of Interior Office of Inspector General. "*Management Of The Coastal Impact Assistance Program, State Of Mississippi*. Report No. ER-IN-MOA-0013-2011. DOI OIG. *Doi.gov/oig*. 27 June 2013. Web. <http://www.doi.gov/oig/news/management-of-the-coastal-impact-assistance-program-state-of-mississippi.cfm>.

[811] U.S. Department of Interior Office of Inspector General. "*Management Of The Coastal Impact Assistance Program, State Of Mississippi*. Report No. ER-IN-MOA-0013-2011. DOI OIG. *Doi.gov/oig*. 27 June 2013. Web. <http://www.doi.gov/oig/news/management-of-the-coastal-impact-assistance-program-state-of-mississippi.cfm>.

[812] U.S. Department of Interior Office of Inspector General. "*Management Of The Coastal Impact Assistance Program, State Of Mississippi*. Report No. ER-IN-MOA-0013-2011. DOI OIG. *Doi.gov/oig*. 27 June 2013. Web. <http://www.doi.gov/oig/news/management-of-the-coastal-impact-assistance-program-state-of-mississippi.cfm>.

[813] Lee, Anita, "Louisiana Firm Takes On DMR Coastal Management Program." *Sunherald.com*. Biloxi Sun Herald, 18 September 2013. Web. <http://www.sunherald.com/2013/09/17/4959591/louisiana-firm-takes-on-dmr-coastal.html>.

[814] Lee, Anita, "Louisiana Firm Takes On DMR Coastal Management Program." *Sunherald.com*. Biloxi Sun Herald, 18 September 2013. Web. <http://www.sunherald.com/2013/09/17/4959591/louisiana-firm-takes-on-dmr-coastal.html>.

[815] Vilsack, Thomas J. "The Impacts of Sequestration." Letter to The Honorable Barbara Mikulski. 5 Feb. 2013. *US Senate Committee on Appropriations*. 14 Feb. 2013. Web. <http://www.appropriations.senate.gov/ht-full.cfm?method=hearings.view&id=17d3dc99-c065-4bec-a7c8-cfd374bf41a3>.

[816] Vilsack, Thomas J. "The Impacts of Sequestration." Letter to The Honorable Barbara Mikulski. 5 Feb. 2013. *US Senate Committee on Appropriations*. 14 Feb. 2013. Web. <http://www.appropriations.senate.gov/ht-full.cfm?method=hearings.view&id=17d3dc99-c065-4bec-a7c8-cfd374bf41a3>.

[817] Stephen, Paul. "N.C. Distillery Turning Leftovers into Sweet-Potato Potable." *Starnewsonline.com*. ," StarNews Online. 14 May 2013. Web. <http://www.starnewsonline.com/article/20130514/ARTICLES/130519850?p=1&tc=pg>.

[818] Alcohol Beverage Control Commission of North Carolina." Legal Sales by County." *Abc.nc.gov*. North Carolina ABC Commission. Web. <http://abc.nc.gov/xo/county.aspx?county=40>, accessed October 4, 2013.

[819] Cheney, Kyle. "POLITICO." *Politico.com*. 19 Sept. 2013. Web. <http://www.politico.com/story/2013/09/fda-social-media-contract-raises-eyebrows-on-hill-97086.html>.

[820] Social Media Monitoring Tool. Solicitation No. FDA-SOL-13-1120182. Department of Health and Human Services, Food and Drug Administration. 15 August 2013. *FBO.gov*. Federal Biz Ops. Web. <https://www.fbo.gov/index?s=opportunity&mode=form&id=59b72a42d9e2720a3254f0a6ad210e22&tab=core&_cview=1>.

[821] Gaffney, Alexander. "FDA to Spend up to $182,000 on Social Media Tool to Shape, Monitor Communications." *Raps.org*. Regulatory Focus. Regulatory Focus. 19 September 2013. Web. <http://www.raps.org/focus-online/news/news-article-view/article/4100/fda-to-spend-up-to-182000-on-social-media-tool-to-shape-monitor-communications.aspx>.

[822] Hope College. "NEH Grant to Support Broader Adaptation of 'Valley Sim' Platform." *Hope.edu*. Hope College. 12 August 2013. Web. <http://www.hope.edu/2013/08/12/neh-grant-support-broader-adaptation-valley-sim-platform>.

[823] Hope College. "NEH Grant to Support Broader Adaptation of 'Valley Sim' Platform." *Hope.edu*. Hope College. 12 August 2013. Web. <http://www.hope.edu/2013/08/12/neh-grant-support-broader-adaptation-valley-sim-platform>.

[824] Hope College. "NEH Grant to Support Broader Adaptation of 'Valley Sim' Platform." *Hope.edu*. Hope College. 12 August 2013. Web. <http://www.hope.edu/2013/08/12/neh-grant-support-broader-adaptation-valley-sim-platform>.

[825] National Park Service. "Glacier National Park, Montana: Fact Sheet." Web. <http://www.nps.gov/glac/parknews/fact-sheet.htm>.

[826] Repanshek, Kurt, "How Might Fatal Attack By Mountain Goat Change Backcountry Dynamics in National Parks?" *nationalparkstraveler.com*. National Park Advocates, LLC. 24 October 2010. Web. <http://www.nationalparkstraveler.com/2010/10/how-might-fatal-attack-mountain-goat-change-backcountry-dynamics-national-parks7117>. A goat-related fatality in Olympic National Park in Washington State in 2010 was the first such incident at the park since its opening in 1938.

[827] Germann, Denise, and Jennifer Lutman. Newsroom. *Mountain Goat Study to Begin at Logan Pass. Nps.gov/glac*. National Park Service. 24 June 2013. <http://www.nps.gov/glac/parknews/media-13-39.htm>.

[828] Repanshek, Kurt, "How Might Fatal Attack By Mountain Goat Change Backcountry Dynamics in National Parks?" *nationalparktraveler.com*. National Park Advocates, LLC. 24 October 2010. Web. <http://www.nationalparkstraveler.com/2010/10/how-might-fatal-attack-mountain-goat-change-backcountry-dynamics-national-parks7117>.

[829] Repanshek, Kurt, "How Might Fatal Attack By Mountain Goat Change Backcountry Dynamics in National Parks?" *nationalparktraveler.com*. National Park Advocates, LLC. 24 October 2010. Web. <http://www.nationalparkstraveler.com/2010/10/how-might-fatal-attack-mountain-goat-change-backcountry-dynamics-national-parks7117>.

[830] Germann, Denise, and Jennifer Lutman. "Mountain Goat Study to Begin at Logan Pass." *Nps.gov*. National Park Service, DOI. 24 June 2013. Web. < http://www.nps.gov/glac/parknews/media-13-39.htm>.

[831] Germann, Denise, and Jennifer Lutman. "Mountain Goat Study to Begin at Logan Pass." *Nps.gov*. National Park Service, DOI. 24 June 2013. Web. < http://www.nps.gov/glac/parknews/media-13-39.htm>.

[832] Devlin, Vince. "Glacier, UM to Study Human, Goat Interactions Near Logan Pass." *Missoulian.com*. The Missoulian, 24 June 2013. Web. <http://missoulian.com/news/state-and-regional/glacier-um-to-study-human-goat-interactions-near-logan-pass/article_1f023f5e-dd11-11e2-82e0-0019bb2963f4.html>.

[833] Repanshek, Kurt, "Olympic National Park's Mountain Goat Plan Warns of Dangers of Urinating on Hiking Trails," *nationalparktraveler.com*. National Park Advocates, LLC. 11 June 2011. Web. <http://www.nationalparkstraveler.com/2011/07/olympic-national-parks-mountain-goat-plan-warns-dangers-urinating-hiking-trails8431>.

[834] See http://www.nps.gov/transportation/maintenance_backlog.html

[835] See http://youtu.be/Eo1ajamoD0A

[836] Institute of Museum and Library Services, Awarded Grants Search, "Long Island." Web. <http://www.imls.gov/recipients/grantsearch.aspx>.

[837] BWW News Desk. "Puppets Take Long Island Festival Opens Today at Children's Museum, Got on a Boat Puppet Theatre." *BroadwayWorld.com*. Wisdom Digital Media. 8 July 2013. Web. <http://www.broadwayworld.com/long-island/article/PUPPETS-TAKE-LONG-ISLAND-Festival-to-Open-78-at-Childrens-Museum-Goat-on-a-Boat-Puppet-Theatre-20130707>.

[838] BWW News Desk. "Puppets Take Long Island Festival Opens Today at Children's Museum, Got on a Boat Puppet Theatre." *BroadwayWorld.com*. Wisdom Digital Media. 8 July 2013. Web. <http://www.broadwayworld.com/long-island/article/PUPPETS-TAKE-LONG-ISLAND-Festival-to-Open-78-at-Childrens-Museum-Goat-on-a-Boat-Puppet-Theatre-20130707>.

[839] BWW News Desk. "Puppets Take Long Island Festival Opens Today at Children's Museum, Got on a Boat Puppet Theatre." *BroadwayWorld.com*. Wisdom Digital Media. 8 July 2013. Web. <http://www.broadwayworld.com/long-island/article/PUPPETS-TAKE-LONG-ISLAND-Festival-to-Open-78-at-Childrens-Museum-Goat-on-a-Boat-Puppet-Theatre-20130707>.

[840] TERC Inc. "Leveling Up: Supporting and Measuring High School STEM Knowledge Building in Social Digital Games." Award Abstract #1119144, National Science Foundation. 19 July 2013. Web. <http://www.nsf.gov/awardsearch/showAward?AWD_ID=1119144&HistoricalAwards=false>.

[841] Bringham Young University "Full-Scale Development: Collaborative Research Advancing Informal STEM Learning Through Scientific Alternate Reality Games." Award Abstract #1323787, National Science Foundation. 17 September 2013. Web. <http://www.nsf.gov/awardsearch/showAward?AWD_ID=1323787&HistoricalAwards=false>.

[842] University of Maryland, College Park. "Full-Scale Development: Collaborative Research Advancing Informal STEM Learning through Scientific Alternate Reality Games." Award Abstract #1323306, National Science Foundation. 17 September 2013. Web. <http://www.nsf.gov/awardsearch/showAward?AWD_ID=1323306&HistoricalAwards=false>.

[843] "Pathways: Large Alternate Reality Games for Education-Assessing Performance and Play." Award Abstract #1224088, National Science Foundation. 11 September 2012. Web. <http://www.nsf.gov/awardsearch/showAward?AWD_ID=1224088&HistoricalAwards=false>.

[844] Fujimoto, Randall. "Designing an Educational Alternate Reality Game." *Shoyu.com*. Shoyu Learning Solutions. Web. <http://www.shoyu.com/education/Research_DesigningAnEducationalARG.pdf>.

[845] TERC Inc. "Leveling Up: Supporting and Measuring High School STEM Knowledge Building in Social Digital Games." Award Abstract #1119144, National Science Foundation. 19 July 2013. Web. <http://www.nsf.gov/awardsearch/showAward?AWD_ID=1119144&HistoricalAwards=false>.

[846] BYU "Full-Scale Development: Collaborative Research Advancing Informal STEM Learning Through Scientific Alternate Reality Games." Award Abstract #1323787, National Science Foundation. 17 September 2013. Web. ‹http://www.nsf.gov/awardsearch/showAward?AWD_ID=1323787&HistoricalAwards=false›.

[847] UMD College Park. "Full-Scale Development: Collaborative Research Advancing Informal STEM Learning through Scientific Alternate Reality Games." Award Abstract #1323306, National Science Foundation. 17 September 2013. Web. ‹http://www.nsf.gov/awardsearch/showAward?AWD_ID=1323306&HistoricalAwards=false›.

[848] "Pathways: Large Alternate Reality Games for Education-Assessing Performance and Play." Award Abstract #1224088, National Science Foundation. 11 September 2012. Web. ‹http://www.nsf.gov/awardsearch/showAward?AWD_ID=1224088&HistoricalAwards=false›.

[849] Brackin, Adam Lloyd. "Tracking the Emergent Properties of the Collaborative Online Story 'Deus City' for Testing the Standard Model of Alternate Reality Games." PhD. diss., University of Texas at Dallas, 2008. Print.

[850] BYU "Full-Scale Development: Collaborative Research Advancing Informal STEM Learning Through Scientific Alternate Reality Games." Award Abstract #1323787, National Science Foundation. 17 September 2013. Web.

[851] Fujimoto, Randall. "Designing an Educational Alternate Reality Game." *Shoyu.com*. Shoyu Learning Solutions. Web. ‹http://www.shoyu.com/education/Research_DesigningAnEducationalARG.pdf›.

[852] Brackin, Adam Lloyd. "Tracking the Emergent Properties of the Collaborative Online Story 'Deus City' for Testing the Standard Model of Alternate Reality Games." PhD. diss., University of Texas at Dallas, 2008. Print.

[853] Jafarinaimi, Nassim, Meyers, Eric, and Nathann, Lisa. "Entertained but Misinformed? Play and Prevarication in Alternate Reality Games." Abstract Presentation. Canadian Association for Information Science, 41st Annual Conference, June 6-8, 2013 Web. ‹www.cais-acsi.ca/proceedings/2013/JafarinaimiMeyersNathan_Submission83.pdf.›

[854] de Freitas, Sara. "Learning in Immersive worlds: A review of game-based learning." JISC e-Learning Programme. 2006. Web. ‹http://www.jisc.ac.uk/whatwedo/programmes/elearninginnovation/outcomes/gamingreport.aspx›.

[855] Szulborski, Dave. This Is Not a Game: A Guide to Alternate Reality Gaming, New Fiction Publishing, 2005. (7).

[856] Fujimoto, Randall. "Designing an Educational Alternate Reality Game." *Shoyu.com*. Shoyu Learning Solutions. Web. ‹http://www.shoyu.com/education/Research_DesigningAnEducationalARG.pdf›.

[857] Fujimoto, Randall. "Designing an Educational Alternate Reality Game." *Shoyu.com*. Shoyu Learning Solutions. Web. ‹http://www.shoyu.com/education/Research_DesigningAnEducationalARG.pdf›.

[858] Boessen. Brett. "This is Not a Game (It's a Class): Lessons Learned from an In-Class Alternate Reality Game (ARG)." *Academiccommons.org*.The Academic Commons, 30 September 2013. Web. ‹http://www.academiccommons.org/2013/09/this-is-not-a-game-its-a-class-lessons-learned-from-an-in-class-alternate-reality-game-arg/›.

[859] National Science Foundation. "Update to Important Notice No. 133." IN-133A. Arlington, VA, 17 July 2013. Web. ‹http://www.nsf.gov/pubs/2013/in133a/in133a.jsp?org=NSF›.

[860] Nagoumey, Adam. "Crowds Return to Las Vegas, but Gamble Less." *Nytimes.com*. The New York Times Company. 31 July 2013. Web. ‹http://www.nytimes.com/2013/08/01/us/as-las-vegas-recovers-new-cause-for-concern.html›.

[861] Shine, Conor. "What's Your Economic Vision for Las Vegas? Grant Offers $800K No-Strings-Attached Prize." *Lasvegassun.com*. The Las Vegas Sun. 7 August 2013. Web. ‹http://www.lasvegassun.com/news/2013/aug/07/no-strings-attached-grant-seeks-spur-economic/›.

[862] Shine, Conor. "What's Your Economic Vision for Las Vegas? Grant Offers $800K No-Strings-Attached Prize." *Lasvegassun.com*. The Las Vegas Sun. 7 August 2013. Web. ‹http://www.lasvegassun.com/news/2013/aug/07/no-strings-attached-grant-seeks-spur-economic/›.

[863] Barron, Richard M. "Who's Got the Bright Idea for Greensboro?" *News-Record.com*, BH Media Group Holdings, Inc. 25 September 2013. ‹http://www.news-record.com/news/local_news/article_2d045b48-2332-11e3-8454-001a4bcf6878.html›.

[864] Barron, Richard M. "Who's Got the Bright Idea for Greensboro?" *News-Record.com*, BH Media Group Holdings, Inc. 25 September 2013. ‹http://www.news-record.com/news/local_news/article_2d045b48-2332-11e3-8454-001a4bcf6878.html›

[865] Treasury Inspector General for Tax Administration *The Internal Revenue Service is Not in Compliance with Executive Order 13520 to Reduce Improper Payments*. Reference No, 2013-40-084. Washignton, DC: TIGTA 28 August 2013. Web. ‹http://www.treasury.gov/tigta/auditreports/2013reports/201340084fr.pdf›.

[866] Treasury Inspector General for Tax Administration *The Internal Revenue Service is Not in Compliance with Executive Order 13520 to Reduce Improper Payments*. Reference No, 2013-40-084. Washignton, DC: TIGTA 28 August 2013. Web. ‹http://www.treasury.gov/tigta/auditreports/2013reports/201340084fr.pdf›.

[867] Treasury Inspector General for Tax Administration *The Internal Revenue Service is Not in Compliance with Executive Order 13520 to Reduce Improper Payments*. Reference No, 2013-40-084. Washignton, DC: TIGTA 28 August 2013. Web. ‹http://www.treasury.gov/tigta/auditreports/2013reports/201340084fr.pdf›.

[868] Payment Accuracy.gov. "Earned Income Tax Credit (EITC)." *Paymentaccuract.gov*. USA Spending. Web ‹http://www.paymentaccuracy.gov/tracked/earned-income-tax-credit-eitc-2012›.

[869] Dinan, Stephen, "IRS Wastes Billions in Bogus Claims for Earned Income Tax Credit." *Washingtontimes.com*. The Washington Times, LLC. 22 October 2013. Web. ‹http://www.washingtontimes.com/news/2013/oct/22/irs-paid-132B-bogus-tax-credits-over-last-decade/?page=all›.

[870] Dinan, Stephen, "IRS Wastes Billions in Bogus Claims for Earned Income Tax Credit." *Washingtontimes.com*. The Washington Times, LLC. 22 October 2013. Web. ‹http://www.washingtontimes.com/news/2013/oct/22/irs-paid-132B-bogus-tax-credits-over-last-decade/?page=all›.

[871] Clark, Patrick, "Sequestration Cuts $92 Million from the SBA's Budget," *Bloomberg Businessweek*, Bloomberg L.P. 6 March 2013. Web. ‹http://www.businessweek.com/articles/2013-03-06/sequestration-cuts-92-million-from-the-sbas-budget.›

[872] Clark, Patrick, "Sequestration Cuts $92 Million from the SBA's Budget," *Bloomberg Businessweek*, Bloomberg L.P. 6 March 2013. Web. ‹http://www.businessweek.com/articles/2013-03-06/sequestration-cuts-92-million-from-the-sbas-budget.›

[873] Clark, Patrick, "Sequestration Cuts $92 Million from the SBA's Budget," *Bloomberg Businessweek*, Bloomberg L.P. 6 March 2013. Web. ‹http://www.businessweek.com/articles/2013-03-06/sequestration-cuts-92-million-from-the-sbas-budget.›

[874] Moylan, Andrew, "Obama's SBA spent $80,000 in Taxpayer Money on Study to promote Internet Sales Tax." *Rstreet.org* R Street Institute. 20 November 2013. Web. ‹http://www.rstreet.org/2013/11/20/obamas-sba-spent-80000-in-taxpayer-money›.

[875] Moylan, Andrew, "Obama's SBA spent $80,000 in Taxpayer Money on Study to promote Internet Sales Tax." *Rstreet.org* R Street Institute. 20 November 2013. Web. ‹http://www.rstreet.org/2013/11/20/obamas-sba-spent-80000-in-taxpayer-money›.

[876] "Bill Summary and Status: Marketplace Fairness Act" Legislative Information Service. Web. ‹http://lis.gov/cgi-lis/bdquery/D?d113:1:./temp/~bd1JmU:dbs=n:|/billsumm/billsumm.php?id=2›.|

[877] Black, Sam, "When Government Real Estate Deals Go Bad." *Bizjournals.com*. American City Business Journals. 7 June 2013. Web ‹http://www.bizjournals.com/twincities/print-edition/2013/06/07/money-pits.html?page=all›.

[878] Black, Sam, "When Government Real Estate Deals Go Bad." *Bizjournals.com*. American City Business Journals. 7 June 2013. Web ‹http://www.bizjournals.com/twincities/print-edition/2013/06/07/money-pits.html?page=all›.

[879] Steward, Tom, "Federal Building Makeover Drives Up Cost Of MN's Biggest Stimulus Project," *Watchdog.org Minnesota Bureau*. Watchdog Minnesota Bureau – Franklin Center for Government & Public Integrity. 27 October 2013. ‹http://watchdog.org/112940/federal-building-makeover-drives-cost-mns-biggest-stimulus-project/›.

[880] The White House. Office of the Press Secretary. *President Obama Signs an Executive Order Focused on Federal Leadership in Environmental, Energy, and Economic Performance*. *Whitehouse.gov* Oct. 2009. Web. ‹http://www.whitehouse.gov/the_press_office/President-Obama-signs-an-Executive-Order-Focused-on-Federal-Leadership-in-Environmental-Energy-and-Economic-Performance›.

[881] Steward, Tom, "Federal Building Makeover Drives Up Cost Of MN's Biggest Stimulus Project," *Watchdog.org Minnesota Bureau*. Watchdog Minnesota Bureau – Franklin Center for Government & Public Integrity. 27 October 2013. ‹http://watchdog.org/112940/federal-building-makeover-drives-cost-mns-biggest-stimulus-project/›.

[882] Steward, Tom, "Federal Building Makeover Drives Up Cost Of MN's Biggest Stimulus Project," *Watchdog.org Minnesota Bureau*. Watchdog Minnesota Bureau – Franklin Center for Government & Public Integrity. 27 October 2013. ‹http://watchdog.org/112940/federal-building-makeover-drives-cost-mns-biggest-stimulus-project/›.

[883] Steward, Tom, "Federal Building Makeover Drives Up Cost Of MN's Biggest Stimulus Project," *Watchdog.org Minnesota Bureau*. Watchdog Minnesota Bureau – Franklin Center for Government & Public Integrity. 27 October 2013. ‹http://watchdog.org/112940/federal-building-makeover-drives-cost-mns-biggest-stimulus-project/›.

[884] Black, Sam, "When Government Real Estate Deals Go Bad." *Bizjournals.com*. American City Business Journals. 7 June 2013. Web ‹http://www.bizjournals.com/twincities/print-edition/2013/06/07/money-pits.html?page=all›.

[885] Kahan, Dan. "Some Data on Education, Religiosity, Ideology, and Science Comprehension." *Culturalcognition.net*. The Cultural Cognition Project at Yale Law School. 15 October 2013. Web. ‹http://www.culturalcognition.net/blog/2013/10/15/some-data-on-education-religiosity-ideology-and-science-comp.html?lastPage=true&postSubmitted=true›.

[886] Kahan, Dan M. (2013) "Ideology, motivated reasoning, and cognitive reasoning," *Judgment and Decision Making*, 8(4): 407-424.

[887] Kahan, Dan M. (2013) "Ideology, motivated reasoning, and cognitive reasoning," *Judgment and Decision Making*, 8(4): 407-424.

[888] Kahan, Dan M. (2013) "Ideology, motivated reasoning, and cognitive reasoning," *Judgment and Decision Making*, 8(4): 407-424.

[889] Kahan, Dan M. (2013) "Ideology, motivated reasoning, and cognitive reasoning," *Judgment and Decision Making*, 8(4): 407-424.

[890] Kahan, Dan M. (2013) "Ideology, motivated reasoning, and cognitive reasoning," *Judgment and Decision Making*, 8(4): 407-424.

[891] NSF Grant Award #0922714.

[892] Suresh, Subra. "Impact of FY 2013 Sequestration Order on NSF Awards." Letter to NSF Grant Awardee Organizations. 27 Feb. 2013. *Nsf.gov*. Web. ‹http://www.nsf.gov/pubs/2013/in133/in133.pdf›.

[893] Darla Cameron, David A. Fahrenthold and Lisa Rein, "Tracking the Predicted Sequester Impacts." *Washingtonpost.com*. The Washington Post. 30 June 2013. Web. ‹http://www.washingtonpost.com/wp-srv/special/politics/sequestration-federal-agency-update/›.

[894] Department of the Interior. National Park Service. *Route 66 Corridor Preservation Program Reauthorized*. *Nps.gov*. National Park Service, 5 Mar. 2009. Web. ‹http://www.nps.gov/history/rt66/news/PressRelease-NPSRT66Reauthorization.pdf›.

[895] Department of the Interior. National Park Service. "Route 66 Corridor Preservatin Program Grant Awards – 2013," *nps.gov*. National Park Service. Web. ‹http://www.nps.gov/history/rt66/grnts/2013GrantAwards.pdf›. Accessed 25 November 2013.

[896] Department of the Interior. National Park Service. "Route 66 Corridor Preservatin Program Grant Awards – 2013," *nps.gov*. National Park Service. Web. ‹http://www.nps.gov/history/rt66/grnts/2013GrantAwards.pdf›. Accessed 25 November 2013.

[897] Decamp Junction facebook page, Web. ‹https://www.facebook.com/pages/Decamp-Junction/331859090210925?sk=info›. Accessed 25 November 2013.

[898] Department of the Interior. National Park Service. "Route 66 Corridor Preservatin Program Grant Awards – 2013," *nps.gov*. National Park Service. Web. ‹http://www.nps.gov/history/rt66/grnts/2013GrantAwards.pdf›. Accessed 25 November 2013.

[899] Department of the Interior. National Park Service. "Route 66 Corridor Preservatin Program Grant Awards – 2013," *nps.gov*. National Park Service. Web. ‹http://www.nps.gov/history/rt66/grnts/2013GrantAwards.pdf›. Accessed 25 November 2013.

[900] Department of the Interior. National Park Service. "Route 66 Corridor Preservatin Program Grant Awards – 2013," *nps.gov*. National Park Service. Web. ‹http://www.nps.gov/history/rt66/grnts/2013GrantAwards.pdf›. Accessed 25 November 2013.

[901] Minutes of the Lincoln County (Montana) Board of Commissioners. *Lincolncountymt.us*. 1 May 2013. Web. ‹http://www.lincolncountymt.us/Minutes/docs/2013/May/May1.pdf›.

[902] Franz, Justin, "Golf Car Assembly Plant May Open in Libby," *Flatheadbeacon.com*. Flathead Beacon. 16 May 2013. Web. ‹http://www.flatheadbeacon.com/articles/article/golf_car_assembly_plant_may_open_in_libby/33420›.

[903] Gerstenecker, Alan Lewis, "Commissioners OK block grant to aid golf-car company at Port Authority," *thewesternnews.com*. The Western News. 3 May 2013. ‹http://www.thewesternnews.com/news/article_9bcb40a6-b40a-11e2-98b3-0019bb2963f4.html›.

[904] Gerstenecker, Alan Lewis, "Commissioners OK block grant to aid golf-car company at Port Authority," *thewesternnews.com*. The Western News. 3 May 2013. ‹http://www.thewesternnews.com/news/article_9bcb40a6-b40a-11e2-98b3-0019bb2963f4.html›.

[905] Franz, Justin, "Golf Car Assembly Plant May Open in Libby," *Flatheadbeacon.com*. Flathead Beacon. 16 May 2013. Web. ‹http://www.flatheadbeacon.com/articles/article/golf_car_assembly_plant_may_open_in_libby/33420›.

[906] Franz, Justin, "Golf Car Assembly Plant May Open in Libby," *Flatheadbeacon.com*. Flathead Beacon. 16 May 2013. Web. ‹http://www.flatheadbeacon.com/articles/article/golf_car_assembly_plant_may_open_in_libby/33420›.

[907] Hintze, Lynnette. "Stinger's Libby Plant Likely to Close." *Dailyinterlake.com*. The Daily Inter Lake. 8 February 2013. Web. ‹http://www.dailyinterlake.com/news/local_montana/article_8a9307b6-726e-11e2-8c9e-0019bb2963f4.html?mode=jqm;›

[908] Hintze, Lynnette. "Stinger's Libby Plant Likely to Close." *Dailyinterlake.com*. The Daily Inter Lake. 8 February 2013. Web. ‹http://www.dailyinterlake.com/news/local_montana/article_8a9307b6-726e-11e2-8c9e-0019bb2963f4.html?mode=jqm;›; Franz, Justin, "Golf Car Assembly Plant May Open in Libby," *Flatheadbeacon.com*. Flathead Beacon. 16 May 2013. Web. ‹http://www.flatheadbeacon.com/articles/article/golf_car_assembly_plant_may_open_in_libby/33420›.

[909] Plungis, Jeff, "Amtrak Serving Free Wine to Steak Loses Millions on Food." *Bloomberg.com*. Bloomberg L.P. 14 November 2013. Web. <http://www.bloomberg.com/news/2013-11-14/amtrak-serving-free-wine-to-steak-loses-millions-on-food.html>.

[910] Jaffe, Eric, "Why Can't Amtrak Get Food Right?" *TheAtlanticCities.com*. The Atlantic Monthly Group. 20 November 2013. Web. <http://www.theatlanticcities.com/jobs-and-economy/2013/11/why-cant-amtrak-get-food-right/7646/>.

[911] Plungis, Jeff, "Amtrak Serving Free Wine to Steak Loses Millions on Food." *Bloomberg.com*. Bloomberg L.P. 14 November 2013. Web. <http://www.bloomberg.com/news/2013-11-14/amtrak-serving-free-wine-to-steak-loses-millions-on-food.html>.

[912] Jaffe, Eric, "Why Can't Amtrak Get Food Right?" *TheAtlanticCities.com*. The Atlantic Monthly Group. 20 November 2013. Web. <http://www.theatlanticcities.com/jobs-and-economy/2013/11/why-cant-amtrak-get-food-right/7646/>.

[913] Plungis, Jeff, "Amtrak Serving Free Wine to Steak Loses Millions on Food." *Bloomberg.com*. Bloomberg L.P. 14 November 2013. Web. <http://www.bloomberg.com/news/2013-11-14/amtrak-serving-free-wine-to-steak-loses-millions-on-food.html>.

[914] Plungis, Jeff, "Amtrak Serving Free Wine to Steak Loses Millions on Food." *Bloomberg.com*. Bloomberg L.P. 14 November 2013. Web. <http://www.bloomberg.com/news/2013-11-14/amtrak-serving-free-wine-to-steak-loses-millions-on-food.html>.

[915] Plungis, Jeff, "Amtrak Serving Free Wine to Steak Loses Millions on Food." *Bloomberg.com*. Bloomberg L.P. 14 November 2013. Web. <http://www.bloomberg.com/news/2013-11-14/amtrak-serving-free-wine-to-steak-loses-millions-on-food.html>.

[916] Plungis, Jeff, "Amtrak Serving Free Wine to Steak Loses Millions on Food," *Bloomberg.com*. Bloomberg L.P. 14 November 2013. Web. <http://www.bloomberg.com/news/2013-11-14/amtrak-serving-free-wine-to-steak-loses-millions-on-food.html>.

[917] "DOJ OIG. *A Review of the U.S. Marshals Service's Use of Appropriated Funds to Purchase Promotional Items*. DOJ OIG Oversight and Review Division. November 2013. Web. < http://www.justice.gov/oig/reports/2013/s1311.pdf>. (ii).

[918] Anderson, Jeffrey. "U.S. Marshals May Always Get Their Man, but They Buy a Lot of 'Swag' Along the Way." *Washingtontimes.com*. The Washington Times LLC. 5 November 2013. Web. <http://www.washingtontimes.com/news/2013/nov/5/ig-marshals-spent-excessively-swag/print/>.

[919] "DOJ OIG. *A Review of the U.S. Marshals Service's Use of Appropriated Funds to Purchase Promotional Items*. DOJ OIG Oversight and Review Division. November 2013. Web. < http://www.justice.gov/oig/reports/2013/s1311.pdf>. (14).

[920] "DOJ OIG. *A Review of the U.S. Marshals Service's Use of Appropriated Funds to Purchase Promotional Items*. DOJ OIG Oversight and Review Division. November 2013. Web. < http://www.justice.gov/oig/reports/2013/s1311.pdf>. (ii).

[921] "DOJ OIG. *A Review of the U.S. Marshals Service's Use of Appropriated Funds to Purchase Promotional Items*. DOJ OIG Oversight and Review Division. November 2013. Web. < http://www.justice.gov/oig/reports/2013/s1311.pdf>. (13).

[922] "DOJ OIG. *A Review of the U.S. Marshals Service's Use of Appropriated Funds to Purchase Promotional Items*. DOJ OIG Oversight and Review Division. November 2013. Web. < http://www.justice.gov/oig/reports/2013/s1311.pdf>. (13).

[923] "DOJ OIG. *A Review of the U.S. Marshals Service's Use of Appropriated Funds to Purchase Promotional Items*. DOJ OIG Oversight and Review Division. November 2013. Web. < http://www.justice.gov/oig/reports/2013/s1311.pdf>. (13).

[924] "DOJ OIG. *A Review of the U.S. Marshals Service's Use of Appropriated Funds to Purchase Promotional Items*. DOJ OIG Oversight and Review Division. November 2013. Web. < http://www.justice.gov/oig/reports/2013/s1311.pdf>. (21).

[925] "DOJ OIG. *A Review of the U.S. Marshals Service's Use of Appropriated Funds to Purchase Promotional Items*. DOJ OIG Oversight and Review Division. November 2013. Web. < http://www.justice.gov/oig/reports/2013/s1311.pdf>. (21). *see also* p. 33, noting the USMS policy as a result of the Attorney General's directive: On January 21, 2011, the Attorney General addressed issued a directive that essentially suspended the purchase of promotional items by the USMS. Attorney General Holder's directive required all components "to reduce expenditures to only mission-essential programs, projects and activities." Six months later, the USMS Chief Financial Officer emailed all USMS management stating the agency was developing a promotional items policy and all expenses for those items were "suspended pending issuance of a formal policy."

[926] "DOJ OIG. *A Review of the U.S. Marshals Service's Use of Appropriated Funds to Purchase Promotional Items*. DOJ OIG Oversight and Review Division. November 2013. Web. < http://www.justice.gov/oig/reports/2013/s1311.pdf>. (22).

[927] "DOJ OIG. *A Review of the U.S. Marshals Service's Use of Appropriated Funds to Purchase Promotional Items*. DOJ OIG Oversight and Review Division. November 2013. Web. < http://www.justice.gov/oig/reports/2013/s1311.pdf>. (41)..

[928] "DOJ OIG. *A Review of the U.S. Marshals Service's Use of Appropriated Funds to Purchase Promotional Items*. DOJ OIG Oversight and Review Division. November 2013. Web. < http://www.justice.gov/oig/reports/2013/s1311.pdf>. (41).

[929] "DOJ OIG. *A Review of the U.S. Marshals Service's Use of Appropriated Funds to Purchase Promotional Items*. DOJ OIG Oversight and Review Division. November 2013. Web. < http://www.justice.gov/oig/reports/2013/s1311.pdf>. (21-22).

[930] See H.R. 933: Consolidated and Further Continuing Appropriations Act, 2013.